Notre Dame Football

Notre Dame Football

The Golden Tradition

Dave Condon, Chet Grant, and Bob Best

Icarus Press

South Bend, Indiana

1982

Notre Dame Football
The Golden Tradition

Copyright © 1982 by Icarus Press

Manufactured in the United States of America.

Icarus Press, Inc.
Post Office Box 1225
South Bend, Indiana 46624

1 2 3 4 5 6 7 8 9 10 85 84 83 82

The publishers gratefully acknowledge the valuable assistance of John Heisler, Jim Langford, and Herb Juliano of the International Sports and Games Research Collection. We are also grateful for assistance from Chet Grant, Jeff Jeffers, The Dome yearbook, the Notre Dame Archives, and Ave Maria Press.

Library of Congress Cataloging in Publication Data

Condon, Dave.
    Notre Dame football, the golden tradition.

    Includes index.
    1. University of Notre Dame—Football—History.
I. Grant, Chet, 1892-   . II. Best, Bob. III. Title.
GV958.U54C66   796.332'63'0977289   81-20240
ISBN 0-89651-510-9   AACR2

Contents

Knute Rockne and the Golden Tradition

Chet Grant

Contemporary football is a far cry from what football was that morning in 1887 when the modern era of the game was initiated at Notre Dame. It came in the form of one "inning" of instruction from an experienced team (champions of the West, no less) from the University of Michigan.

But an earlier type of football, a variant of rugby, existed on campus long before that. Father Arthur Hope records in *Notre Dame: One Hundred Years* (Icarus Press) a pick-up game of old-fashioned football in the fall of 1876 in which two teams fielding forty-three players to the side played four "innings" to a tie, the final period lasting forty-five minutes with no time-outs—all for sheer sport garnished by "a couple of barrels of apples" which "they divided evenly."

Meanwhile Harvard University at Cambridge had been introduced to the game of rugby by McGill University of Montreal. The reported etiquette adopted for this international event I found inveigling, as chronicled by Frank Menke in his *Encyclopedia of Sport*

The first ND varsity team photographed in 1887.

(1917): "American football exists today as the ultimate spinoff from the McGill-Harvard get-together in the spring of 1875. In a pre-game workout the McGills were kicking the ball or picking it up and running with it. 'That's our game, rugby,' the McGill captain explained to the puzzled Harvard captain, who countered, 'our game is kicking and nothing else. But you're our guests. We'll play your game if you'll explain the rules.' Not to be outdone in sportsmanship the McGill captain proposed a half-and-half arrangement. . . . It was so agreed. . . ."

It would be more than a decade after this exhibition of sportsmanship before "rugby" was introduced at Notre Dame by the University of Michigan. By this time, I think, the name of the football game being played at Notre Dame was soccer. At any rate, it came to pass the morning of November 23, 1887, that the Wolverines, on a short tour of the Midwest, stopped off long enough to induct Notre Dame's athletes into the rules of rugby, taking time to inflict an 8–0 lesson in the one inning their time-table allowed. They enjoyed a hearty meal on campus and then were sped on their way by Father Walsh, who was then president, with an invitation to continue the series thus begun. They responded in the spring of 1888 by returning to defeat Notre Dame 26–0 on April 20, and 10–4 on April 21.

Nevertheless Notre Dame claimed the championship of Illi-

nois and Indiana after beating Harvard School of Chicago 20–0 at Notre Dame on December 7, the third and last game of that season.

Since I historically had identified these states with Western Conference institutions, I shared in my first reaction the skepticism of the students' magazine, *The Scholastic*, in early 1889: "Since Harvard had been acclaimed the champions of Illinois, Notre Dame went them one better and claimed to be the champions of Indiana and Illinois. How Notre Dame became champion of Indiana is something of a mystery since Notre Dame did not play an Indiana team that year [1888]."

Indiana University wouldn't field a representative team until 1895. Purdue's eleven were not available in 1888 after a 48–0 walloping by Butler in 1887. As for Illinois, since the University of Illinois and Chicago University did not field football teams intercollegiately until 1890 and 1892 respectively, who was there to challenge Chicago's Harvard School!

The spring of 1889, the Notre Dame footballers looked forward to meeting Michigan again, this time equipped in uniforms padded for the first time, jackets bearing the letters ND on the breast ("the one in old gold, the other in sky-blue"), and caps also sporting the college colors. According to the aggressive *Scholastic*, Michigan "backed squarely out when asked to play that spring." The first game ever played away from Notre

Dame resulted in a 9–0 victory over Northwestern in November of that year, a contest for which the team seems to have trained by running around the lake (St. Joseph's, one presumes) every morning. No games were scheduled for 1890 and 1891. Intercollegiate competition was unimpressively resumed in 1892 with a 56–0 defeat of South Bend High School and a 10–10 tie with Hillsdale College. Notre Dame would win four games in 1893, the last played in snow, and lose a fifth game with Chicago, 8–0, played in Chicago January 1, 1894.

It was only in 1894, according to Notre Dame historian Father A.J. Hope, C.S.C., that football took on some of the aspects associated with later stages of intercollegiate play. "What the football eleven needs most," he quotes the *Scholastic*, "is a coacher. . . . If a good man were obtained for two or three weeks there would be a great improvement." One James L. T. Morrison, left tackle on the Michigan team of 1893, was the man. "Under him," Father Hope records, "regular training was inaugurated as well as a training table, possibly as much to incite the men to go out for the team as to 'condition' them, for part of the coach's problem was to get twenty-two men out to practice. Morrison's period of coaching was brief. He came in time to prepare the team for a game with Hillsdale and a week after the victory left Notre Dame to go to Hillsdale to coach. The *Scholastic* calmly advised the abandoned team, 'It rests now with the captain and his men to continue practice on the lines mapped out by the coach.' The advice seems to have been heeded: in the following four games only one, the last, was lost. The five-game season, against Hillsdale, Wabash, Rush Medical of Chicago, and two games with Albion was the first in which a regular schedule was followed. It was," Fr. Hope concludes, "the beginning of a great football tradition at Notre Dame."

Anticlimax followed in 1895, under one H. G. Hadden, in the nature of the opposition, although Notre Dame won three of four games. Northwestern Law, Illinois Cycling Club, Indianapolis Artillery, and Chicago Physicians & Surgeons seemed to bespeak scheduling expedience.

In 1896 Frank E. Hering would coach, captain, and quarterback the Notre Dame football team, besides teaching English. He had been a quarterback at Chicago under A. A. Stagg and coached at Pennsylvania's Bucknell College. He would be the only Notre Dame coach to serve three years until the advent of Jesse Harper in 1913. His overall record consisted of fourteen wins, six losses, and one tie.

Assisting Frank Hering in 1898 was his antithesis in background, build, and bearing. James J. McWeeney had been a heavyweight wrestler, a one-time member of the Chicago police department. He

was said to have worked on the Notre Dame farm. I can't vouch for the chronology. I remember him as South Bend's chief of police, who appeared at a high-school practice. I was a bystander one afternoon about 1908 when he dispensed some rugged psychological technique for the benefit of ball carriers. "Go into the line with your free fist doubled," he recommended. "You won't have to use it. Your opponents will get the message."

Jim McWeeney was Notre Dame's head coach in 1899. His 6—3—1 record included defeats by Chicago (6—23) and Michigan (0—12), victory over Indiana (17—0), and a tie with Purdue (10—10). His successor was Pat O'Dea, noted Wisconsin kicker, in 1900 (6—3—1) and 1901 (8—1—1)—two seasons most distinguished by the discovery in an interhall football game of one Louis (Red) Salmon and his emergence as Notre Dame's first nationally recognized football star. His four-year record for most touchdowns individually scored still stands at thirty-six and was established when the rules deterred offensive effectiveness more than at any time since.

Father Cornelius Hagerty, C.S.C., my instructor at Notre Dame in ontology, as a student sat next to Salmon in class. Red's cheeks were so smooth, the color so solid, that his skin appeared translucent, according to Father Hagerty. The blue of his eyes was "startling." Quiet, reserved, he

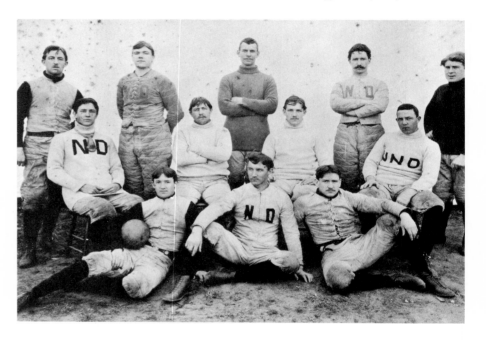

Below, the 1893 team. To the right, the 1896. The player holding the ball is Frank Hering, ND's first fulltime coach.

was what an opponent described as "red-headed, blue-eyed, apple-cheeked so & so on the football field." He blasted the line with the impact of a heavyweight, although standing less than 5'10" and weighing between 165 and 170 pounds. Born a little later, he would have been an ideal triple threat. He punted, kicked off, and drop-kicked from the field and for points-after. He was a breakaway potential on

kickoff and punt returns. He was a first-rate blocker. He was reputed to be the only linebacker able to stop the great Willie Heston of Michigan consistently, even as the Wolverines dominated the scoreboard. A western press association circulated his half-tone with the caption, "Greatest Back in the West." At a time when it was a red-letter event for even a Western Conference or a nonconference

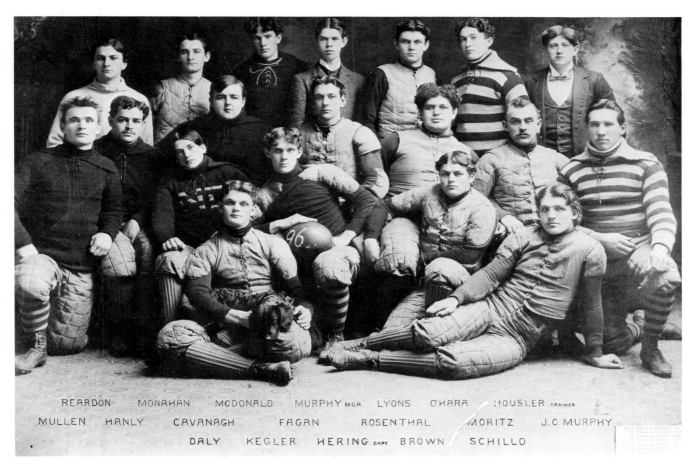

REARDON   MONAHAN   MCDONALD   MURPHY MGR   LYONS   O'HARA   HOUSLER TRAINER

MULLEN   HANLY   CAVANAGH   FAGAN   ROSENTHAL   MORITZ   J.C. MURPHY

DALY   KEGLER   HERING CAPT   BROWN   SCHILLO

Michigan star to breach the envied walls of Walter Camp's All-America lineup, Red Salmon of tiny Notre Dame of the West made the third team.

In 1903, both captained and co-coached by Salmon, Notre Dame was unbeaten and unscored-on in nine games and was tied once. The 0—0 standoff was with the Northwestern Wildcats, who had played Wisconsin and Chicago even and had defeated Illinois. The Notre

Dames thought they had won and would have rejoiced in an immediate rematch with traditional confidence.

To acquire his degree in engineering, to which he had transferred from arts and letters in his sophomore year, Red Salmon returned to Notre Dame in 1904 and coached the football team formally. That season the Gold and Blue, absorbing a 58—0 pasting by Wisconsin, conference powerhouse, and a 36—0

affront by Purdue, receded from the 9—0—1 peak of 1903 to a 5—3 record. Succeeding Salmon was a brilliant back, who had been Red's teammate for four seasons—Henry J., better known as "Fuzzy," McGlew. The nickname was inspired jointly by his great head of tightly curled hair and the prominence in the current newspaper headlining of the British war in Africa with native warriors descriptively dubbed the "Fuzzy-Wuzzies."

Fuzzy McGlew's '05 team held Wisconsin 21—0, lost to Purdue 32—0, and finished with a 5—4 record. He was replaced by Tom Barry of Wisconsin. Barry's records for 1906 and 1907 were 6—1—0, 6—0—1. Wisconsin was not on his schedule. The Barryites shaved the margin of Indiana's 22—5 scoreboard superiority of 1905 to 12—0 in 1906, and defeated Purdue 2—0. In 1907, they tied Indiana and turned back Purdue, 17—0.

The Notre Dame athlete I knew most about was our most famous redhead after Salmon. Harry Miller was not only a great himself but the brother and father of Notre Dame greats. Red hit hard on offense; he had great legs and he also punted. If he forward-passed for Notre Dame I didn't know it.

My first game-action memory of Notre Dame football features Pete Vaughan breaking through the line in 1908 when Victor Place (Dartmouth, '03) was coach. Place was as rugged in person and coaching methods as the New England setting of his playing days. Red Miller, captain in 1908, would recall that Place had two well-matched teams he goaded into battering each other so fiercely in intrasquad drills that they were not always up to physical par for games.

But back to Vaughan. The 1909 *Dome*, reviewing the 1908 season, summed up Pete Vaughan's football showing as a freshman in these words: "Not since . . . Salmon has Notre Dame had a man for all-around ability who could measure up to Vaughan. His terrific line plunges, remindful of the famed leader of '03, were irresistable [sic], and his skill in handling the forward pass yielded many a long gain for the varsity." These passes, incidentally, were chiefly thrown to Chief Bob Mathews, lurking with Indian stealth and wile along the sideline.

Vaughan as a linebacker undoubtedly contributed trenchantly to the Notre Dame defense in 1908

that kept the Michigan offense from crossing the Notre Dame 30-yard line. The Wolverines won 12–6 by resorting to the air . . . but not with forward passes: Coach Yost practiced forward passing but distrusted its reliability at game time. The great Allerdice accounted for all their points with his toe. Pete Vaughan charged fifty yards for Notre Dame's touchdown. P. A. McDonald broke loose for another TD but was charged with stepping out of bounds. Captain Red Miller had followed McDonald down the sideline, a little behind and a little to the outside. He never withdrew his opinion that the referee had confused his cleatmarks on the sideline with McDonald's.

Frankly, the so-called Notre Dame mystique didn't begin with Knute Rockne. Win or lose, it really began with that aborted indoctrinating defeat by Michigan in 1887 and attained its virtually unanimous recognition after a game with Michigan in 1909, when the winner emerged with the championship of the West and an arguable title to national eminence. A significant step had been taken in that direction the week before when the *South Bend Tribune* reported that Notre Dame's "Coach Longman was one in a hundred who was willing to predict success against Pittsburg [sic]. Odds," according to the *Tribune's* sports editor, "favored Pittsburg two to one and every angle pointed to a good score in favor of the Smoketown team. The game itself

was a revelation to the 7,000 Pittsburg fans (5000 of whom were Notre Dame partisans). All were surprised to find the westerners adept at the modern game." A dispatch from Pittsburgh recorded that "Notre Dame's great football machine was a big surprise to its supporters, yet praise goes to the visitors for their great exhibition of the game. In fact, Pittsburgh is to be congratulated that the score was low as six to nothing. Never since the days of the great D. C. & A. C. and Homestead elevens . . . has a team presented such a bewildering mass of plays. . . . Line-smashing Vaughan and Dimmick were voted wonders by the Pitt linemen."

Everybody understood that Miller's running against Pittsburgh had been sensational. But powerhouse Michigan was coming up. It was assumed that concentration of pregame emphasis on Pete Vaughan's role had set up the scene for "Longman's new plays," featuring Miller. Red Miller carried the ball ten straight times—to the 2, the 8, or the 4; from *wherever*, Pete Vaughan took it over. The score was 5–0 when Michigan recovered a fumble deep in Notre Dame territory. Unable, as throughout the 1908 game, to break through the Notre Dame defense, Allerdice place-kicked for three points. Score, 5–3. Only once again was the Notre Dame goal menaced, when the Wolverines recovered a fumble on the Notre Dame 2-yard line. Unable to crack Notre

Above, the great Red Salmon.

1902 varsity captain Red Salmon in the center, wearing monogram.

Luke Kelly and George Philbrook.

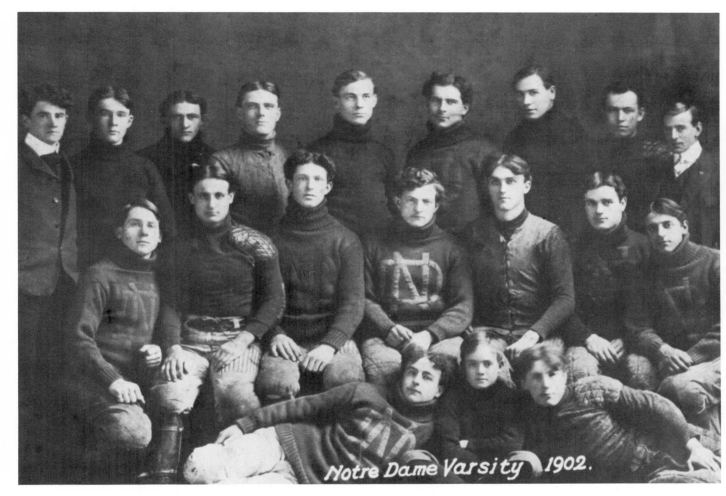

Notre Dame Varsity 1902.

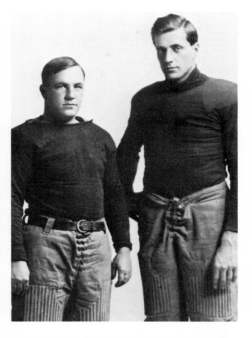

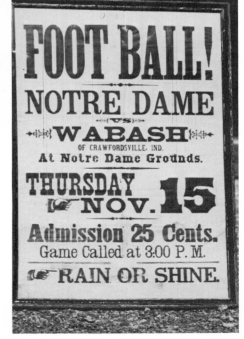

FOOT BALL!
NOTRE DAME
vs
WABASH
OF CRAWFORDSVILLE, IND.
At Notre Dame Grounds.
THURSDAY
☞ NOV. 15
Admission 25 Cents.
Game Called at 3:00 P. M.
☞ RAIN OR SHINE.

Dame's goal-line stand on the first two downs, the Wolverines lined up for a field-goal attempt. There had been an onfield discussion. Quarterback Wasmund, it would be learned later, had wanted to go for it. Captain Allerdice overruled him. The students in the stands called for the toe that had been good for all Michigan's scoring on Notre Dame in 1908 (four kicks, twelve points). Three points here would have put the Wolverines out in front 6–5. It looked like a sure thing.

The whole line ready to rush: Mathews, Edwards, Philbrook, Lynch, Dolan, Dimmick, Collins. Red Miller draws the picture: "Each man was set, like a tiger about to spring, his body taut, his face grim, his lips drawn back, his teeth flashing: a picture of power and determination." Then, the snap; the entire Notre Dame line charging. Boom. Boom. Kick and block. The ball bounds back thirty-five yards. Sam Dolan falls on it. It's almost anticlimactic when, soon after, Billy Ryan runs thirty yards through a broken field for the second touchdown. Notre Dame, 11; Michigan, 3.

That's the way it stood at the end of the game, but it was Notre Dame all the way home. Red Miller al-

The 1908 team, Rockne middle row, second from right.

Sam (Rosey) Dolan, left, and Harry (Red) Miller, 1909.

The 1909 all-Western champs. Three players are mislabeled. The man labeled Schmitt is Vaughan; "Maloney" is Schmitt, and "Vaughan" is Maloney.

most broke loose for another score. Quarterback Wasmund, playing safety, nailed the Notre Dame flyer by the ankle. Later Miller had a clear field ahead but lost Pete Vaughan's forty-yard pass in the sun. Chief Mathews, running with Miller, got his hands on the ball and carried it across the goal, but the throw was ruled incomplete.

Newspaper writers as far east as Boston in various forms corroborated the judgment of a Cleveland expert who classed the 1909 Notre Dame team as "probably the cream of the country."

In the cold light of the Monday after, when he realized that Notre Dame had been both expertly and popularly awarded the distinction he coveted for Michigan, "Hurry-up" Yost said, according to the *Chicago Record-Herald*, "You must recognize that we went into the game caring little whether we won or lost."

But when his more honest emotions prevailed he testified as Notre Dame's most qualified, if reluctant, booster. In this mood he made the following remarkable, perhaps hysterical, admission:

"What makes me so doggone

mad is that we might have won. These are the worst kind of games to lose. They leave a worm in the heart to gnaw and gnaw. O, I don't know. I'm sick and tired of the whole business. It certainly is discouraging. I take off my hat to the Irishmen. They are regular Indians. I was afraid of them because they have all the qualities of great players." The implication of this last remark might be that he had underestimated his former pupil's ability to take advantage of exceptional playing talent.

Coach Yost's discomfiture was aggravated by non-conference Michigan's subsequent 7–6 defeat of Western Conference champion Minnesota, leaving Notre Dame incontestable champion of the West.

Next was a newcomer on the schedule, Miami of Ohio, disposed of 46–0. Wabash followed, for the fourth game in a series that began in 1903 with a 35–0 Notre Dame victory. Thereafter the Little Giants had played up to their name: losing 12–4, winning 5–0, losing again 8–4. Playing without Pete Vaughan, Billy Ryan and Pete Dwyer, Notre Dame won in a 38–0 game against Wabash College in which Red Miller was in my view the outstanding offensive star.

Despite Red's continued heroics on offense, Notre Dame was held to a 0–0 tie in Milwaukee by Marquette. This I would explain partly by a number of factors in support of the Hilltoppers' basic merit and their will to win; namely, a grassless, sandy, heavy-footed gridiron, continued absence from the lineup of Ryan, Dwyer, and Vaughan, an unprecedented number of penalties for blocking infractions, not to mention that linebacker Sam (Rosey) Dolan played most of the game with a broken collarbone.

The name of the football game at Notre Dame in 1910 was anticlimax. Michigan backed out of its scheduled October 22nd date, this time charging Notre Dame with using ineligible players. Notre Dame could have countercharged while presenting a tenable defense against the Michigan indictment.

Lowlight was a 0–17 upset by the Michigan Aggies. A 5–5 tie with Marquette was typical of a relationship beginning in 1908. Only Notre Dame's seasonal point spread, thanks to four patsies on the schedule, looked familiar: 192–25. In retrospect, the season of 1910 looms most critical in Notre Dame football history, not because a freshman candidate named Knute Rockne quit the football squad but because he almost quit Notre Dame.

Jack Marks of Dartmouth would replace Frank Longman as coach. His teams in 1911 and 1912 posted thirteen wins and two ties, running up in the process 611 points to 26. The summer of 1912 I had managed to survive a rookie season (incognito) in the Class D Michigan State League, having quit my sportsediting and general reporting job with the *South Bend Tribune* in order to do so. When I returned home, a friend told me Jesse Harper of Wabash College had been asking for me. I had occasion to assume that his curiosity had been pricked by some of my former high-school mates, by then on the Wabash football squad.

For a number of reasons, including economic, I had never considered going to college—hypothetically, college meant at some point farther away than Notre Dame (maybe Wabash)—even if solicited. The urge to see my words in print, long-felt, was being allayed, far from being satiated, by my newspaper involvement. Notre Dame sports were covered in both local newspapers by campus correspondents. I don't recall seeing a Notre Dame football game in 1911. I do remember vividly the 1912 Wabash game on Cartier Field for several reasons, among them the fact that three of my ex-high-school teammates were with the Little Giants. For the first time since 1903, featuring a varied ground attack, Notre Dame would run up the score (41–6). But the unsuccessful forward passes thrown by quarterback Skeets Lambert are etched most distinctly in my memory by the consequence of their incompletion. Again and again, under extreme pressure from defensive pass rushers, Skeets grounded beautifully spiraling passes far downfield. One of the game officials was the great Chicago ex-quarterback, Walter Eckersall, who covered football for the *Chicago Tribune*. Eckie's eloquent tribute in the *Trib* to Lambert's evasive tactic

soon precipitated establishment of a conventional penalty, loss of down for incompletion!

In 1912, Notre Dame had acquired an athletic director and football-basketball-baseball coach from Wabash College in the person of Jesse Harper, who had sought and achieved a new varsity eligibility rule at ND: one year of residency. At the same time he had dramatically jacked up the Notre Dame schedule with new opponents, featuring Army and including also new opponents South Dakota, Penn State, Christian Brothers (St. Louis), and Texas. Only two breather games moderated this pressure.

I've read varied accounts of Notre Dame's approach to the first (1913) confrontation on the West Point plains, many of them inconsistent with my own contemporary feeling of confidence. A presumption of ridiculous odds favoring Army is implicit in Frank Menke's reference in the *Encyclopedia of Sport* to Notre Dame as a "pipsqueak team" made up of "pint-size" players. He was not without company in erroneously implying that quarterback Dorais and end-captain Rockne in 1913 were pioneer users of the forward pass, although it had been in Notre Dame's offensive repertoire at least as early as the 1908 Pitt game. Eddie Cochem of St. Louis University had made sensational use of the new gadget the very first year of its authorization, 1906. It's a fact that Army had one advantage more

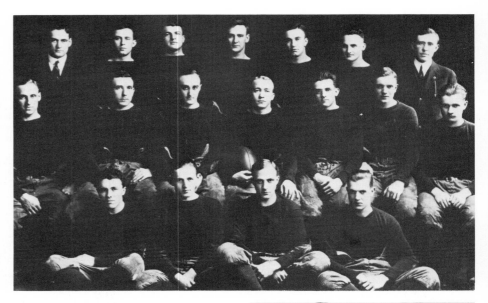

important than weight; i.e., the recruitment of cadets from among graduated college stars. On the other hand, academic and military education cut down on the allotment of their time to football practice. As for weight, Notre Dame's average of 180 well-conditioned pounds was not to be sniveled at. Nor can there be doubt that Dorais and Rockne, while employed at Cedar Point, the Lake Erie resort at Sandusky, Ohio, found occasion and leisure to rehearse their forward-passing combinations.

Notre Dame had three games to warm up for Army, two of them breezers (the other, South Dakota, providing a 20–7 challenge). Harper also was well aware of the individual capabilities of his inheritance, having had the opportunity to oppose the current Notre Damers with his Wabash Little Giants

The 1913 team, Captain Knute Rockne holding the ball.

Roy Eichenlaub, left, and Charles (Gus) Dorais.

The 1917 team, last one coached by Jess Harper, upper left. Assistant coach Rockne is upper right. George Gipp is absent, but was on the team.

in bad weather at Crawfordsville and in good at Notre Dame. Notre Dame gridders long had been notable for almost professional poise and savvy in game competition.

The Notre Dame-Army game of 1913 constituted a fair match in all the fundamentals; the differential factor was Notre Dame's apparently unexpected accent on the forward pitch in which the receivers of quarterback Gus Dorais' passes included left-half Joe Pliska and right end Fred Gushurst, as well

as left end and captain Knute Rockne. Off-tackle slashes by Pliska and left-half Sam Finegan, alternating with crushing inside plunges by the great fullback, Ray Eichenlaub, set up the Notre Dame aerial attack. (Score? Oh, yes: ND 35; Army 13.)

The 1913 team set another Notre Dame football record and a scheduling precedent in distance traveled, racking up miles by the thousands in contrast with previous seasons in which travel had been confined to total seasonal distances measurable in hundreds of miles.

The season of 1914 opened auspiciously. Alma and Rose Poly were typical openers, but a combined scoreboard of 159–0 had to be more than mildly impressive considering that Gus Dorais' replacement, Alfred H. (Big Dutch) Bergman,

was in absentia and that conventionally ND didn't use the backfield shift in warmup competition. Bergman's continued absence from the lineup in the third game, with Yale in New Haven, was coincident with, if it did not precipitate, a rout of the Gold and Blue by the Yale Blue, intrinsically less authentic than the 28–0 score seems to suggest. Big Dutch was well established as Notre Dame's greatest all-around athlete, lettering in all the major sports of football, basketball, track, and baseball. Compactly built (5'9", 160 lbs.), he was Notre Dame's best broken-field runner. His teammates seemed to gain at will on the ground that horrendous day. But fumbles cost them possession again and again on promising drives. Dutch could have made the

difference in ball handling. I associate with Yale's offense that day an extraordinary resort to *lateral* passes, most if not all completed. I can't place with certainty the perspective of my recollections of what I'm sure Notre Dame followers considered an upset, I among them.

South Dakota and Haskell Indians succumbed on Cartier Field next, successively and respectively 33–0 and 20–7. Army, in the middle of a 214–20 perfect season on the scoreboard, set Notre Dame down 20–7 at West Point. The following Saturday (November 14) I took the interurban train to Chicago, traveling for the first time west of Hammond, Indiana, to see Notre Dame play Carlisle in Comiskey Park. By that time there was no great Jim Thorpe with the Carlisle Indians. Notre Dame won, 42–6. I remember distinctly one play: guard Charlie Bachman's long return of a short Carlisle kickoff for a touchdown, a feat influencing Charlie's shift to fullback in 1915.

Notre Dame wound up the 1914 season at Syracuse, New York, with a 20–0 win over Syracuse University.

Early in the following June, I chanced into Frederick B. Barnes in the company of one of his playground directors: a tow-headed, broad-faced, bulky-chested man who might have been years older than his true twenty-seven years without diminishing the impact of a dynamic personality. As we shook hands I was struck by the searching intentness of his blue-eyed fix on my brownish eyes—an impression that would be shared by countless persons from diverse perspectives. I'm sure I intuited at that time and spot that Knute Rockne, assistant Notre Dame football coach and head track coach, was registering, for infallible future reference, my face and name, probably in context with a character evaluation to which he could adjust, if indicated, for better or worse.

At that time, Notre Dame sports were still reported by campus correspondents. Since school wouldn't open until some time in September, the city editor of the South Bend *Tribune*, Duff Horst, suggested that I telephone head-coach Jesse Harper for an interview about the 1915 football prospects. The city room was located on the second floor of the Tribune Building, and I had not the slightest premonition that the man climbing the dark narrow stairs that afternoon would, within the hour, usher me into another world to which I would be bound in multifarious ways the rest of my life. Our interview completed, Jess Harper posed a startling and provocative question: How would I like to come out to Notre Dame that fall? My immediate reaction was incredulity. I couldn't afford to scrap my job. I wouldn't have to do so, he assured me. I could continue to get out my sports section and substitute coverage of campus athletic activities for my general reportorial beat. He also

was in a position to set me up as a correspondent for an Indianapolis newspaper. The rub, I thought, would be the approval of F. A. Miller, *Tribune* editor and co-owner of The Tribune Publishing Co. I didn't think he would go for it. It happened that the foxy Mr. Harper had already made the necessary arrangements. When I went to see Mr. Miller, he said. "I didn't go to college myself, but if I can help someone else do so, I want to help." Me—a college man? It didn't seem tenable, but it was. I thought I was being recruited for basketball. When Coach Harper said I wouldn't have to go out for freshman football *that fall*, I grasped the message. My classes would begin at 11 A.M. with journalism, followed in the afternoon with English, distributive justice, and torts & claims: a schedule sandwiched between most of the morning at the *Tribune* and late-afternoon football practice. Assistant football coach Rockne and I chanced to meet in the Main Building the day I was assigned my schedule of classes. How about English I? Who was to be my instructor? Told it was Father Crumley, Rock nodded and snapped: "Good. He's great with words." I was not aware then that Father Crumley had been university vice-president and chairman of the athletic board in 1905 and that he'd had occasion to defend Notre Dame's athletic eligibility standards and did so with eloquence but without avail when the big western colleges voted to

oust smaller members of the Western Conference in favor of a restricted "Big 9," which would be expanded to a "Big 10" with the induction of Ohio State.

Head coach Harper had offices in both the Main Building and the Big Gym. One day he handed me a hot potato. Charlie Bachman, shifted from guard to fullback, was suffering from what had the appearance of chronic fumbleitis. On both T and shift formations, the fullback mainly either blocked or plunged. On the shift, the center timed an arched pass to enable the fullback to receive the ball and tuck it away in accelerating stride. Charlie, I'm sure, was somewhat older than the average of his teammates. On and off field he manifested relative maturity in perspective and deportment. In undergraduate approach to both football and track and field, he was already a pedagogue. Both paid coaches, Harper and Rockne, used uncharacteristic kid gloves in dealing with Charlie Bachman. This is how I became acquainted with him before I myself went out for football. Harper asked me, as campus sports correspondent, to apply the needle to Charlie's tendency to take the center's pass on his chest, whence in turn it tended to bounce. I think the coaches had in mind a minimum of pointed sentences—preferably one; at most, a very brief paragraph. But as captain of coachless athletic teams since I was a high school junior, I allowed myself to be carried away. In the

next edition of the *South Bend Tribune's* sport columns, Charlie's problem rated a virtual essay. On my way to or from an academic commitment early the next afternoon I met the head coach. With a small wry grin, he warned me that I had gone much farther than intended and suggested that I not divulge his instigative role. Of this situation I recall only Charlie's shrugging off of the whole matter. "I know Harper put you up to it," he volunteered.

That's the way non-Catholic Charlie Bachman was—then and thereafter in an impressive career as collegiate football coach and athletic director—understanding and tolerant, as our contacts intermittently have exemplified for more than sixty years.

Notre Dame's opening football games in 1915 were more or less conventional breezes, both played on Cartier Field as Notre Dame routinely defeated Alma College in the opener (32–0) and the Haskell Indians (34–0). The third game was played at Lincoln, Nebraska; the Cornhuskers prevailed by kicking two points after touchdown to Notre Dame's one, to account for the

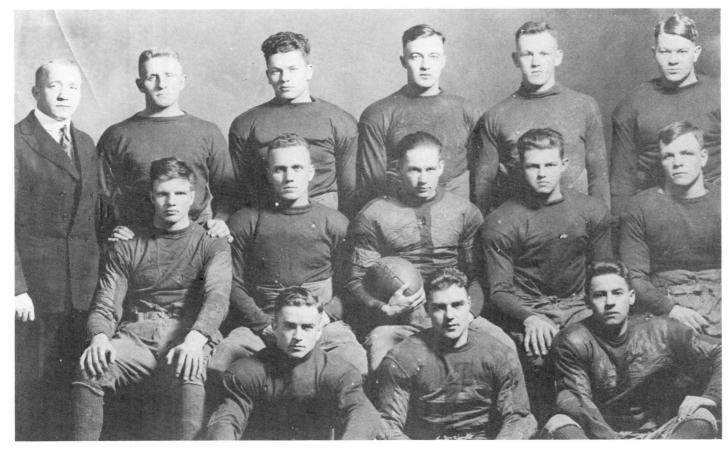

which I was watching as a reporter. I also was becoming acquainted with Knute Rockne as track coach while training for track interhall competition in the Big Gym. I remember annoying Rock by breaking into a run while supposed to be jogging to develop high knee action.

In the spring of 1916, I didn't realize at first how green I would appear to be as a football candidate at Notre Dame with a background all-told of only fourteen sixty-minute games. Fortunately, someone else recognized my dilemma—no less than Ray Eichenlaub (1911-14), Notre Dame's Western fullback. Eich possessed a formidably comprehensive list of the do's and don'ts of Notre Dame football, which, I was led to believe, he had acquired clandestinely and was passing on to me under the same cloak of privacy.

Group practice was far more detailed and sophisticated in college than I had found it in my one season of high-school football. For backs, punting and punt returning began each day as soon as that exercise could be manned. Warm-up for the squad as a whole usually followed. Respective group drills came next, including daily individual backfield dodging practice. Team signal drill was a daily must, sometimes topped by squad wind sprints to wind up the day. That first season I recurrently experienced difficulty in backfield-shift timing, tending to get ahead of the hip!-one-two count

regrettable tune of 20–19. I seem to recall an understandable expression of chagrin by a future teammate, cool halfback John Miller, whose toe could have tied, even won, this major contest. The last home game was with South Dakota. Outpointed in 1914 at Sioux City 33–0, the Dakotans held Notre Dame on Cartier Field in 1915 to a 6–0 margin.

Time would come in my Notre Dame football affiliation when I would be identified as the quarter-

back who lost the Iowa game (1921), costing us the national championship. From a later perspective I would be identified with having called a last-minute winning play against Army at West Point back in 1915: old "54," a long forward pitch up the middle by left-half Stan Cofall to right-half Bergman (little Dutch) for a long run and a 7–0 victory. Another old Notre Dame teammate of mine would credit me in a nationally syndicated article years later with calling that

play. Fact: I was back home in 1915; a Notre Dame freshman ineligible for varsity competition!

The 1915 season wound up on the road: Creighton, 41–0, at Omaha; Texas at Austin, 36–7; Rice at Houston, 55–2.

During the winter of 1915-16, I played one game of basketball, with Notre Dame Day Students v. the Knights of Columbus at Fort Wayne, Indiana. Once, when Jess Harper was short-handed, he drafted me for a basketball scrimmage,

transition from tight-T formation into the backfield box, and causing penalties incurred by this defect in rhythm.

During the earliest stage of fall practice in 1916 I was still a long shot as a football prospect at ND. Joe Dorais, brother of the great Gus, was my rival for second-string quarterback. I certainly wasn't going to play football simply for fun: football was a stage toward the higher academic education I had previously shunned. While at it, of course, I was anxious to play it as well as I should, if not better. I got off to a misleading start in the opener against Case Tech of Cleveland, the first time I got hold of a punt behind our own 20-yard line whence, in a time when offensive play was constricted by ideas not in force today, the strategy was to let the ball roll out of bounds to the end zone and take over on your 20.

I caught the ball instead, surveyed the field, thought I saw daylight on my left, only to be shut off in that direction. I reversed, and again an apparent break in the defense was plugged. I reversed once more, thinking to myself that at least "I'll get credit for trying." At that moment the field opened wide except for the Tech safety. Right end Harry Baujan sprinted across from the right flank to dispose of that threat with a nifty rolling block. I still felt guilty about violating strategy, even after I later read in *The Scholastic* I'd returned the ball from our 5-yard line. That

ninety-five-yard punt return for touchdown has stood as the ND record for sixty-four years.

Favoring a groin strain, I sat out an anticipated warm-up with Western Reserve at Cleveland. Reserve frustrated our offense the first half, but the final score duplicated our 48–0 margin over Case.

The Haskell Indians were scheduled next for Cartier Field. I still remember my sense of frustration in that affair. No long punt returns that day. Our relative futility on offense was reflected in the modest margin of our victory, 26–0.

Wabash was next. Notre Dame hadn't played the Little Giants since walloping them 41–0 in 1909. Scouting the Little Giants against Purdue in 1916, Rock had come back profoundly impressed by their upset potential in size and speed despite a 28–7 defeat by the Boilermakers. This was his third coaching year, but I doubt that this was his first pre-game pep talk, even though it was an unforgettable first for me. Head coach Harper, remembering that the Wabash Crimson in his time had given the Gold and Blue more than one scare, turned his exhorter loose. Of Rock's address in the locker room in the Big Gym I recall most vividly the intensity and power of his phraseology, rather than the text, with a singular exception: his last piercing injunction to "go out there and kill 'em, crucify 'em!"

That language had been inspired by Rock's understanding that Coach Paul Sheeks had invested

the impending confrontation with the character of a Holy War, Methodist vs. Catholic, despite the fact that both of ND's coaches were non-Catholic as well as four of the first-string players. I answer only for my own physical and emotional reaction. If my feet touched the cinder path en route from the Big Gym to Cartier Field I was unaware. My conscious physical sensation was a head-to-foot tingle. We first possessed the ball on our 40. I sent LH Cofall on a cutback off tackle that was good for a sixty-yard romp. That was the first of enough TDs to give us 60 points to the Little Giants' 0.

Next, West Point. Despite the infamous rout we endured, my most lingering memories were of toasted home-made bread and rich whole milk before the game, and a sly chat with Charlie Bachman under the cover of a wooded section of the Point's riverbank. At the end of the first half Notre Dame led 10–7. In the second, Army opened up a devastating forward passing attack. The score was 10–27 when the beleaguered Jess Harper, with about five minutes to go, sent me in to redeem the situation from a starting point on our own 20. Charlie Bachman had a tide-turning inspiration which he slipped to me sotto voce: "Take it yourself." I signalled a short punt formation with Grant back. I took the ball and raced for the cutback point. But out of the twilight, a demoniac form: Bang! I'm hit, ball-high. I'm being wrenched into two sec-

tions. The ball flies clear and Army recovers. We hold for three downs and Oliphant boots for three points. Score: 30–10.

Football at Notre Dame, 1917, marked the swan song of Jesse Harper. While I was immersed in military duty at Camp Shelby, Miss., Notre Dame lined up with only seven 1916 monogram men, of whom quarterback and captain Jim

Alfred (Big Dutch) Bergman.

The great George Gipp, All-American left half.

Phelan would show up during the season at Camp Taylor. Of this group only George Gipp, Maurie Clipper, and Joe Brandy would be on deck when I came back in 1920. The team record in 1917 was 6–1–1: the loss was to Nebraska, 7–0; and the tie with Wisconsin, 0–0. It was hardly in my horoscope that Joe Brandy would play football at Fort Sheridan, Ill., in 1918, acquire a commission, return again as alternate Notre Dame quarterback in 1919, and remain as number one upon my return in 1920.

In 1918, Notre Dame played its first football season under Jess Harper's successor as head coach, Knute Rockne. The only familiar name on that season's squad was George Gipp, sophomore. But six newcomers to the 1918 lineup would notably be around when I got back to ND in 1920: Hunk Anderson, Ojay Larson, Clipper Smith, Eddie Anderson, Johnny Mohardt, and Chet Wynne. The 1918 schedule was trimmed to six games. Notre Dame beat Case Tech (26–6), Wabash (67–7), and Purdue (26–6), tied Great Lakes (7–7) and Nebraska (0–0 in the snow), and was upset by Michigan State in rain (7–13).

Returning to South Bend in late October, I managed to see the 1919 squad play Indiana at Indianapolis and Purdue at Lafayette. I recall being only mildly impressed by George Gipp's running in his third year at left halfback when measuring him against such greats as Red Miller, Gus Dorais, Stan Cofall, and the Bergmans, Big and Little Dutch. The 1919 season seems to me, in retrospect, most impressive as a coaching challenge for Rockne. That year, Rock was confronted with a squad that conglomerated experience, talent, and personality spanning seven years of peace and war. Players who had started in 1915 and 1916 returned to the squad in 1919 and 1920.

It was no surprise to me that Rock had emerged triumphant with this mixed bag. Of the genius of his leadership there was no question in my mind, although he would be dead for some time before I would recognize him clearly as a "man for all seasons," his strength rooted in the virtue of humility. That image was obscured to my view by the immediacy of current events and crises attending his first undefeated season (9–0). The 1919 team beat such significant opponents as Nebraska (12–9), Indiana (16–3), Army (12–9), Michigan Aggies (13–0), Purdue (33–13), and Morningside (14–6).

By the time I reported to Rock, the opening football game of 1920 had been played, but I had already got into training in the form of a fifteen-mile hike from a point south of the Bend where a B & O passenger train out of Akron had deposited me and my ditty bag. At Notre Dame Rock had tabbed me to share a "subway" room in Sorin Hall with Frank Reese, of Robinson, Illinois, freshman quarterback prospect. I hadn't been in a football uniform since Thanksgiv-

Good Luck
from

ing Day, 1917, at Camp Shelby.

I was twenty-eight years old. I stood five feet-seven inches and weighed 138 pounds. I'd never had to do much blocking. In his senior year at Notre Dame the great Paul Hornung might have done more tackling in a single game than I did in my whole collegiate career. By this time my arm seemed to have become calcium-bound in the shoulder. I wasn't as fast as I used to be, and while playing basketball I had slightly cracked a knee cap. On the other hand, I was not as specifically stupid tactically as suggested by Archie Ward's résumé of my brief and only appearance in game action with Gipp the Great at the tail end of our 16–7 defeat of Nebraska at Lincoln in October, 1920.

Although I recall no details, I'm sure I had watched the second game of 1920 from the Cartier Field stands. Notre Dame licked Western State Normal, 40–0.

My first day out, I was lined up to take my turn with Joe Brandy, Mickey Kane, and other quarterbacks receiving punts when George Gipp arrived at Cartier Field late. He paused with us long enough to receive three or four kicks before joining the kickers. I was uncomfortably conscious of having thought of him as a World War slacker before hearing that he had failed to pass the Army physical examination.

The Nebraska game still had at least five minutes to go; we enjoyed a comfortable 16–7 lead when

Rock sent me in to "play it safe" the rest of the way. In the interest of stipulated safety I asked for center Harry Mehre off the bench because center Ojay Larson's then-unconventional one-hand snap to the quarterback challenged my smallish grip. A fumble, or blocked kick, gave us possession on Nebraska's 10-yard line. I sent Gipp off tackle for five yards to the Nebraska 5. It was second down and five and I meant to repeat. As we were lining up on the T, Gipp said, "Give it to me again." That intrusion on the sovereignty of the quarterback eliminated Gipp. Fiery Norm Barry at right half enjoined me to call his number. I was tempted to choose fullback Chet Wynne because he held his peace, but feared that the other backs would check signals and cost us a down if Mehre moved the ball. A sure shot was a quarterback sneak but its potential under the circumstances was a yard and third down, four yards to go. So I called play 77—a fake split-buck eventuating in a quarterback forward pass to the right end, down and out: a decision resolved in almost the wink of an eye. Whirling to make my first fake, to the right halfback, I found no one to fake to. All three backs were knocking heads in place. Bumping into Barry as I faded back, foregoing perforce the fakes, I lost momentary control of the ball. By the time I recovered, fading laterally to my right, Eddie Anderson (RE) had drifted so deep into the end zone, nobody near him

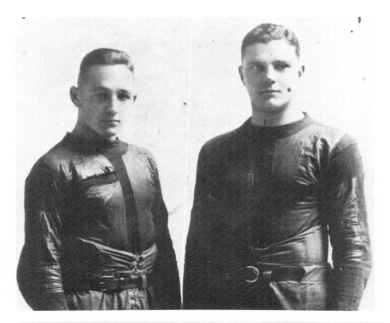

I was fearful of overthrowing the endline. Eddie made a desperate but fruitless dive to redeem my underthrow and the ball went over to the Cornhuskers on their 29. O Death! The sting was not cerebral. My *mechanical* failure shamed . . . me. It didn't bug me to hear Eddie Anderson sing out, "What happened, George?" or Hunk Anderson passing counsel: "Next time ask George what to do!" I didn't realize, until Nebraska had to punt, and we repossessed deep in our

Arthur (Little Dutch) Bergman, left, and Stanley Cofall, 1916 captain.

1921 backfield. John Mohardt, LH, left; author Chet Grant, QB; Danny Coughlin, RH; and Chet Wynne, FB, at right.

An unpublished and rare photo of George Gipp, circa 1919, at Cartier field, with John Mohardt in background.

own backyard, how much that extra TD meant to Gipp. Again he sought to influence my choice of play. He wanted to pass, although the game was snug in our bag with only two minutes or so to go. I yielded to his importunity when we were reassembling in our T-formation and he indicated we needed another touchdown to make good the points he had given in order to get down a bet for some friends. Actually, the risk was minimal when I called a throw down and out deep to right-end Anderson: an interception would be as good as a punt. It was too long by inches. Gipp didn't have to ask me for a repeat crack at it. Center Harry Mehre reminded me we had come in to play it safe. I hadn't forgotten. "That's all, George," I said.

Gipp was satisfied. He'd had the chance to play his hand. For the first time, and perhaps the last, I had encountered a Mississippi riverboat gambler-type of the old school wearing a football uniform, playing his cards to the limit in a football game, losing gracefully. He punted us well out of serious threat. A half hour or so later in the hotel he was offering to buy me a Coke, as outwardly cheerful as if I hadn't jeopardized his and his friends' investment by forward passing on second down when line-plunges, especially his, had been obviously indicated.

Valparaiso, next on our home schedule, was coached by Notre Dame's future and highly successful basketball coach, George Keogan. Harvard, which was 9–0–1 in 1920, had had a tough time downing Valpo.

That 1920 season witnessed introduction of the shock-troops strategy at Notre Dame. I was the quarterback of the second team, assigned to soften up the opposition with hard-nose fundamentals for exploitation by the first-string team, quarterbacked by Joe Brandy. My personal experience will exemplify our group futility during that first period. First of all, we'd been working out with used footballs only. The extreme contrasting hardness of the game ball embarrassed me, to start with, on a quick-opener hand-off which was rightly interpreted as an illegal forward pass because my insecure

grip caused me to hand it off *forward*! Then, I thought I was on my way off short-punt formation when wingback Earl Walsh literally flattened Valpo's left end, encouraging me to change course to the outside—and get slammed for an embarrassing loss as one Eklund, who later would become an All-American at Minnesota, uncoiled from his prone position like a spring. Before the first quarter was over I was sure I should have stayed in bed. The Valpo center on certain plays was assigned to deal with the opposing safety—in this case, me. Prior to a final occasion he had stopped short as our defense smothered the Valpo play. What he did the last time should be recorded in the Guinness book of records. The play was over when he ran up to me, blithely kicked me in the shin, and darted away laughing at my belated accusation that he was a no-good so-and-so.

The first team bumped into its share of frustration in the second quarter and had to battle all the way to a 28–3 finale, to which Gipp made the most dramatic contributions, probably minimized in my memory by his spectacular showing against Army the following Saturday: the game that would move Walter Camp to make room for halfback Gipp on his 1920 All-America first team by positioning him at fullback.

The action of this game might have been plotted for movie or TV, taken by quarters:

First Quarter: Ball on Army 35.

Plebe fullback Walter French (ex-Rutgers) appears to be touchdown bound. Quarterback Brandy, defensive safety, maneuvers him out of bounds on the Notre Dame 23. Halfback Lawrence fights his way to a touchdown. Right guard Breidster kicks point after. Score: Army 7, Notre Dame 0. Notre Dame moves ball on ground and in air from deep in own territory to Army 5. Right halfback Johnny Mohardt scores on off-tackle cutback. Gipp makes point after. Score: Army 7, Notre Dame 7.

Second Quarter: Gipp passes to left-end Kiley on Army 30; Kiley scores. Gipp kicks point after. Score: Notre Dame 14, Army 7. Gipp punts to French, who executes the most dramatic long-gainer of the day. I've never witnessed a more dazzling demonstration of open-field running in all my years. Breidster delivers extra point. Score: Notre Dame 14, Army 14. French kicks field goal from the Notre Dame 15. Score: Army 17, Notre Dame 14.

Third Quarter: No scoring.

Fourth Quarter: Notre Dame has ball on Army 20-yard line. Gipp makes five yards in two shots at the line. Notre Dame regroups in the T-formation. Joe Brandy snaps out the signal: "45-14-93 Hip!" The backs shift into the box right. The ends shift laterally, in two counts. Mohardt half pivots to the inside. Gipp starts right, slips the ball under his left arm to Mohardt who reverses to the left and cuts inside or outside the Army right tackle

to score. Gipp kicks point after. Score: Notre Dame 21, Army 17. Notre Dame holds Army on the following kickoff. According to historian Jim Beach, Gipp takes French's punt and "skyrockets fifty yards straight up the middle." I visualize that return more esthetically, as describing a weaving course that unostentatiously impaired the timing of would-be tacklers whom Jim Beach graphically identifies as "sprawling cadets littering his wake, arms pawing in air." Jim Beach again: "It's a pass by Gipp that connects with 'Rog' Kiley who thunders along for fifteen yards to the West Point 20 before he is stopped."

Fullback Chet Wynne made Notre Dame's fourth touchdown of the day, kicker Paul Castner missed the point after, and the final score was Notre Dame 27, Army 17; with just enough time left for No. 2 Quarterback Grant to stick his neck out.

The heroic dimensions of the great Gipp's greatest performance are attested by Jim Beach's compilation of Gipp's yardage gained v. Army October 30, 1920: 124 yards from scrimmage, 96 yards from forward passing, 112 yards from kickoffs and punt returns, for a total of 332 yards all before the rulemakers of collegiate football got around to making rules drastically favoring the offense.

The 1920 Army game climaxed the great George Gipp's football career. The denouement began to unfold the following Saturday (No-

vember 6) in a homecoming day with Purdue on Cartier Field. Special guest of the University was Gipp's great predecessor, Louis "Red" Salmon, returning for the first time since graduation in 1905. It didn't take long for Gipp to reel off two long touchdown runs, one called back, before Rockne retired him for the day.

Indiana at Indianapolis (November 13) stopped him for three quarters on the ground and intercepted his passes. The score was 7–10 in the fourth quarter when Gipp returned to the game, with left arm taped, to slant off tackle and make the score 13–10. Gipp sat out most of the Northwestern game on a fateful November 20. When Rock finally sent him in it was by popular demand shared, I'm sure, by even some Wildcat supporters. I think he completed at least one pass for a touchdown. He uncharacteristically fumbled a punt. In the shower I overheard his casual remark that he had been trying to pivot while making the catch, presumably to protect his injured left arm or shoulder. At a football dinner in South Bend's Oliver Hotel Gipp sat across the table from me. He borrowed a handkerchief before excusing himself from our company. I thought he might be keeping a date to play billiards or cards. The next I heard he was confined in St. Joseph's Hospital with a strep throat while we finished the season at East Lansing, defeating the Michigan Aggies 25–0, Thanksgiving Day, November 25.

In the aftermath of Gipp's death December 14 there evolved a not necessarily apocryphal story about a Northwestern player reputed to be found any night in the corner of a Chicago speakeasy confiding remorsefully that his tackle in Gipp's last game had sped the great one to an early grave!

In the late summer of 1950 *Collier's Weekly* published in serial form Knute Rockne's memoirs. Following his fatal airplane crash March 31, 1931, this material appeared in book form as his autobiography. Conspicuously missing from both publications is any significant allusion to the 1921 10–1 season. I presume herewith to substitute for Rock in recall of our bizarre upset by Iowa, the Western Conference champion. After all, for at least thirty years not a Notre Dame commencement passed without my being introduced to some old head who ejaculated, "Oh, yeah! You're the quarterback who lost the Iowa game!"

I did have the opportunity in 1921 to contribute to that negative distinction for the first fifty-plus minutes of the only major Notre Dame

1919 Western champions. Rockne at left, George Gipp center of top row.

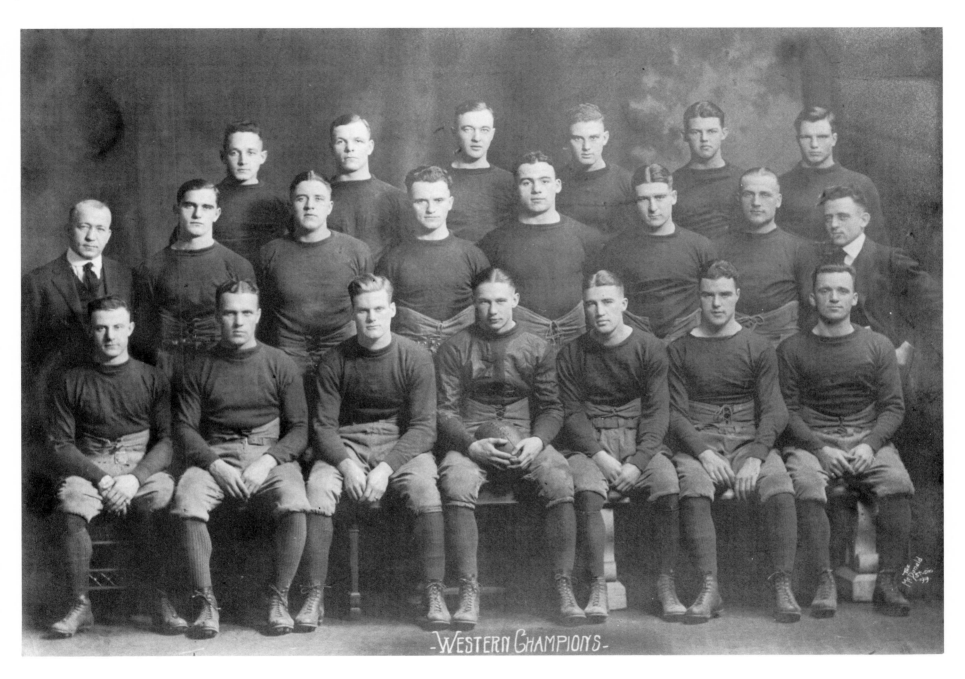

-WESTERN CHAMPIONS-

football game I had started in three seasons; that is, the Iowa affair that cost us both the national championship and an unconditional invitation to the 1922 Bowl. Nobody, under Heaven, could have foreseen that we could roll up 420 yards by land and air against Iowa's 240 on the ground and wind down with 7 points to the Hawkeyes' 10.

Intrinsically, we could afford to spot Iowa the touchdown and field goal that left us in arrears 0—10 at the end of the first quarter. To start the second period I had an immediate chance to convert Aubrey Devine's not very long, not really high punt into a zigzagging return for TD from our 40-yard-line. Perhaps it was ominously prophetic that it seemed to me the wobbling pigskin would never get down before the Hawkeyes would swarm upon me. Actually, it came down in time to wobble out of my shaky grasp and bounce so far as to require eons to scoop it into my embrace.

Now we begin to romp. To the right *off tackle* with left-half Mohardt, to the left *around end* with right-half Coughlin (repeat as prescribed) all the way to Iowa 6. Fullback Wynne high-knees it to second down, one to go. All then required to acquire a TD without risk is to call right-half Danny Coughlin straight ahead from T-formation and—too bad! You're still eighteen inches short of your first points. But, of course, you've noticed, all the way from your 40-

yard-line take-off, an inviting hole opening right of center as you have shifted and maneuvered to scoring range. So you call a quarterback sneak from the shift. You step back from the box to take the ball from the inside of your snapback's near leg, and there's no place to go —you'll swear ever after that eleven Hawkeyes were stacked against your advance more than half of 18 inches. (That's your story and you'll stick to it.) What now? Watch! Listen, rather. The setup is ideal. The signal is 77. "Hip!"

You double fake into the line with your backs . . . Oh, no you don't! Once again your backs (remember the Nebraska game, 1920) are knocking heads (it's the Cornhusker charade with a different cast). Whereupon, instead of eating the pigskin and leaving Iowa in awkward possession on its goal-line, you drop back, bump the ball loose on the elbow of your right halfback, and make a desperation heave which Iowa linebacker Glen Devine retrieves on the six-inch line, six inches off the turf, and runs

back to the ND 40. Would you try that again if you were I? I'm sure you would if I were you.

As it went we soon retrieved possession on about our 35 or 40. All right! I yip "35-57-19! Hip!" Right halfback Coughlin slants from tailback left, transfers ball under left arm to left halfback Mohardt, who pivots from wing position to receive his charge, fakes a run, drops back to legal forward-passing depth, and pitches to left-end Roger Kiley down and across for sudden TD and point-after. Score:

Even then, anything for publicity. That's Miller on the left, Layden, Crowley, and on the right, Stuhldreher.

Your guess is as good as ours. That's Stuhldreher on the left, Crowley, Captain Adam Walsh holding the ball, Layden, and Miller on the right.

Still on horses in later life: Layden, Crowley, Stuhldreher, Miller.

7–10. Fourteen years later in 1935, old 57, Mazziotti to Shakespeare to Millner, will beat Ohio State in the *"Game of the Century."*

The future Four Horsemen and Seven Mules were working out on the dirt floor of the Big Gym one winter's afternoon in 1922 as I dropped by and Rock asked me to check out the timing of a group quarterbacked by Harry Stuhldreher, my roommate who, in my judgment, was bound to beat out both senior Frank Thomas and sophomore Frank Reese, who had been my roommate the year before. During the fall I had scrimmaged against the freshmen at least once when three of the future Horsemen were involved: Stuhldreher, Don Miller, and Jim Crowley. My recollection of James Crowley is defensive. He was called on an off-tackle play to the longside of the field and forced wide so that I had an early crack at him. I embraced only air while forcing him to run wider. Still on his feet at the sideline, he reversed his field. I was still on my knees when he fell over me. That day or another, I scrimmaged on offense against the 1921 freshmen when Stuhldreher was at safety and Don Miller at defensive right half. When I called myself to my right off-tackle, Don was explosively reactive. As I cut through the hole I knew all I had to do in order to get clear was head-fake right and cut sharply left. Sure enough, Don took himself out of position. He was so

fiercely eager he literally ran past me; I could hear him sharply condemning his overcommitment, a tendency he would learn to control. It was a must now to get past Stuhly, as an antidote for his natural cockiness. I didn't have the speed to outrace him. Instead of trying to maneuver me to one side or the other he tried for a head-on tackle. For a dark fraction of a moment I thought I was a goner. But his neglect to hold his head back enabled me to contact the top of his helmet with my free hand and pump my knees, almost in place, again and again it seemed, in order to be rid of him. This was rather a social gesture than technical, as I've hinted: to keep him tolerable as a roommate!

The circumstance that sold me on Stuhly's prospects physically was a scrimmage of which I was an observer. He completed a forward pass with an authority and precision I envied, then called a running play to his right for which he was a blocker. His target was a sophomore or junior end of some substance. Never before or after did I see anything on a football field resembling what happened to that end. Stuhly made contact about shin high, literally laid his man flat on the ground, and rolled over him foot to head as if he were a rug.

As for Don Miller, he was considered by the Miller family to be the best football player of his generation. This day Don Miller didn't gain an inch on a significant drive

inated the statistics. Notre Dame might have won *them* too but for a foot-injury that hampered Stuhldreher's resort to passes. The degree of that deprivation is more than suggested by his 1924 passing record: thirty-three attempts, twenty-five completions, for an average of .788, a fabulous percentage I have never seen or heard expressly recognized in pertinent commentary.

Off field I once had painful occasion to regret Stuhldreher's pregame optimism. Notre Dame had been upset by Nebraska in 1922. The Rockneites were en route in 1923 to a perfect season and championship acclaim again. They had only to defeat Nebraska and the title was assured. At Hullie & Mike's you had to give eighteen points in order to get a bet down. I caught Stuhly at the railroad station in time to be infected by his manifest optimism. Back at Hullie & Mike's I laid down a week's salary, giving the eighteen points on the board. In 1924 it would be Notre Dame 34, Nebraska 6. In 1923 the score was

off tackle I witnessed. Nonetheless, the way he slammed into a wall of opposition persuaded me that *I* had just spotted the greatest football Miller since the immortal Red, and so reported to Tedo (Ray) Miller of my own generation.

The Horseman I bore least acquaintance with, Elmer Layden, would designate me as one of his assistants when he became athletic director and head coach in the 1930s. Elmer was the scoring star when the Four Horsemen and Seven Mules crowned their national championship with a sensational victory in the 1925 Rose Bowl. Stanford's Pop Warner could point out that his Cardinal and White dom-

The great Miller brothers. At left, Don (1922-24), Gerry (1922-24), Walter (1915-19), Ray (1911-12), and at the right, Harry "Red" Miller (1906-09).

Cheyenne, Wyoming, after the 1925 Rose Bowl victory in Pasadena.

1929 national champs. Top row, from left, Carideo, Brill, Mullins, Elder. Front row, from left, Conley, Donoghue, Law (captain), Moynihan, Cannon, Twomey, Caldrick.

Nebraska 14, Notre Dame 7. That made the Cornhuskers thirty-two points better than I had been influenced to calculate.

But it appeared almost worthwhile when I heard about Rock's Monday morning session with his favorite downtown coach, big Bod Singler, East side butcher and son of a butcher. Big Ed Weir, Cornhusker tackle, had played havoc with the Notre Dame offense. Without naming Weir the butcher's boy bearded the Notre Dame coach in his office the Monday-morning-after with a scathing exposition of how to keep opposing tackles out of the sacred precinct of a prima donna backfield. Rock's temper appropriately crackled. He challenged his baiter to take the stance of a defensive tackle. Bulbous Bob struck an awkward pose. "You look like an overstuffed scarecrow stuck on a crooked stick," Rock jeered. Big Bob countered, "You shouldn't laugh, Rock. That's the way Weir lined up last Saturday." Wherewith and whereupon exit baiter Bob without ado, leaving building contractor Tom Hickey, a Rockne buddy, to observe and report the backlash. For a moment or two, Tom once related to me, Rock spit shredded unsmoked cigar tobacco in frustration—then relaxed with the famous smile that lighted up his broad features with indescribable charm. He looked forward, of course, to his next tour de force with Big Bob. If Bob hadn't shown up soon again at Notre Dame Rock would drop off at the east side

Singler shop enroute downtown.

Recognizing that the pressure got to Rock in the mid-20s, one might understandably identify that occasion with the 1928 season (5—4—0) unless authentically aware that he passed a crisis in earlier years that conditioned him to weather such a near-losing record. Adversity of the 1928 season converted it into the most dramatized interlude in Rockne's career, climaxing in the "Win one for the Gipper" tradition. It was also the curtain-raiser, of course, to successive national championships, in 1929 and 1930, both the subject of many-angled historical examination. For me the negative distinction of the Carnegie Tech game on Cartier Field in 1928 (7—27), as Notre Dame's first home defeat since 1905, had been esthetically eased by the superb passing spectacle staged by Carnegie's Howard Harpster.

I watched a 1927 game (ND 7, Southern Cal 6) in Soldier Field with opera glasses, so remote was my seat from the action. The generality of my recall of these games reflects, I think, the relative unspectacularity of even brilliantly played games of that era because the rules were defense-oriented. Notre Dame played all its games on the road in 1929. The rich, hardy turf of the Cartier Field gridiron had been transplanted to the site of the Notre Dame Stadium, then under construction. Wisconsin, Drake, and Southern California were played at Chicago's Soldier

Frank Carideo, All-American 1929-30.

Jack Cannon, All-American 1929.

Field. I retain vivid images of the Southern California game in Chicago. I still can visualize All-American guard Jack Cannon racing down under kickoffs bare-headed. (Helmets thereafter became required game equipment.) Then there was left-tackle Ted Twomey, defending his area (and Jack's too) like a lion rampant.

There was a pass play that remains in my memory. The passer was left-half Jack Elder, and the receiver, right-end Tom Conley. There was an unconventionality in the execution of that long, long pass in Soldier Field, down and out, that cinched a 13–12 Notre Dame margin. At the time, I was sensitive to Jack's limitations as a passer and Tom's shortage of breakaway speed. It was only in delayed perspective that I was able to appreciate the expedience that led to

that historic touchdown. First of all, Jack never did sight his prescribed receiver. Tom Conley was a decoy. Jack began to fade as Tom faked this way and that, ever deeper on a staggered course. Presently, in desperation, Jack turned his burden loose with all his strength, hoping for the best. The best was to find Tom Conley so far down field that he was able to make the catch and amble the rest of the way to the winning touchdown.

The 1929 ramblers were 8-0 when they closed the season with Army on a cold day in the Yankee Stadium. The Cadets had a ball in the air tagged TD until Jack Elder picked it off on his 4-yard line and sprinted ninety-six yards to a touchdown which, with point-after, weathered two quarters and tamped down Rock's second perfect season: this time during a rel-

ative stage of absentia imposed by a disabling case of phlebitis, compelling his representation on the field by assistant coach Tom Lieb.

It can be said that the 1929 season served as a kind of precursor to Rock's last seasonal triumph (10–0) in 1930, when he reappeared on the practice field. I had occasion to contact him on old Cartier Field early that fall. He had dismissed the squad, except for some backfield combinations. The scene was touched with a kind of unreality for me because Rock was dressed in civilian attire. He seemed markedly less animated than I recalled from other occasions as player and ex-player. It may have been that his catapulting fame was beginning to grip him.

While taking in the opening game in the brand-new Notre Dame Stadium, I found myself beguiled and

more than a tinge depressed (I do confess) by the Southern Methodist Mustangs: their wide-open attack (featured by lateral as well as forward passes) made Notre Dame look relatively stodgy though eventually victorious by 20–14. Navy's distinction as participant in the official dedication of the Stadium in the second game was dimmed by a 25–2 rebuff on the beautiful turf drafted from Cartier Field. Carnegie Tech, Pitt, and Indiana were disposed of almost conventionally. The big rout of the season was a 60–20 defeat of Pennsylvania in Philadelphia, an action some identified as *Marty Brill's Revenge.* Philadelphia was Marty Brill's homestead. He had won a football letter at Penn in 1927, but relatives and friends persuaded him to transfer to Notre Dame where his talents would be more justly ex-

1930 national champs. Rockne, left; Hunk Anderson, left, top row.

Right tackle Cliff Brasey (facing camera) about 1930.

Tommy Yarr, Bert Metzger, "Hunk" Anderson, Frank Carideo, "Moon" Mullins, 1930.

ploited, in their opinion. In his 1930 homecoming on Franklin Field Marty ran wild for Notre Dame touchdowns.

I was in the sellout Northwestern crowd in Evanston that saw left-halfback Marchmont Schwartz demonstrate the efficacy of our tried and true No. 51 play to the tune of 14–0. Marchie made five out of seven All-America teams in 1930. Quarterback Frank Carideo's all-around skills, often most dramatically demonstrated with his toe, made him unanimous choice for the second straight year. Bert Metzger, Notre Dame's all-time "watch-charm guard" (5'9", 149 pounds) was picked No. 1 by the most prestigious experts, representing the AP and UP; Bert rated selection across the board.

Rain and snow prevailed the afternoon of the 1930 Army game at Chicago's Soldier Field. Spending the first half in a cab enroute from the Loop, I was in the stand throughout the second-half buildup to the final result in a series of off-tackle trials which left-half-back Schwartz crowned with the "perfect play," a fifty-four-yard touchdown run. Kicker Carideo made it 7–0. Time remained for Army to block a Carideo punt deep in Notre Dame territory and cover it in the end zone for a touchdown. A muddy field and a fierce Notre Dame rush against attempt for the point-after preserved a Notre Dame one-point margin of victory.

At this stage Notre Dame approached the season's finale at Southern Cal with a 9–0 game record and statistics of 268 points to 66. The Trojans' game record was 8–1 but statistically they swamped Notre Dame with 382 points to opponents' 66. Rock resorted to leger-demain during the Irish stopover in Tucson, Arizona, anticipative of a pre-game visit by Los Angeles football writers, if not some scouts. His pawns were right half Bucky O'Connor (5'9", 175 pounds) and third-string fullback Dan Hanley (6'2", 190 pounds). No. 1 fullback Moon Mullins was disabled. No. 2 fullback Joe Savoldi was not available. O'Connor, swift and shifty, was slated to play fullback against Southern Cal. Dan Hanley, less fleet and evasive, was the decoy. At various stops enroute to Tucson O'Connor was rehearsed in his new role. What observers from Los Angeles observed in Tucson workouts was Hanley running at full-back wearing O'Connor's number. Well . . . Bucky broke the game wide open with two long touch-down runs. Finale, 27–0, tanta-mount to a second national championship in a row. (This is the way I understood the plot worked; I owe more recent confirmation to Hunk Anderson's book with Emil Klosinski: *Notre Dame, Chicago Bears and "Hunk"*).

The Rocknes had a son in a school near Kansas City in the late winter of 1931. They were visiting him when I chanced to be in Kansas City as press agent for the Chicago entry in the American Hockey League. Rock came into

our dressing room after the game with Kansas City. Again I had the feeling that some of the zest had gone out of it all for him. About a month later I was visiting an old South Bend friend and teammate in Chicago when Rock's fatal plane crash was announced over the radio. As reality superseded my shocked incredulity I was doubly grieved by the thought that I had had so much to clear up about our relationship, and would have used the opportunity at Kansas City had he been there alone.

In the fall of 1933—never mind how I had been employed, or not employed, at the time of Knute Rockne's tragic plane crash March 31, 1931, or since, for that matter—I found myself back in a newspaper city room as sports editor of the *South Bend News-Times*. That was my position at the close of the 1933 season when Notre Dame replaced Jesse Harper as athletic director and Hunk Anderson as head coach with Elmer Layden in both roles. End coach Tom Conley was retained. Acquired was Joe Boland, mid-20s tackle, replacing Nordy Hoffman. The post vacated by Hunk's backfield assistant, Marchy Schwartz, remained one kind of question mark and became another on a day in early 1934 when Elmer Layden picked sports editor Chet Grant as a link with pre-Rockne Notre Dame football. Perhaps I had impressed him favorably with a talk on field general-ship Rock had invited me to make to the 1921 freshmen in the spring of 1922. A good friend of mine with

ROCKNE ENROUTE TO LOS ANGELES

Coach in Chicago; Says Irish Weaker than In 1930.

By United Press:
CHICAGO, March 31.—Knute Rockne made a brief stopover here Monday en route to Los Angeles for a conference regarding his motion picture contract.

Rockne said the 1931 Notre Dame football team would not be as strong as the 1930 undefeated team.

"The squad looked all right," said Rockne, "but it's not as good as last year's. I may have to teach it the Warner system."

While here Rockne made a sales talk record to be used at conferences of salesmen for the Studebaker company with which he now is associated.

First game in the new Stadium, 1930.

Knute Rockne's funeral. His son, Bill Rockne, and daughter Jean, are at the right. His widow, face obscured by her hat, is being supported by Bill. Frank Carideo is at extreme left; Larry "Moon" Mullins stands to the right of Jean Rockne.

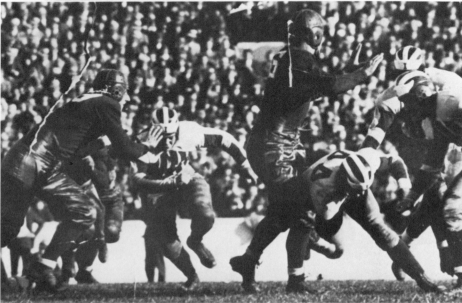

Jesse Harper, athletic director, 1931-33; and Hunk Anderson, head coach, 1931-33.

J. J. Kurth and "Moose" Krause.

Action circa 1933. ND versus Southern Cal. Moose Krause at left; Tom (Kitty) Gorman, co-captain, in center of photo.

Jesse Harper in later life. He was head coach and athletic director from 1913 to 1917; and athletic director again in the 1930s.

Quick kick against Army, 1934. Bill Shakespeare punting. Defending Shakespeare is fullback Don Elser.

NOTRE DAME'S "QUICK KICK" AGAINST ARMY, 1934

A tense moment for Coach Elmer Layden, smoking cigaret.

Left, Bill Shakespeare, LH, 1933-35; center Andy Pilney, LH, 1933-35; right, Wayne Millner.

some football savvy, a subway alumnus, understandably exclaimed, "What the hell was Elmer thinking of?" I appreciated that friend's concern as I undertook to compose a pertinent press release for circulation by Notre Dame sports publicity director Joe Petritz.

For the next seven years I coached, scouted and recruited, collaborated with the head coach in two articles for the *Saturday Evening Post* and ghosted during the last three seasons three syndicated articles weekly. Meantime we'd had our Saturday afternoon ins and outs, ups and downs, in a pattern I appreciate more in retrospect than at the time. The Victory-over-All esprit seemed to have been diluted by an it's-all-right-if-you-win-over-all-but-you-don't-have-to administrative attitude.

It is not my intention here to delve into the respective essences of the Anderson and Layden head-coaching tenures at Notre Dame. Both were victims of pressures from within and without, aggravated by expectations good and bad, multiplied in Elmer's case by his investiture as athletic director. In his book, Anderson tells all, in collaboration with Emil Klosinski. **Elmer Layden, in his book** (*It Was a Different Game*) with Ed Snyder, is faithful to his commitment to the promotion of goodwill.

As the only survivor of the Layden coaching personnel (which included Tom Conley, Joe Boland, John O'Brien, Joe Benda, and Bill Cerney), as worshipper of Notre Dame football heroes until I finished high school, as a downtown fellow athlete, as a Notre Dame football player, coach, scout, recruiter, and demi-historian who authored a book about Notre Dame football before Rockne, and a fictional takeoff (*Fumblestumble Sandy*) on Notre Dame's 1935 *Game of the Century* published in book form: from all these sundry perspectives combined I might round off this essay with a prejudiced evaluation of the Layden coaching experience based on the proposition that his winning percentage of .783 (47 won, 13 lost, 3 tied) could well have been .933 (58 won, 5 lost, 0 tied), transcending all recorded percentages based on the records of more than two seasons. But herewith I plan to let Rock's .897 record stand unchallenged and confine my testament to the explication of certain situations in which facts and factors as I encountered them were not always as they might have appeared to others (say I!). If this proce-

dure, however, eventuates into a replay of certain incidents, so be it.

For immediate example of this policy, take our opener with Texas in 1934, an unregistered "upset" by all accounts if our scout, Tom Conley, were alive to testify. We lost by the skinny margin of 7–6. In his book head *football coach* Layden intimates that *athletic director* Layden was responsible for the liberal substitution of untried personnel in the name of sportsmanship or something. This was the first sacrifice on the altar of athletic de-emphasis. Accorded a reasonable portion of game-time, halfback Andy Pilney could have reversed a 6–10 decision with Navy, as suggested by his part in the 14–0 overturn of the Middies in 1935.

We were 5–0 when we played Ohio State at Columbus November 2, 1935, in the *Game of the Century.* Our 18–13 victory—glorified by the fact that we entered the last quarter 0–13 underdogs—is recorded as an upset in our own publications. I, along with some fellow scouts, accorded Notre Dame a two-touchdown margin of superiority at game-time—a prognosis in my case rooted in the assumption that our second-string linemen had earned in the Navy game a major role against the Buckeyes, plus the condition that second-string Andy Pilney was going to be accorded the first-string time to capitalize on his unplumbed potential. We spotted the Bucks their thirteen points in the first half with Pilney

and the No. 2 line on the bench. In a final brilliant run, setting up a Shakespeare to Millner victory TD, Pilney was done in for the season by a mass of out-of-bounds tacklers.

I think Shakespeare was already compromising with a troublesome ankle when we went into the Northwestern game 6–0 and crossed the Purple goal-line the first two times we possessed the ball. A penalty robbed us of the second touchdown for a holding violation, later refuted by our motion pictures. There ensued a let-down and a genuine 7–14 upset, followed the next Saturday by an unsetting 6–6 tie with an Army we should have beaten *without* Pilney or a wholly healthy Shakespeare. Consolation prize for 1935 was a spirited 20–13 win over Southern Cal, featuring quarterback Wally Fromhart on the offense.

The season of 1936 opened with victories less decisive than we anticipated, respectively over Carnegie Tech, Washington, and Wisconsin. Pittsburgh was next. In 1935 we had squeezed through with a 9–6 edge over Pitt's Panthers, thanks defensively to a brilliant display of delay tactics downfield to thwart a ball-carrier with an escort of two blockers, again featuring Wally Fromhart. In 1936 we were more decisive underdogs against Pitt, spearheaded by a great sophomore who would be a 1937-38 All-American; namely, Marshall Goldberg.

Having scouted the Panthers I knew we had to play over our heads and to do that we had to become profoundly aroused. I was invited to address a student pep rally outside St. Joseph's Hall the night before we would take off to Pittsburgh. I had occasion to assume there would be players among those present when I put my all into a fight, fight, fight theme. Their absence confirmed my apprehension that they did not appreciate what they were going up against. By predictable coincidence the Panthers rudely blasted us that weekend, 26–0. Slim six-foot halfback Bob Wilke appeared in peril of being broken into pieces! By my suggestion head-coach Layden substituted sturdier Jack McCarthy. Later it became apparent that we had underestimated Bob's wiry durability.

After the Pitt debacle we came back at home with a 7–2 brush over Ohio State at Notre Dame; then collapsed into an alarming 0–3 concession to Navy at Baltimore. First assistant coach Joe Boland, stationed in the press box as observer and advisor, was so upset he influenced the induction into our playbank of a system of spinner plays proposed, I understood, by Johnny (One-Play) O'Brien, who had succeeded Tom Conley as end coach. I retained confidence in our standard T, box and punt formations if utilized more imaginatively and aggressively. Nevertheless I welcomed the spin stuff after being indoctrinated in its function and exe-

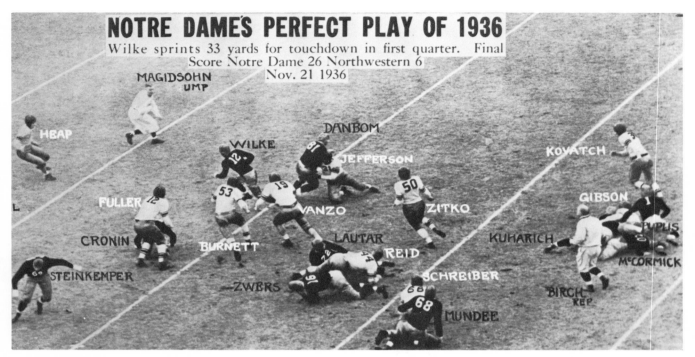

NOTRE DAME'S PERFECT PLAY OF 1936
Wilke sprints 33 yards for touchdown in first quarter. Final Score Notre Dame 26 Northwestern 6 Nov. 21 1936

Actor Pat O'Brien, and Coach Elmer Layden, and ND players doing a film approximately 1939.

Ed Beinor, All-American 1936-38.

cution. The Army was in for a shock the following Saturday when we used the new spinoff to flummox the Cadets, 20—6.

Next on our schedule was Northwestern, whose undefeated status already had clinched the Western Conference title. Prior to the game I was contacted by a certain downtown coach, a respected lawyer and substantial citizen. D. S. contacted me because I was the only one he knew on the coaching staff. He had a trick play up his sleeve for us, capitalizing on our endpunter Joe O'Neill's practice of laying his headgear on the ground when he punted. The squad was hot; but not too hot. We were persuaded that Northwestern hadn't

caught on to our man-in-motion innovation. We had a tackle-trap play we hadn't disclosed yet. It was part of our strategy to maintain a low profile all week. I was personally on the spot: I had assured D.S. we would work on his worthy proposal and give him a report, which turned out to be the game itself. Twice we let the opposing tackle through to be sideswiped by guard and quarterback as Bob Wilke executed a sharp cutback and picked up a convoy of blockers while weaving his way to two touchdowns from Northwestern's 40. There is a picture of one of these plays in which every Wilke teammate is a blocker. The score was 26—0 going into a fourth quarter

which Elmer Layden flooded with substitutes down to the fourth A-squad team who allowed the Wildcats 6 gratuitous points.

Enroute to close the 1936 season in the Los Angeles Coliseum with Southern Cal, we stopped as usual in Tucson, Arizona. Watching us run through signals on the Wildcats' campus, Arizona U. coach Tex Oliver confessed that he couldn't keep tab of the ball in our spin series, the three-option sequence. Southern Cal had the same experience that weekend. Interspersed with Bob Wilke cutbacks, our man-in-motion tactics garnered eighteen first downs and thirteen points. The Trojans matched us with two tainted touch-

downs. Inadvertently, I like to assume, but literally, a game official ran interference for a Trojan pass-interceptor from deep in Trojan territory all the way to one Trojan touchdown. On fourth down around our 40-yard line a Trojan back *crawled* to a first down (as indisputably registered in our game film), enabling Troy to convert that illegal break into a second touchdown, and the one and only Notre Dame tie in seven years I could endure with a measure of grace as partisan scout and coach.

We opened a weird 1937 season with an unimpressive margin over Drake (21–0). Then we were tied 0–0 by Illinois in what amounted to *reductio ad absurdum*. Ditto 9–7 in

favor of Carnegie Tech. Then Navy 9–7, a fantasy of black and white played in a snowstorm. Then we upset Minnesota 7–6 and lost to Pittsburgh 6–21. We beat Army (rain), 7–0, and Northwestern 7–0, and Southern California, 13–6. If I hadn't privately influenced Quarterback Andy Puplis to capitalize on his open-field running skills from punt formation and in punt returns (as demonstrated against Minnesota, Northwestern, and Southern Cal), we might have wound up 3–5–1.

The 1938 season began well. By the week of October 29 we were 4–0, looking forward to the Army game in Yankee Stadium. Brushing up my recall of this occasion

I referred to *The Big Game* (the Notre Dame-Army series, 1913-1947) and came upon the following reminder of that critical event in our closest bid for a national championship, authored by Jim Beach: "Notre Dame was worried after hearing a lot of talk around New York about Army power. Chet Grant, the backfield coach, left the Westchester Country Club, where the team was billeted Friday evening, and spent the night in town since he planned on going to Philadelphia the next day to scout Navy. But Saturday morning he phoned Layden and told him he thought he'd better stay over for the game in Yankee Stadium that afternoon."

As I will exemplify down the line the author rhetorizes in the following vein: "Chet Grant took Steve Sitko, the Rambler quarterback, aside in the dressing room and cautioned him about sticking to formula field generalship. He told him to call a few early down passes, because it was reasonable that Army expected him to pull his punches as he had in the past."

The score is 7–0, Army, going into the third quarter. We have the ball about midfield, first down. A ground play fails to gain. Jim Beach records: "Army is playing for another shot along the ground—and Sitko remembers Chet Grant's instructions before the game: 'Don't stick to formula on calling plays.'" That isn't the way it went, Jim!

First of all, I didn't say anything

to Sitko about anything until the end of the first half. Bill Cerney and I had scouted Army. We'd seen the Cadets run up the score on inferior opponents, who in turn were able to pass almost at will against the Army's relatively short defensive backs. Joe Boland, I knew, would be reeling off a score of plays, most of which we'd never get around to using. To spare Steve any confusion attending an optional selection I took him aside and said, "Steve—I don't give a damn what anybody else tells you—I'm telling you to start the second half with a first down pass!" It was still out of our pattern for him to cut loose a long one on *second* down. It was short, but there still was time for Earl Brown to slow down and retrieve for a touchdown and six points. It was clear enough then that we might pass on any down.

It isn't long before halfback Benny Sheridan, an all-time open-field runner, cuts back over the Army right guard on a spin-and-keeper from about the Army 30-yard line and maneuvers his way with speed and grace to the goal area, and sneaks over on the next play to make the score Notre Dame, 12–7. Time is running out when fullback Joe Thesing breaks through the right defensive side and cuts right. I was intrigued by Jim Beach's account of Thesing's run: ". . . Saggau spins, slapping the ball in Thesing's mid-section. The fullback lowers his head and the rested linemen lower the boom.

Joe is tagged as he plows inside left tackle [Jim means *right* defensive tackle] but he shakes the Soldier off and cuts to his right. A backer-up dives at him and is left in a dazed condition by a stunning smack from an upswung thigh. A third Army man attempts to lurch in under a stiff-arm and finds himself on the seat of his pants at the 40 near the sideline. Thesing pounds on toward the goal with 'Huey' Long the only obstacle to a touchdown by the classiest runner on the field. Long throws himself at the target at the 1-yard line —but it's another six-pointer for Notre Dame!"

This time the point-after made it 19–7 just before the final gun.

Minnesota was Western Conference champion when Andy Puplis' running upset the Gophers in 1937. We took them over again in 1938, 19–0. Coach Bernie said we were "lucky." It took more than Irish luck to score on a long pass by Saggau and a weaving seventy-yard run by halfback Lou Zontini off a spinner. The following Saturday we edged out Northwestern 9–7 and were so favorably rated that Professor Frank Dickinson of Illinois awarded us a "Rockne Memorial Trophy" before we closed our season with Southern California in Los Angeles.

In my book, we lost our ninth game in 1938 at Tucson. Wintry weather had confined football workouts for a week to the Big Gym. In my retrospective view we began losing to Southern Cal the

first day under Tucson's bright blue sky, relieved by snowwhite clouds. The players were jumping with ginger. Presently one player after another sat down and pulled off his shoes. The tawny grass turf of the practice field was deceivingly soft to the eye. Underneath the ground was tough. The players' feet were killing them because, for some reason I choose not to pinpoint, they were working out in long-cleated game shoes. Hindsight would dictate calling off that day's program. Instead we recessed to change to practice shoes, an anticlimactic gesture devastatingly depressive as it transpired.

If there was one member of the squad immune to this spiritual letdown it was Benny Sheridan, one of the most gifted ball carriers in Notre Dame football history. On the second day of practice during a pass-defense drill Benny was benched by an ankle sprain. Most of the first half Saturday neither side had seriously threatened the other's goal. With about two minutes to go we had the ball on about our 45-yard line on fourth down, six, with triple-threat Bob Saggau back in punt formation. I was surprised but not displeased when Bob began to run. He was fast enough to go the whole way if the Trojans were as surprised as I was. But in an evasive maneuver he stepped out of bounds just short of a first down. Southern Cal took over and on second down scored with a pass to the left end, down and across. I privately condoned our departure

from orthodoxy. The second half drably justified my support of the expediency of the first-half gamble when we failed dismally to get going and the "underdog" Trojans padded their lead with a second touchdown. Final, 13–0. Quarterback Steve Sitko was a goat without guilt in this situation. Head coach Layden had used a time-out to circumvent the rule against communication by an incoming substitute (except another quarterback) until one play had been run. Trainer Scrapiron Young served as messenger. Elmer disclosed to me later that he'd planned to clear quarterback Sitko publicly of the stigma attached to the gamble that backfired, but he had been dissuaded from making this concession to ethics by another quarterback, Knute Rockne's old teammate Gus Dorais, then coaching at the University of Detroit.

The championship at stake in our game with Southern Cal had attracted Gus to Los Angeles. He pointed out to Elmer the risk of having a unique evasion of the code mistaken as an example of strategic *policy*. Gus was reminded of what happened to him when asked how Rockne would have adjusted to certain posthumous changes in the football rules trenchantly favoring the offense. Rock would have done anything he considered appropriate to keep ahead of his contemporaries, Gus had assured a newspaper interviewer. Presently he began to receive voluminous hate messages from real and syn-

thetic Notre Dame alumni charging him with veritable slander of their hero. These outraged partisans obviously had read only as far as a headline that read: ROCKNE OUTMODED TODAY, DORAIS SAYS. "Football coaches," Coach Dorais reminded Coach Layden, "take enough abuse without volunteering for it."

In 1969, there was published a book, of which the jacket bears the following intimations of the content:

IT WAS A
DIFFERENT GAME

Elmer Layden with Ed Snyder

A Nostalgic Picture of a
Bygone Era, By One of the
Four Horsemen of Notre Dame

This book should be in every Notre Dame football follower's library. I could take issue with what I deem to be personal and historical misrepresentations, some if not all attributive to collaborative authorship. But in general I've been impressed not only by this book's readability but also by its overall authenticity. Whenever the collaborative text appears to conflict with my recollections I find it incumbent not to hold author and collaborator wholly responsible. Rather, I tend to assume that the classical butler of literature and drama might have had a hand in it. It irked me when I first read this book to find myself misrepresented as presuming to teach Andy Pil-

The All-America arbiters of the 30s. From left, Elmer Layden, Christy Walsh, Pop Warner of Stanford, Howard Jones of Southern Cal, and Frank Thomas, head coach at Alabama.

On the set of Fox's "Good News." At right, Johnny (one-play) O'Brien, end coach; the film's director (unidentified);

Loretta Young; author Chet Grant, backfield coach; Slim Summerfield, and Tyrone Power.

1936 coaches. Front, left, Elmer Layden, head coach, with player Bill Smith, captain-elect. Back row, Chet Grant, backfield coach; Bill Cerney, B-Squad coach; Joe Boland, line coach; and Johnny O'Brien.

ney, one of Notre Dame's greatest naturals at halfback, how "to catch a punt on the run." There are other misleading implications that the hero of the 1935 Ohio State game had been "brought along" to that point by his coaches. Actually, Pilney had been held back because we had another excellent back in Bill Shakespeare whose super-punting cut more ice with head-coach Layden than with assistant-coach

Grant. I had first seen Andy Pilney in scrimmage action in 1933 prior to the opening of the season. By whimsical and fortuitous chance I was back with the *South Bend News-Times* as a sports reporter, presently to be advanced to the editorship. I saw Andy Pilney run once that fateful afternoon. My hands trembled with excitement when I sat down to my mill to indite a prose paean to the occasion.

In Hollywood, doing The Spirit of Notre Dame, *are, from left, Elmer Layden, Adam Walsh, Frank Carideo, Jim Thorpe, Harry Stuhldreher, Don Miller, and Jim Crowley.*

Publicity for Warner Brothers' Knute Rockne, All-American. *With Kate Smith are, from left, Steve Juzwik, Bob Hargrave, Milt Piepul, and Bob Saggau.*

The following paragraph exemplifies prosaically the exalted emotions of my reaction to the spectacle of Andy Pilney cutting back off tackle: "I didn't expect to find the Pilney I'd heard about. As he functioned in Saturday's practice he is the greatest compound of compact power and co-ordination Notre Dame has ever seen. He is dynamite under perfect control. Never have *I* seen such a straight-arm on Cartier Field: greater than Red Miller's, greater than Cofall's. Swift, precise as a piston rod, ruthless as a mule's kick. He sidesteps, crosses over, pivots, fights his way with the sure expertness of a master boxer, with consummate skill uniting grace with terrible strength."

That Andy would complement in the air this genius on the ground I had yet to witness. It has been both illuminating and gratifying to chance in my muddled files on the clipping of an article appearing in the *News-Times* after the 1935 "Game of the Century" with Ohio State, under the heading of CALLING THE TURN and subheading *What Sports Editor Chet Grant*

Wrote in 1933 about Backfield Coach Chet Grant's Pilney. In my view, head coach Layden had tended to over-react negatively to Andy's fumbles and stumbles for which, in my judgment, Andy was bound to compensate, and then some, given the time and call. The Ohio State game of 1935 had provided the ultimate example. In his book Elmer Layden assigned a chapter to this event in which he paradoxically renders graphic all-out tribute to Pilney's spectacular running and passing, a phenomenon it was my privilege to view on the spot from the players' bench and review many times on the game-movie screen.

Another source of faulty witness in the case of Andy Pilney is titled *With Rockne at Notre Dame*, ostensibly authored by Gene (Scrapiron) Young whom I knew as trainer under Elmer Layden. My personal relations with Scrap were invariably cordial. I hope his testament can be charged against a literary ghost if not the butler, with particular reference to the absurd representation that backfield coach Chet Grant "went so far as to require that Andy Pilney carry a football wherever he went," as a recommended cure for alleged fumbleitis. Both coach and trainer pass over the fact that in this last game, against Ohio State, Andy Pilney's super-performance was punctuated with his conventional one stumble and one fumble.

Since we had grounded Northwestern's championship balloon in 1936 (26–6) the Wildcats had cramped our victories to respective margins of 7–0 and 9–7. In 1939 they stymied us repeatedly in unfavorable field position. Our last and best break found us on their 40, first down, fourth quarter. With five minutes to go we capitalized on a pre-charted series of intricately timed spin plays, perfectly integrated and executed by what I recall as the sterling combination of quarterback Steve Sitko, left-half Ben Sheridan, right-half Steve Juzwik, and fullback Joe Thesing, all fast, shifty, and potentially explosive. With 3:30 left on the scoreboard we squeezed through with a climactically earned 7–0 decision.

Fielding in 1939 its best team since 1933, however, Southern Cal (6–0–2), spearheaded by a dramatically potent back named Lansdell, outplayed a first-rate Layden team (20–12): it was the first time in six seasons. In my diversified view of the caliber of our competition, this game was a credit to the series, without reconciling me to the defeat! Nor was I comforted by the fact that the 1939 Iowa coach had been a Notre Dame teammate in 1921 and the captain of that team. In any case, Eddie Anderson's natural satisfaction by this upset of his alma mater should have been qualified by his awareness that our Benny Sheridan, after sitting out the whole game even unto the last play, had changed back from sneakers to cleats and come within a half-step of breaking loose from punt formation into a long

touchdown run and last-moment Notre Dame victory!

In his book, Elmer Layden points out to his second guessers how in 1939 he was criticized for having played Harry Stevenson while Benny Sheridan virtually sat it out. This was the prelude to Elmer's statement that he was again the subject of criticism "the next year" when he went the whole way with Benny against Iowa and his critics thought he should have played Harry! There happens to be a factual flaw in this author-collaborator-butler projection, a non

sequitur. In 1940, "the next year," halfbacks Sheridan and Stevenson weren't around any more while Iowa short-changed us again, this time by 7–0.

Northwestern was overdue to beat us in 1940 on percentage and on its seasonal record (6–2–0). The Wildcats had held western champion Minnesota (9–0) to a 12–13 margin—and Michigan (7–1) (defeated only by champion Minnesota) by a margin of 13–20. Based on my scouting observation of Northwestern v. Michigan at Ann Arbor I might have rated it as an

upset if we had beaten the Wildcats on the following Saturday. As it was, we succumbed 20–0 and needed a 10–7 decision over Southern Cal in the season's finale in Los Angeles to wind up 7–2–0 again. From Elmer Layden's book (published in 1961) I would learn he was shocked some weeks after the turn of the year to be offered a one-year renewal of what had been a four-year contract. He resigned to accept a newly created role of commissioner of professional football. End-coach Benda returned to his prior coachship at St. John's University, Minnesota. Line coach Joe Boland lined up pro tem at Purdue as assistant to head coach Mal Elward, a Notre Dame end when Rockne was player. B-squad coach Bill Cerney (a Fifth Horseman) eventually went into sales promotion. I finished working on a manuscript for the *Saturday Evening Post* entitled *They All Coach at Wabash*. All were maintained on the monthly payroll until September, 1941.

The zenith of my seven coaching years with Elmer Layden, of course, was reached that afternoon in Columbus, Ohio, when Andy Pilney more than rewarded my never-waning faith in his triple genius. The nadir of my total football association under Elmer Layden at Notre Dame was reached about midway of our last season, 1940, when we defeated Army 7–0 in a game that should have been a relative walkaway as suggested by Army's 1940 record: 1–7–1, 54 points to opponents' 187. We scored

on a pass-interception in the first quarter which Steve Juzwik converted into a hard-earned eighty-four-yard touchdown run. This, with point-after, was it for all day, 7–0, despite the horrendous statistical inferiority of our side, specified as follows:

	Notre Dame	Army
First downs	4	15
Yards gained rushing (net)	69	167
Passes	8	19
Passes completed	1	6
Yards gained, passes	2	78
Passes intercepted by	4†	1
Punts	13	9
Average distance, punts*	44	38
Runback of punts	29	95
Fumbles	3	1
Loss of ball, fumbles	2	0
Penalties	5	1
Yards lost on penalties	65	15

*From lines of scrimmage
†Juzwik intercepted one and went for TD (84 yards)

Notre Dame's administrative leadership had undergone a significant change following the 1939 football season. The president, Father John F. O'Hara, had been "appointed bishop, as military delegate to the armed forces of the United States." His successor was Father J. Hugh O'Donnell, vice president, whom I'd known since he was a senior varsity football center and I an older freshman football candidate. Succeeding Father O'Donnell as vice president and chairman of the faculty board for athletic control was prefect of religion Father John J. Cavanaugh; I'd known him since my undergraduate days and much

more recently as a handball opponent. These adjustments of authority connoted a more realistic approach to football at Notre Dame.

Upon the team's return from New York I contacted Bob Hargrave, quarterback whom I had recruited. He said the Cadets were wild men. "Why didn't you pass!" That was my first challenge. The answer was both naive and convincingly enlightened. "They wouldn't let us!" Bob explained. Army was always super-physical whatever the score. But there seemed to be no precedent for the ferocious defense in 1940 even by a team destined to wind up with a

Action with Southern Cal, 1940. That's Milt Piepul with ball, Steve Juzwik on ground, foreground.

More action against Southern Cal, 1940. Bob Saggau carrying ball. Steve Juzwik, 19, background.

for all species and seasons of sport, varsity and intramural: he head-coached varsity football impeccably, with one exception—he didn't use enough forward passes, especially on early downs, according to backfield coach Grant. After signing as Notre Dame director and coach in December 1934, Elmer had wound up his connection with Duquesne University in the New Year's Festival of Palms at Miami, Florida. It was 0–0 at the half. Then Duquesne hit the air. Final score: Miami University 7, Duquesne 33. Except for our 1935 Ohio State spectacular, passing had not been integrated strategically or tactically with our ground game as I'd anticipated. Toward the close of our Notre Dame coaching association, more than just once Elmer and I were close to physical argumentation, without impairing our personal relations then or thereafter.

I think the last time we enjoyed a chat it was in the presence of a social drink to bear witness, following a Chicago Notre Dame Club affair. Out of context with whatever we'd been talking about, I like to recall, Elmer paused to reflect. "You know," he reflected, "if I had it to do over again I think I would use more passes."

1–7–1 season; that is, until I heard that at one of the pre-game parties Elmer had divulged to a select group that my scouting report had made him fearful of embarrassing the West Pointers because of their relatively small pass defenders. Right-guard Joe Weidner of Army had spent a year at Notre Dame, following his brother Fred, before going to West Point. Some years later he would return to Notre Dame as an instructor in the cadet military courses there. We recalled the 1940 game. One of Elmer Layden's confidants had passed the word to West Point. That was

enough to make crusaders of all concerned.

Elmer's book gives the impression that his resignation came as a shock to everybody concerned with Notre Dame football. Not all. I'd had an early hint in a chance meeting with Father Cavanaugh soon after the Army game of 1940, which he considered "a travesty of traditional Notre Dame football."

I didn't appreciate the singularity of the Army-Notre Dame game of 1940 until I read about it in Jim Beach's *The Great Game*. After the game was over, Notre Dame fullback and captain Milt Piepul,

benched most of this game with a bad leg, led the rest of the Notre Dame squad in autographing the game ball they had won conventionally on the scoreboard. Inscribing it "morally this is yours," they presented it to the Army captain, Will Gills, for submission to Harry "Dutch" Heffner, who had played in the 1939 Army game and was hospitalized with polio at the time of this most unpredictable event in a classic series going back to 1913: a testimonial to esprit de corps on a rampage.

As director of athletics at Notre Dame, Elmer Layden was a man

The Leahy Era, and Terry Brennan

Dave Condon

Leahy, in November, 1952.

"We accept the challenge of the appointment. Perhaps we can make in a small way a return on the tremendous debt we owe our alma mater . . . We know we never will be in a position to contribute as much to football as Knute Rockne. We will be most happy if we can come close to the wonderful record made by Elmer Layden."—Frank W. Leahy.

A new gridiron golden era dawned beneath the shadows of the Golden Dome as Frank W. Leahy, ND '31, appeared in the offices of the Rev. J. Hugh O'Donnell, Notre Dame's president and 1914-15 football letterman, to sign the contract officially making him successor to Elmer Layden. The man who was to be known as The Master had returned home less than ten years after receiving his diploma; less than ten years after Rock's fatal plane crash.

Frank Leahy was born in O'Neill, Nebraska, on Aug. 27, 1908. Later he lived in Roundup, Montana, before the family settled in the new railroad town of Winner, S.D., where Frank Sr. had homesteaded. The future ND coach learned his first football from brother Gene, who was starring at Creighton. Frank was left halfback and captain as a senior at Winner, which Coach Earl Walsh directed to an unbeaten season. Walsh, who had played for the 1919-20-21 Knute Rockne teams that won twenty-eight while losing only one, was impressed by the determined

young Leahy. Though some thought Leahy's dreams of playing for Notre Dame were grandiose for a frontier youth, Walsh encouraged him. Walsh also wrote Rock. Leahy was a reserve left tackle (shifted from center), behind Capt. Fred Miller and Jerry Ransavage, on the 1928 Rockne team that lost four games and had the skeptics suggesting the world had caught up with Rockne's football. Caught up? The 1929 and 1930 Irish elevens were national champions and Frank Leahy, now at right tackle, won two monograms. Leahy had his shot at the starting assignment in 1929, and though handicapped by injury to his right arm and elbow, saw his share of action. Through his life, Leahy was handicapped by physical woes, and he missed his entire senior year, though touted to be a regular, after injuring a knee in preseason practice. The injury influenced Frank's career—he now could study from the sidelines, picking up strategies from the ailing Rockne and Rock's shrewd assistants. He made the trip for the season windup at Southern California, and aggravated the knee injury in a freak bit of horseplay.

Rockne, scheduled for a checkup at the Mayo Clinic during the Christmas holidays, asked Leahy to accompany him to Rochester and have the medics examine the knee. They roomed together and Rock asked about the future plans of the winner from Winner. Leahy said he would like to coach—if he

could find a job. Rockne produced four letters asking him to recommend assistants for jobs and said: "Frank, take your pick."

"I'd like the Georgetown job," Leahy decided, finally. Georgetown was coached by Tommy Mills, who not only had been a Rockne assistant when freshman Leahy arrived on the campus, but had been brother Gene's coach at Creighton. So Frank coached the Georgetown interior line in 1931. Georgetown's foes included Michigan State, then directed by Jimmy Crowley, of Four Horsemen fame. Michigan State won and, after the season, Crowley—who knew coaching talent when he saw it—invited Leahy to join the staff at MSU. Come the end of the 1932 season, and Fordham was looking to replace Coach Frank Kavanaugh, the ill Iron Major. Fordham chose Crowley, who invited Leahy to come along. There Leahy developed Fordham's Seven Blocks of Granite line, which included Vince Lombardi. Years later, with Lombardi of Green Bay the toast of pro football coaching, many would attribute much of Lombardi's success to Leahy's disciplines. The two were much the same, each a man dedicated to winning, and each a rugged individualist. Once, at Fordham, Leahy and Lombardi exchanged words and settled it with a post-practice fist fight. Early in 1939, Boston College tabbed Leahy to succeed Head Coach Gloomy Gil Dobie.

Leahy's 1939 Boston College team lost only to Florida in the regular season and earned an invitation to meet Clemson in the Cotton Bowl. Clemson won, 6—3. In 1940 Leahy's B.C. Eagles were unbeaten and upset Tennessee in the Cotton Bowl. It was Frank Leahy's first unbeaten campaign (11—0) in big time coaching. Boston College offered a new long-term contract. Leahy signed after receiving verbal agreement that he would be free to leave if Notre Dame ever beckoned. The beckoning was immediate.

Layden had resigned to become commissioner of the National Football League. Notre Dame narrowed the list of potential successors to a pair of excellent alumni: Buck Shaw of Santa Clara, one of Rockne's first pupils, and young Frank Leahy, one of Rock's last. When Shaw asked that his name be withdrawn, the automatic choice was Leahy.

Leahy appeared before the student body in March, 1941, and introduced his assistants—Johnny Druze, Joe "Captain Bligh" McArdle, and a smiling Texan, Edward C. McKeever. Druze and McArdle had not attended Notre Dame, but McKeever had been a freshman there in Leahy's time before financial difficulties forced him to go to Texas Tech. Leahy had been impressed with McKeever's ideas on offense—particularly passing—at a coaching clinic, and they had developed mutual respect for each other. That respect even-

Angelo Bertelli, 1943 Heisman Trophy winner and All-American.

tually was to give Smiling Ed a stint as head coach at Notre Dame.

When the new staff sized up the talent left behind by Layden, they despaired because of lack of depth, and planned some changes. Bernie Crimmins, a fullback, was shifted to guard and became a 1941 All-American. Harry Wright, another fullback, became regular quarterback although he was to share duties with Bob Hargrave and, in 1942, would replace Crimmins at right guard. Wally Ziemba, a strong right tackle in 1940 behind 1941 Capt. Paul Lillis, was switched to center. Fred "Dippy" Evans went from left half to fullback, leaving the halfback job open to a talented freshman passer from West Springfield, Mass. Other veterans who were to carry heavy loads that first year included halfback Steve Juzwik and end Bob Dove, both All-American candidates; Jim Brutz, Bob Maddock, Lou Rymkus, George Murphy, John Kovatch, Matt Bolger, Bob McBride, and Creighton Miller.

Only 19,567 were in Notre Dame Stadium for the opener against Arizona and the unveiling of Angelo Bertelli, the Springfield Rifle, who subsequently became ND's first Heisman trophy winner. Arizona was stubborn until the intermission, and trailed only 12—7. Notre Dame's second-half assault provided a 38—7 victory. Bertelli, throwing from a special protective-brush blocking pocket perfected by Leahy, completed eleven of fourteen aerials for 145 yards. A 19—6 win over Indiana followed. The Irish went to Georgia Tech for a 20—0 decision, and that brought up Carnegie Tech, a long-time Notre Dame foe then de-emphasizing football. Campus jokes were that an interhall team would meet Carnegie's hapless eleven. Notre Dame found an inspired Carnegie in the battle ending the series, and squeezed out a 16—0 conquest when a 60—0 margin had been predicted. Bob Zuppke brought his last Illinois team to Notre Dame and was routed, 49—14, after the Irish became infuriated at what they considered unsportsmanlike play by an Illini stalwart.

With the running of Juzwik and Evans supplementing Bertelli's passing marksmanship, Notre Dame was 5—0 heading for the traditional Army game in Yankee Stadium. A rain had been pouring down for more than twenty hours as Notre Dame dressed, and Juzwik said to Bertelli: "I'm afraid you're not going to be much help today." Though the downpour had let up by intermission, the players thought they were competing in a rice paddy. Both lines played aggressively; Ziemba, Crimmins, and Captain Lillis the ND standouts. Notre Dame's closest penetration was to the Army 18 in the same second quarter that found the Cadets probing to the ND 11. With the clock running out, ND had first down on the Cadet 25. Juzwik gained five in two rushes. With time for only one more play, Evans lost five on a high pass from center. Army made five first downs in the 0—0 tie, Notre Dame one less. Hundreds of students greeted the team when it returned. One group carried a banner: "STILL UNDEFEATED." Undefeated, yes, but close calls were ahead.

Unbeaten Navy was confident of triumph in greeting Notre Dame in Baltimore. Notre Dame rose to the occasion, with standout play by Bertelli and Little Norm (Jack) Barry—son of Big Norm Barry, a Golden Dome immortal—pacing ND to a winning 20—13 thriller. It was even tougher next week at Northwestern's Dyche Stadium, though there were heroics galore in Notre Dame's 7—6 decision. Otto Graham plunged four yards for the Wildcats' touchdown. Dick Erdlitz's kick for the extra point was blocked by Ziemba, on a special play designed by Leahy, so the margin was Juswik's extra point following Bertelli's sixteen-yard touchdown pass to Bolger. Crimmins recovered a

fumble by Don Clawson, who had sparked Northwestern's 20—0 victory in 1940, to set up the ND touchdown. Northwestern tried to salvage the game in the fourth quarter, but Erdlitz missed a field goal shot from the 21. Yet the Cats furiously stopped Notre Dame at the NU 2 in the waning moments. Juzwik personally stopped two serious Wildcat thrusts, one with a goal-line interception, the other on a picturebook defensive maneuver: Northwestern's great Bill De Correvont broke loose in the second quarter and had three blockers in front of him with only Juzwik guarding the goal. Juzwik wove between the blockers and drove DeCorrevont out of bounds after a thirty-four-yard gain. Now only Southern California stood in the way of Notre Dame's first unbeaten season since 1930 and the Trojans were at full strength, for the first time all year, when they hit South Bend. It was the usual SC—ND classic.

The Trojans opened scoring after blocking Evans' quick kick at the ND 3. Ralph Heywood took a TD pass over Juzwik, but Ziemba blocked the extra-point attempt. The lead didn't stand long. Notre Dame began moving as soon as the Trojans punted out of bounds on the SC 32. Juzwik raced twenty-six yards to the 6. The touchdown came as Evans raced five yards when given the ball by Creighton Miller on a reverse. Juzwik's kick made it 7-6. Juzwik ran for the next ND score, set up by Evans'

fumble recovery. USC retaliated with a touchdown pass to Bill Bledsoe, and now Kovatch blocked the extra point preserving a 13—12 Notre Dame lead. The victory was assured with a fifty-three-yard Irish drive climaxed when Bertelli, passing from the SC 18, bulls-eyed to Evans, who scored behind George Murphy's key block. Juzwik again kicked the point, 20—12. The Trojans made a consolation touchdown and, fearing the aggressive ND line, tried to pass for a conversion. Bertelli—who completed thirteen of his twenty-one passes—batted down this aerial. Final: ND, 20; USC, 18. An unbeaten season at last, but the scoreless deadlock with Army was responsible for Notre Dame finishing third —behind Minnesota and Duke—in the final Associated Press rankings. Greater days were ahead. And Pearl Harbor was much closer.

Notre Dame students were serious, sober-minded, returning from the 1941 Christmas break. Life no longer was as simple or as carefree as before the sneak Japanese attacks plunged a poorly prepared United States into World War II. Some students had enlisted immediately after Pearl Harbor; hundreds upon hundreds were awaiting the call to service; a few had friends or relatives already killed or wounded in the hostilities. Soon the students would be doubling up in the residence halls to make other residences available for the

first influx of naval trainees to be sent to the campus. Eventually the dining halls would go cafeteria style. But the students were advised to try to carry on university life much as usual while they waited and prepared.

Leahy had been impressed with the dynamite potential of the Chicago Bears' T-formation from the first time he had watched the Monsters of the Midway. Prior to the 1941 season, Leahy had told the Rev. John J. Cavanaugh, then vice-president and top executive in the athletic administration, that though he respected all of Notre Dame's traditions and revered them, he wanted to abandon the storied Rockne shift that moved the offensive backs into a box. Leahy said that though successful with a man-in-motion at Boston College, he had much to learn about the T, and could not possibly install it for the 1941 campaign. But if Father Cavanaugh did not object, Notre Dame would attack from the T-formation in 1942. Given the go ahead, Leahy set out to master the intricacies of the T. He had long sessions with Coach George Halas of the Bears, and extracted what he could from the Bears' great T-quarterback, Sid Luckman. Leahy visited Maryland coach Clark Shaughnessy, who had created T-formation powerhouses at Stanford prior to the war. The quarterback, of course, was the key in successful execution, and Leahy was confident he had a candidate with the potential of becoming another Luckman, the best. Leahy's candidate was Angelo Bertelli.

Notre Dame's first T-party was no howling success. The Irish opened at Wisconsin and perhaps it was ominous that Bertelli missed train connections and did not arrive at Camp Randall Stadium until shortly before game hour. ND lost four of five fumbles. Final score was 7—7, not entirely embarrassing because Harry Stuhldreher's Badgers were to wind up Number Three nationally. Georgia Tech's visit to Notre Dame *was* embarrassing enough though the Engineer-Yellow Jackets were to finish the season rated Number Five, a niche ahead of the Irish. Tech, paced by Eddie Prokop and freshman Clint Castleberry, dealt Leahy his first defeat as Notre Dame coach, 13—6. The scoreless first half ended with Bertelli stifling a Tech threat by intercepting on the ND 2. Opening the third quarter, the Irish rolled to the Tech 10, where a Bertelli pitchout was intercepted. Jimmy Mello's fumble was grabbed by Tech on the Irish 28. Ralph Plaster plunged a foot for the touchdown on this Tech drive, and kicked the point. The end of the third period found Tech at the Notre Dame 24 and moving. Plaster missed conversion following Castleberry's TD aerial to Pat McHugh, leaving the Georgians' lead at 13—0. The Miller brothers, Creighton and Tom, sparked a seventy-three-yard march for No-

tre Dame's lone touchdown. Tom scored by sprinting fifteen yards. Bertelli's kick failed. Notre Dame's last-ditch threat was terminated on interception of Bertelli's attempted bomb. In mid-evening, an upperclassman found four of us sophomores crying at the Washington Hall movie. He looked, then said. "That's right, this is the first time you have seen Notre Dame lose." The next Saturday brought in Stanford, coached by Marchie Schwartz, ex-Rockne great. Leahy was in the Mayo clinic, so Ed McKeever directed Notre Dame. Bertelli completed fourteen of twenty passes, four going to Bob Dove, Paul Limont, George Murphy, and Bob Livingstone, for touchdowns in the 27—0 victory. Schwartz, desolately trudging to the dressing room, tipped his hat to the Notre Dame stands. The Irish grad was rewarded with an oceanic "He's a man! He's a Notre Dame man!" cheer.

Bernie Bierman's potent Iowa Pre-flight School Seahawks had whipped Kansas, Northwestern, Minnesota, and Michigan, by the time they arrived at Notre Dame. In the Rev. John O'Brien's religion class on game morning, soph tackle Ziggy Czarobski said: "We're not going to lose big, we're going to win big." The Irish won big, 28—0, over the favored service team. Leahy assistant McKeever again was in charge as Notre Dame posted one of its most magnificent victories ever; it was, up to that time, the most one-

sided defeat suffered by Bierman, who had wholesaled national championships at Minnesota.

The Irish marched past Illinois (21—14), Navy (9—0), as Leahy returned to the helm, and Army (13—0) to gird for its first game with Michigan since 1909. Fielding H. "Point A Minute" Yost, coach of the Wolverine team that lost to ND in 1909, was at Notre Dame for this renewal. So was Harry Miller, father of Creighton and Tom, and hero of the 1909 11—3 triumph. Also present were the governors of Indiana and Michigan. This was a natural!

Bertelli passed to Bob Dove, then added point, to propel Notre Dame in front, 7—0. Going into the second period it was 7—7, on Capt. George Ceithaml's sneak for a Wolverine TD. Michigan faked a field goal attempt, Don Robinson running for a touchdown. Jim Brieske failed the extra point, so Michigan had a 13—7 advantage. ND Capt. George Murphy recovered Tom Kuzma's fumble to touch off the drive leading to a Creighton Miller plunge for two and a touchdown. Bertelli's extra point sent the Irish into the intermission with a 14—13 advantage after they had held Michigan four downs inside the ND 4. No Irish eyes were smiling when a nineteen-point blitz gave Michigan a 32—14 lead after three periods. Creighton Miller, taking the ball on a Statue of Liberty play, made the third Notre Dame touchdown, but Bertelli missed point. A goal-line interception stopped the

final Irish attack, and Michigan headed home 32—30 victor. The loss of 1909 was avenged.

Notre Dame defeated Northwestern, 27—20, won the last duel with Southern California (13—0) until after the war, then headed to Chicago Soldier Field to conclude against the Great Lakes Bluejackets, who, like the Iowa Seahawks, were loaded with great college players. Great Lakes, following a shaky start, had won six consecutive games without yielding a point. The Bluejackets so completely dominated the first half that they should have run up more than their 13—0 lead. Were they—and 35,000 fans braving freezing weather—due for a surprise!

Bob Livingstone returned the third-quarter kickoff from goal to the Notre Dame 18. Bertelli faked to Livingstone and handed to Clatt, who smashed outside defensive left tackle, and, with picturebook blocking, was untouched on an

Leahy and his 1942 team.

eighty-two-yard touchdown romp. Bertelli missed the conversion. Great Lakes received and punted to Tom Miller at the Irish 32. Notre Dame immediately duplicated its scoring maneuver, but this time Creighton Miller carried on the play. Creighton cracked the right side of the Bluejacket line, reversed his field, and ran sixty-eight yards to score. John Creevey kicked the point to make the score 13–13, and that's the way it ended. The season: 7–2–2. Dove and Bertelli earned spots on some All-Americans. Wright received a second-team mention though he deserved more.

The championship season! Bolstered only slightly by some military transferees, the 1943 Irish began with decisions over Pittsburgh and Georgia Tech, 41–0 and 55–13, prior to invading Michigan with revenge in mind. The game drew 86,408, then a Michigan record. Creighton Miller ran sixty-six yards for a touchdown, Angelo Bertelli kicking point, to send the Irish off in front.

The Irish entered the third quarter with a 21–6 lead and were headed for more. In that elongated period (it took some while before officials noted the clock had stopped), Notre Dame added another fourteen points. Bertelli sneaked for one touchdown, passed to Miller for a second, and kicked both conversions. Michigan's consolation touchdown in the shortened last period was a last-play pass, Elroy Hirsch to Capt. Paul

White. Pregulman missed the conversion, Notre Dame winning 35—12.

The Irish scored routs against Wisconsin, 50—0, and Illinois, 47—0, before engaging Navy at Cleveland in the last game for the Marine-bound Angelo Bertelli. The Middies were stubborn in the first half. Julie Rykovich, the ex-Illini, took a twenty-four-yard pass from Bertelli, and streaked another twenty-five yards, for a ND touchdown as the first quarter was closing. Bertelli's kick was blocked. A seventeen-yard Bertelli pass clicked early in the second period, receiver Creighton Miller taking the ball the final thirty-five yards to the end zone. Bertelli added point, 13—0. After Hillis Hume intercepted a Bertelli pass at Navy's 48, the Middies eventually reached the goal on Hal Hamberg's twenty-nine yard aerial to Bill Barron. A poor center snap frustrated the conversion attempt. With Notre Dame leading, 13-6, Rykovich returned the third-quarter kickoff to the ND 31. Jim Mello broke loose for thirty-eight yards and Creighton Miller jaunted another twenty-three. Navy braced and eventually Notre Dame faced fourth down two yards from the end zone. Notre Dame attacked from the single-wing instead of the T, Bertelli passing to John Yonakor in touchdown land. Later in the period Mello ran forty yards after intercepting a Hamberg pass to pave the way for a fourth Irish TD and Bertelli's third extra point. Then Vic Kulbitski, a transfer from Minnesota, was aided by George Sullivan's block in scampering seventy-one yards before being stopped. Successive bolts by Rykovich and Lujack carried to Navy's 2, where Bertelli plunged for the final Notre Dame touchdown of his career.

With Lujack taking over the quarterback controls, Notre Dame moved on to New York to whip Army, 26—0. After three seasons, an Army team coached by Col. Earl "Red" Blaik still had not scored on any Notre Dame team directed by Frank Leahy. The Irish won at Northwestern, 25—6, leaving only the two strong service squads, Iowa Pre-Flight and Great Lakes. Leahy's warriors still were unbeaten after entertaining the Iowans, but it was close. The Seahawks were nothing but trouble.

The Iowans grabbed a 7—0 first quarter lead on Art Guepe's eight-yard standup touchdown and Bernard McGarry's conversion that culminated a drive beginning with

Ziggy Czarobski, 1947 All-American.

1943 backfield, with backfield coach Ed McKeever. From left, Jim Mello, Bob Kelly, McKeever, Creighton Miller, John Lujack, Herb Coleman.

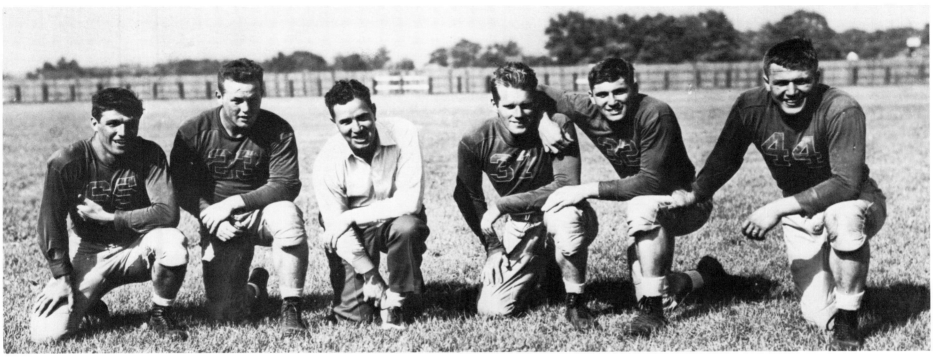

Lujack's punt out of bounds on the ND 37.

The Seahawks third-quarter kickoff sailed out of bounds, so Notre Dame started scrimmage from its 35. Now the great back-field combination—Jimmy Mello, Creighton Miller, Kelly, and Lu-jack—began rolling behind the mighty forward wall of Paul Li-mont, Jim White, Pat Filley, Herb Coleman, transfer John Perko, Ziggy Czarobski, and Yonakor. Mello rushed for three and Miller added five. Lujack advanced to Iowa's 48. Mello rammed ahead seventeen yards. Two carries by Creighton Miller made it first down at Iowa's 17. Several plays later Kelly cracked the line for a

touchdown and Fred Earley's ex-tra point tied it, 7—7. The Irish fury started to strike again, the Sea-hawks finally digging in at their 18. Iowa responded by sledging to the Notre Dame 6 before surrend-ering on downs. The respite for ND was only momentary. Lujack fum-bled, and then Dick Todd, from Texas A & M, immediately passed to Dick Burk, who needed only one step to cross the TD stripe. McGarry's extra-point kick hit an upright. Pre-Flight, 13; No-tre Dame, 7.

Now the victory march: Mello lugged the kickoff to Notre Dame's 45. After several plays, Creighton slashed to a first down at the Iowa 6, then smashed through tackle

for the tying touchdown. This put the pressure on extra-point kicker Earley. Fred's marksmanship was perfect and Notre Dame players, with a 14—13 advantage, rallied around Fred for a half-minute. The Seahawks had one gasp left when Perry Schwartz, former star with the Brooklyn pros, recovered Creighton Miller's fumble at the Irish 33. Four desperation Seahawk passes missed target, Notre Dame then running out the clock with two plays. So, wind-ing up at Great Lakes, the Mighty Irish were 9 and 0, and scenting their first unbeaten, untied cam-paign since 1930.

The battle at the naval training station was a classic for the ages.

Johnny Lujack carried the Blue-jackets' kickoff to the ND 33. Then Lujack mixed up his running and passing plays, befuddling the Sail-ors, in a seventeen-play assault on the goal. Creighton plunged for required yardage when Notre Dame was confronted with a fourth-and-two situation. Eventu-ally, ND had first down only four yards from goal. The Bluejackets turned stubborn. Lujack sneaked for the TD on fourth down, Fred Earley's point giving ND a 7—0 bulge at halftime.

The Bluejackets charged seventy-one yards, on eleven plays, following the second-half kickoff. They were at the ND 24 when they sent Dewey Proctor faking a smash into the line, decoying the defense as Emil Sitko, a 1942 Notre Dame freshman and ticketed to play on the unbeaten 1946-47-48-49 Irish elevens, carried the football around defensive left end and jaunted the necessary twenty-four yards. Capt. Pat Filley blocked the extra point kick by Steve Juzwik, former ND star, so Notre Dame still led, 7—6.

Play ensued, the ball being exchanged twice before Great Lakes began cruising from its 20. Proctor sprinted fifty-one yards from inside defensive left tackle to put the Bluejackets in front, 12—7. Juzwik missed the kick. With the Irish failing to score in the third quarter for the first time all year, it remained 12—7 going into the fourth.

One writer called Notre Dame's eighty-yard attack, to take the lead, "irresistible." ND controlled the ball for eight minutes, running twenty plays, in this surge. Earley's extra point had ND ahead 14—12. One minute and six seconds stood between the Irish and a perfect season.

Julie Rykovich purposely kicked out of bounds so Great Lakes started from its 35. Cecil Pirkey took Lach's aerial at the Irish 46, as the clock was creeping through the final minute. Sitko and quarterback Paul Anderson streaked downfield as potential receivers when Lach again drifted back to pass. Irish defenders stampeded Lach's protectors. Steve ducked one tackler, sidestepped, moved to his left, and saw Anderson had far

NOTRE DAME 1943 FOOTBALL TEAM

Front Row: Vic Kulbitski, Bud Meter, Jim Snyder, Bob Palladino, Jim Flanagan, Fred Earle, Bob Kelly, Jim Mello.

Middle Row: John Lujack, John Perko, Zig Czarobski, Frank Szymanski, Pat Filley (Capt.), Creighton Miller, Herb Coleman, Ray Davis, Paul Limont.

Top Row: Jim White, Joe Signaigo, Jack Zilly, Julie Rykovich, George Sullivan, John Adams, John Yonakor, Gasper Urban, Bob Benson.

outdistanced the ND secondary. Lach fired the bomb, Anderson collected it between the ND 8 and 5, and scored the touchdown. With Juzwik kicking point, Great Lakes had to protect its unbelievable 19—14 lead for only thirty-three seconds.

Great Lakes kicked out of bounds. Johnny Lujack, moving

back from his 35, aimed a pass downfield. Sitko intercepted and a naval siren signalled the contest's conclusion. Joe Boland, immortal Irish broadcaster, sobbed in his mike. Yet the 9-1 campaign provided Leahy his first national championship. The Saturday wasn't a total loss, though; it brought news that the departed

Bertelli had been named Notre Dame's first Heisman trophy winner. All-American recognition went to Bertelli, Creighton Miller, John Yonakor, Jim White, Pat Filley, and Herb Coleman. And coach Leahy could hear the war drums beating louder.

*"New York, Nov. 11—A coura-
geous team from Notre Dame, made
up substantially of seventeen and
eighteen-year-old boys, today ran
afoul of the powerhouse that mas-
querades as the Army football
team, and, fortunately, no one was
maimed. The score was 59—0, the
most one-sided defeat Notre Dame
[ever] has suffered."*

—Arch Ward
Chicago Tribune

Edward Clark Timothy McKeever, an affable Texan and a canny
football mind who was instrumental in the development of such outstanding passers as Charlie
O'Rourke at Boston College and
Angelo Bertelli and Johnny Lujack at Notre Dame, moved from
top aide to head coach when Leahy
was sworn in as a full navy lieutenant on May 1, 1944. After a
freshman stop at Notre Dame,
finances forced McKeever to transfer to Texas Tech, where he served
three years as quarterback and
also starred in basketball and
baseball. Classmates related that
although McKeever had a dish-
washing job at Texas Tech, and
made a few nickels selling rattle-
snake skins, he was in such dire
need that often he could afford only
one meal a day. Now, in 1944,
McKeever had inherited his first
big coaching post. He also inherited headaches.

All-American Creighton Miller,
perhaps Notre Dame's greatest

running back ever, had graduated.
Lujack led a vanguard of Irish
who, with eligibility remaining,
moved on to military service for
the duration. On the bright side,
Pat Filley had returned for a second year as captain and starting
left guard.

McKeever's Irish opened awe-
somely, not yielding a point in
crushing Pittsburgh, 58—0; Tulane
26—0; and Dartmouth, 64—0, as Mc-
Keever briefly returned to Boston,
his original stomping grounds with
Leahy. Chicago sports editor Warren Brown observed "that Notre
Dame will bowl over everything
until it runs into Army and Navy,
those two powerful service acad-
emies, and just might take care of
Army and Navy, too." The Irish
continued on, beating Wisconsin
and Illinois, 28—13 and 13—7, respectively, to bring up the engage-
ment with Navy in Baltimore. But
Navy scuttled the Notre Dame victory cruise, 32—13. Kelly led the
Irish runners against Navy with
thirty-nine yards. Four Middies—
Bill Barron, Bob Jenkins, Clyde
"Smackover" Scott, and Ralph
Ellsworth—each scrimmaged for
more yardage than Kelly's total.
Topping it off, Fred Earley, the
point kicker at ND in 1943, was in
a Navy uniform and made a ten-
yard dash and two conversions
against his old mates.

At halftime, Navy had ham-
mered out a 12—0 lead. Following
intermission, Navy battered Notre
Dame's defense with heavy artillery for a sixty-five-yard scoring

advance. On the eighth play, Jenkins ran five yards for the TD. Fred
Earley had lost none of the touch
perfected at Notre Dame and
kicked Navy's first extra point.
The Irish, beginning deep in their
own territory, took the overhead
route, but the attack fizzled.

The Irish began anew as Steve
Nemeth recovered Jenkins' fumble at Navy's 48. Dance-
wicz clicked on passes to Bill
O'Connor and Guthrie. Angsman
ripped for eight yards and Guthrie
nabbed Dancewicz's aerial at Navy's 5. Kelly made those five, and
the touchdown, hitting over his
right guard. Nemeth's extra point
left Navy leading, 19—7, going into
the last quarter. Ellsworth soon
picked up another Navy touchdown, Earley missing point. Then
Kelly scored for Notre Dame on a
three-yard plunge, leaving Navy in
front, 25—13. The Middies quickly
drove eighty yards for a fifth
touchdown. Earley's extra point
accounted for the final 32—13. It
was Navy's first victory over the
Irish since the 3—0 success in 1936.

Despite the lopsided loss to Navy,
Irish hopes were high when
they invaded Yankee Stadium to
challenge the Army blitzkreig.
Frank Szymanski, a mighty center
first enrolled at Notre Dame in
1941, had returned from service
and was to start against the Cadets. But on a day when Notre
Dame needed the luck of the Irish
more than anything, they had only
pluck.

A crowd of 75,142 was awed by

the Army power from the instant
Bill O'Connor was downed
on the ND 13 after accepting Felix
"Doc" Blanchard's opening kickoff.
With Doug Kenna, Dale Hall, and
John Minor leading the blitz, the
"Black Knights of the Hudson"
thrust to the Irish 5. Kenna
went seven yards around right end
for the only touchdown Army had
scored on Notre Dame since 1938.
Dick Walterhouse's first of five
successful conversions made the
score 7—0. Army kicked off again
(Notre Dame had no kickoffs) and
immediately Kenna intercepted a
pass by Frank "Boley" Dancewicz
and returned to the ND 26. Minor
raced twenty-six yards to score
and it was 14—0. Army's Ed Rafal-
ko got ahead of Bill Chandler, the
defending back, and took Kenna's
aerial for the touchdown, giving
Army a 20—0 lead at the quarter's
end.

Glenn Davis, the Army speed-
ster paired with Blanchard, the
howitzer, registered both second-
quarter touchdowns on short runs,
though he had set up one by returning an intercepted pass forty-
six yards. In the fourth quarter,
Davis scored on a fifty-six-yard
run and Walterhouse's conversion
made it 52—0.

Before the game, Coach Mc-
Keever had attempted some Rockne psychology, telling the Irish
that his seriously ill father was
listening to the broadcast and that
a ND victory surely would save
his father's life. When Notre Dame
had its first huddle after Army's

margin mounted to 52—0, Szymanski told his mates: "Well, we sure took care of McKeever's old man."

Army's final TD came when Joe Gasparella's screen pass, from behind the goal, was intercepted by Harold Travel. Later, Leahy, who had heard the broadcast, said: "Notre Dame, Coach McKeever and his staff, and the athletes, made a great showing. Naturally, I was disappointed over the score, but McKeever and his quarterbacks did the right thing. What difference if the score had been 159—0? There was only one thing to do—McKeever and the team did that; tried every trick in the book to score even if their efforts only meant a bigger score for Army."

The 1944 Fighting Irish wound up the season with conquests of Northwestern (21—0), Georgia Tech (21—0), and with vengeance, Great Lakes (28—7).

At the football banquet the following January 8, Notre Dame's president, the Rev. J. Hugh O'Donnell, announced that Frank Leahy had a long-term contract starting after the war. McKeever actually had agreed to terms for 1945, but soon accepted the head-coach position at Cornell. The 1945 team was to be in charge of Hugh John Devore, the 1933 co-captain, who had returned as a Leahy assistant in spring, 1943.

"Notre Dame faces its most critical football campaign this fall since the Rockne era ended fourteen years ago. With a new head coach, an almost complete change in coaching personnel, and with only eight monogram men, the Irish will play a typically difficult schedule which includes Army and Navy, the only teams to beat Notre Dame last year."

—Wilfrid Smith,
Chicago Tribune

Hugh Devore, one of the greatest Fighting Irish, was appointed on March 6 "to serve until Lt. Leahy's return from the Pacific." The choice was popular because Devore had become a legend in his playing days. As a freshman, he so savagely tackled Frank Carideo that Rockne admonished, "A nice play, Devore, but at Notre Dame we tackle them, not murder them!" Old grads delightedly recalled how Hughie had taken out three Pitt Panthers on one block. He served as a freshman coach in 1934, then moved to Fordham to serve as end coach under Jimmy Crowley and line coach Frank Leahy. Devore later coached at Providence and in 1942 became an assistant at Holy Cross. One of his assignments that 1942 season was to scout Boston College, then being called "the greatest college team ever assembled—a team that should be playing the Chicago Bears instead of colleges." Hugh did his scouting so thoroughly the Holy Cross, beaten four times, routed unbeaten Boston College, 55—12, in as dazzling an upset as football has seen.

When Leahy summoned Hugh back to Notre Dame, the thirty-four-year-old Irishman challenged all his ends to try to block him. One accepted the dare and was knocked flat. So when Hugh became interim head coach, critics said "if nothing else, these Irish will block and tackle like demons." Assistants Adam Walsh, Clem Crowe, and Wally Ziemba were to be retained by Devore, but Walsh soon departed to become head coach of the Cleveland (now Los Angeles) Rams and lead them to the National Football League championship, and Crowe had taken over at University of Iowa. When Devore sized up his squad in mid-summer practice, there were only eight lettermen in the group of one hundred: Frank Dancewicz, Joe Gasparella, Marty Wendell, Elmer Angsman, Pete Berezney, John Mastrangelo, Bob Skoglund, and Frank Szymanski. Promising players with some experience were Frank Ruggerio, George Ratterman, Jim McGurk, and John Fallon. Szymanski did not play the 1945 campaign, and Wendell soon was at Great Lakes, but by the time the Irish opened at home with a 7—0 victory over Illinois, Devore had spotted some other athletes who eventually were to delight Notre Dame fans, including Phil Colella, Bill Flynn, Ed Mieszkowski, Steve Oracko, Fred Rovai, Bill Walsh, Frank Tripucka, Bill Gompers, John Panelli, Coy McGee, Floyd Simmons, and a spirited freshman, Terry Brennan, whose 155-pound brother, Jim, had lettered in 1944. Plus a reserve, Joe Yonto, who much later was to become one of the school's most loyal assistant coaches.

Colella scored a touchdown on the first scrimmage play of his first game for ND, and that seventy-six-yard sweep around Illinois left flank, plus Stanley Krivik's drop-kick conversion, got Devore's green (and green-shirted) squad off to a 7—0 victory. The run was behind "perfect blocking," headed by Angsman and Ruggerio as they fanned in front of Colella the instant he took the football. Eddie Bray, the Illini safety, was the only foe who came close to touching Colella,

Six coaches. Brennan, Leahy, Anderson, Layden, Devore, and a portrait of Rockne.

and Phil faked him into a false lunge. The victory was assured by superb Notre Dame defensive play. The Illini were at the ND 5 when the half ended. In the third quarter, "Boley" Dancewicz caught an Illinois runner from behind at the ND 8. Illinois was halted at the ND 4 early in the last period. The Illini made one final desperate drive to tie and gained a first down at the Irish 9. After four plays, they had been halted at the 1.

Conquests of Georgia Tech (40–7), Dartmouth (34–0), Pittsburgh (39–9), and Iowa (56–0) followed, and the Fighting Irish were ranked third nationally as second-rated Navy loomed. Both teams remained unbeaten after the haze cleared on that 6–6 standoff in Cleveland, but the tie ranks as one of the all-time spirited performances by a Notre Dame football team. The Middies, heavy favorites because of their veteran squad and one-sided decision in 1944, were almost scuttled.

The Irish came knocking early in the game as Ruggerio intercepted a pass by Bob Hoernschemeyer, who had gone to Navy from Indiana, and returned to the Navy 33. Ruggerio and Angsman each pounded for three yards. Ruggerio carried three times, Angsman once, to a first down at the 11. Colella lost a yard and then picked up seven. Ruggerio, carrying two Middies on his back, banged over for the TD. Stanley Krivik's attempted kick was blocked and ND led, 6—0. End Bill Leonard was clear at the Navy 10 in the second period, which was marked by a timely pass interception by Dancewicz, but dropped the aerial lofted by Boley. In the fourth quarter, another Irish bid to add to the 6—0 lead was frustrated when they lost the ball on Colella's fumble at the Navy 12. Navy was outplayed keenly through the first fifty-three minutes and it appeared the one touchdown lead would hold up. That picture changed on a single play.

Facing third down and eight near midfield, Dancewicz passed. Navy's Clyde "Smackover" Scott intercepted and ran sixty yards for the tying touchdown with no Devorite putting a hand on him. Jack Currence's conversion attempt was wide, leaving it 6—6. Now the fun began. With less than two minutes left, Notre Dame began from its 23. George Ratterman, making his only pass of the game, hit Leonard at the Navy 40. Bill ran to the 17 before being tackled by Anthony Minisi. The Irish moved five yards closer as Navy was penalized for too many times out. Dancewicz passed to Colella and victory was assured if Phil could go all the way. But the field judge ruled that Colella had stepped out on the 1. Dancewicz's sneak left ND eight inches short. Time for one more play, and another Dancewicz sneak netted only two more inches. Confusion was everywhere as the players were untangled on both sneaks,

and there always will be those who allow that Boley scored on one of the sneaks before he was pushed back by Navy's dreadnoughts.

The confusion was compounded when Bill Blake, the veteran referee, brought together the opposing captains, Dancewicz and Minisi, and flipped a coin to see which team carried off the game ball. A veteran radio announcer shouted into his microphone, "I can't believe this—they're flipping a coin to see if it's a Notre Dame touchdown." A nationally syndicated sports writer, inspired by tonic to ward off the cold, ran to the site to study the footprints. Even with the tie, it was a superb Notre Dame performance.

Next Saturday it was Army. The Irish, victimized in the previous year's 59—0 defeat—the worst loss ever by an ND team—were smarting and eager for another crack at Blanchard, Davis, & Co. But too much had been spent against Navy, physically and emotionally.

Yankee Stadium was packed with a capacity 74,621 and officials said 250,000 tickets could have been sold.

Army's howitzers hit as soon as Arthur Gerometta recovered Angsman's fumble at the ND 31. Blanchard, who was to score two touchdowns, started it with a four-yard run. Davis faked a pass, then sliced through the line for twenty-seven yards and the first of his three touchdowns. Notre Dame fired back as Dancewicz returned

the kickoff to the ND 45. This drive fell a half-yard short of a first down inside Army's 27. The Cadets moved to a 14—0 lead, yet at the end of the opening period Notre Dame faced second down and two at Army's 23. After Dancewicz plunged once, and Ruggerio twice, Notre Dame was no closer, and Army took over. Army's halftime edge was 28—0. Army won, 48—0, with Notre Dame failing to avert a shutout after surging to within six inches of the goal, where a fumble by Gompers was snatched in midair by Bob Stuart, a University of Tulsa gift to Army.

The third consecutive road game found ND at Northwestern's Dyche Stadium. Frank Leahy had returned from naval service and suggested he might sit on the Irish bench against the Wildcats. Coach Devore vetoed this idea and Leahy did not mix with the team through the remainder of the year because Devore, as always, was very much his own man.

In the early going, the NU Wildcats were as fired up as the Irish had been against Navy. The Wildcats had thirty rushing plays in the first ten minutes while Notre Dame handled the football only three times, including a punt by Dancewicz. Twice ND turned back the clawing 'Cats in touchdown territory. Then, everything changed. Angsman reeled off a fifty-yard run, and subsequently made the two-yard TD plunge that terminated a ninety-yard march. Krivik drop-kicked the

extra point and ND was in front, 7—0.

Jim McGurk's touchdown and another Krivik extra point made it 14—0 at halftime. It was 21—0 after three, following a touchdown by Simmons, an Irish recruit from St. Mary's Pre-Flight, and Krivik's third consecutive kick. Krivik finally missed after Gompers had scored on a pass interception pitched by Jim Farrar. Northwestern's consolation touchdown came on Hap Murphey's three-yard end run against a jammed Irish line. The victory march then proceeded with Ratterman flipping a forty-eight-yard TD pass to Gompers.

A 32—6 triumph at Tulane followed before the windup at Great Lakes. It was to be the last game for, among others, Angsman, Ruggerio, Dancewicz, and Berezny. It also was the finish for the Ross Field stadium at the naval training station, as postwar dismantling began two days after the Notre Dame game. A newspaper account stated "Great Lakes scarcely hopes to upset Notre Dame." The Bluejackets reported quantities of athletes injured or ill. Grover Klemmer, Marion Motley, and Frank Aschenbrenner were reported "definitely out" and, three days prior to the game, Wilfrid Smith of *The Chicago Tribune* told his colleagues: "Great Lakes may have to cancel the game." Surprise! The Bluejackets showed up healthy enough to invade Russia.

NOTRE DAME 1946 NATIONAL CHAMPIONS

Klemmer, Motley, and Aschenbrenner each played fifty-four minutes. Great Lakes led, 6–0, eight plays after the kickoff, with Terlep sneaking over from the 1. Bob Sullivan's extra-point attempt failed. In the second quarter Ruggerio recovered Motley's fumble at the GL 21, and soon scored through defensive left tackle. Krivik drop-kicked Notre Dame to a 7–6 lead. Great Lakes came back with a ten-play touchdown salvo immediately. Terlep's twenty-nine-yard pass to Klemmer left the ball on ND's 1. Aschenbrenner scored, Sullivan kicked point, and at the

intermission it was 13–7. Final score: GL 39, ND 7.

A disappointing way to end a season. But the Irish were not to lose again until Oct. 7, 1950. The veterans and "The Master" were coming back.

The seasons from 1946 through 1949 were to bring Notre Dame one of the most glorious eras ever known in college football. During this span the Fighting Irish were undefeated through thirty-eight games, winning thirty-six and tying two. They were national

champions in 1946, 1947, and 1949, and runner-up to Michigan in 1948. Johnny Lujack and Leon Hart would win the Heisman trophy. Lujack, Hart, George Connor, Ziggy Czarobski, Emil Sitko, Marty Wendell, Bob Williams, and Jim Martin were All-Americans, some in more than one season. More than a dozen others, at least, were worthy of All-American recognition, but their greatness was not truly recognized because of the vast numbers of outstanding football players—so many of them service veterans—that massed on college campuses after World War II.

The 1946 opener was at Illinois. The Illini had started a week previously by routing Pittsburgh to begin a season that would take them to the Western Conference championship and a Rose Bowl victory. Johnny Lujack, Jimmy Mello, and Emil "Red" Sitko, later renowned as "Six Yards Sitko," were the ND offensive aces in this duel. Sitko set up the first Irish touchdown, in the second quarter, with an eighty-three-yard run to the Illinois 2.

Tom Gallagher, Illini punter, set back the Irish early with a wind-blown kick that sailed over the safety men. Pete Ashbaugh retrieved it on the roll and returned to the ND 5. Livingstone couldn't gain but Ashbaugh and Mello carved a first down at the 15. Sitko ran wide to his left to accept a long underhand lateral, then turned on the steam as blockers cleared a route down the sideline. Jack Zilly was unable to make a total block on Rykovich, last remaining Illini defender, and Rykovich drove Sitko out of bounds on the 2. Mello plunged a yard. Bob Livingstone thrust through the eight-man Illinois line for the game's first touchdown. Fred Earley missed point.

The Illini had to punt after failing required yardage following kickoff. Livingstone returned twenty-one yards to the Irish 33. Eight plays later Mello crossed for a TD, Earley converting to establish Notre Dame's 13–0 half-time edge.

Mike Swistowicz fumbled in the third period, following his long gain on a pass from Lujack, and Dwight Eddleman—all around Illini sport star—recovered on the Illinois 1. Notre Dame challenged soon again, Earley missing a field goal. Gasper Urban joltingly tackled Paul Patterson, another of the dangerous Illini runners, in the fourth quarter, to force the fumble Ziggy Czarobski recovered at the Illini 28. This break led to Terry Brennan's short touchdown plunge and Earley kicked the ND lead to 20–0. Moments later Joe Signiago knocked the ball from

the hand of Perry Moss, who was trying to pass, and Bill Russell recovered at the Illinois 25. Frank Tripucka's pass was partially deflected by an Illini, but the alert Swistowicz still snared the ball for a nineteen-yard gain to set the stage for Cornie Clatt's TD plunge. Earley's kick was blocked. A pass from Rykovich to Bill Heiss was a touchdown play covering sixty-three yards and enabled the Illini to avert a shutout in Notre Dame's 26–6 victory.

Terry Brennan and Jim Mello each scored two touchdowns, and Bob Livingstone tallied one, in the 33–0 rout of Pittsburgh. Gerry Cowhig contributed some effective rushing. Jack Zilly caught three passes, the first a thirty-nine yard gainer that the dauntless Lujack threw from deep in the end zone.

Seven different Irish—Jim Mello, Cornie Clatt, Terry Brennan, Bill Gompers, John Panelli, Jack Zilly, and Bob Skoglund—each scored a touchdown, with Fred Earley kicking all extra points, during the 49–6 decision against visiting Purdue. Iowa City was next call for the Notre Dame tornado. In the game's third minute, John Lujack and receiver Terry Brennan pulled off a thirty-three-yard scoring pass play. Fred Earley's conversion gave Notre Dame a 7–0 advantage, one point more than the Hawkeyes posted all day. Emil Sitko registered two touchdowns. John Panelli, Bill

Gompers, and Lujack himself, also carried over the Hawkeye goal. Iowa's sole touchdown, the last score that would be yielded by the Irish until the season final against Southern California, left Notre Dame with a 14–6 margin. In Baltimore, Navy found these 1946 Fighting Irish a far different bunch than the ND team that had been routed, 32–13, in the same arena two years previously. Gerry Cowhig recovered a fumble at Navy's 30 in the opening period and carried for a touchdown on the next play. Floyd Simmons ran for two touchdowns in the second quarter, the later one arranged by Simmons himself through recovery of a Navy fumble at the ND 48. The third period saw the Middies sail sixty-nine yards, only to be contained twelve inches from the ND goal line. Bill Gompers collected a last-quarter touchdown. Fred Earley kicked all extra points in Notre Dame's 28–0 success. Through the contest, eastern writers in the press coop amused themselves by making dire predictions of what Army's Black Knights would do to Notre Dame's defense the following Saturday in New York's Yankee Stadium. Army might not roll up quite as embarrassing margins as in 1944 (59–0) and 1945 (48–0), conceded the eastern scribes, but those touchdown twins, Felix "Doc" Blanchard and Glenn Davis, would create havoc in their final duel against the Irish.

Army had won twenty-five con-

secutive games, and had not been held to fewer than nineteen points in any contest through three seasons, as it took the field to engage Notre Dame's big boys, not the teen-agers and inexperienced who had formed the bulk of Notre Dame's 1944-45 squads. The Irish basically employed a 5-3-2-1 defense to check Arnold Tucker's passing, the howitzer inside-running of Blanchard, and Davis's wide forays. Blanchard averaged near three yards in twenty carries; Davis carted the ball seventeen times for an average gain of one-and-one-half yards. Notre Dame held Army scoreless; in return the stubborn Cadets refused to yield a single point to the usually potent Irish offense. The 0–0 game was dominated on both sides by the usually unheralded linemen.

The Cadets received an early break with recovery of Emil Sitko's fumble at the ND 25. Davis and Blanchard divided four running assignments and missed a first down by less than a yard, the Irish taking over.

Terry Brennan, who averaged five yards in his eleven carries through the afternoon, then sparked ND to a pair of first downs. Lujack had no great luck taking to the air and finally punted, Davis returning fourteen yards to Army's 35. Army also picked up two first downs before being forced to punt. Early in the second quarter Lujack started an eighty-four-yard advance by passing to Bob Skoglund on Army's 41. Bill Gompers picked up nine before Gerry Cowhig thrust to the Cadet 13. Lujack passed to Cowhig for two and Gompers plunged to the 6-yard line. Lujack failed to gain and the threat terminated when Gompers was chased out of bounds, at Army's 4, on fourth down. The Titans dueled on. Army recovered a Terry Brennan fumble on the ND 35. Blanchard smashed for two. A pair of passes by Tucker, and one by Davis, were futile against a dogged defense, so Notre Dame again took over.

The Irish had their chance with a Mastrangelo fumble recovery at Army's 34. Sitko and Brennan rushes produced only three yards; Lujack took to the air. Tucker intercepted at the Army 12 and returned thirty yards. Blanchard smashed Notre Dame's right side and suddenly found himself clear except for Lujack, who made the tackle at the Irish 47. Tucker's pass to Foldberg gained twenty-seven yards, but Tucker went to the air once too often, and Terry Brennan intercepted on the ND 8. Terry then scampered twenty-two yards on the first scrimmage play, subsequently catching a Lujack aerial on the ND 44 as the third quarter ended. Cadet Jim Enos claimed Gerry Cowhig's fumble but after four plays Army yielded on downs. Neither team made another dangerous assault; the game concluded with Army in possession at midfield. Notre Dame had ten first

downs, Army nine. The Irish held the edge in net rushing yardage, one hundred seventy-three yards to one hundred thirty-eight. Each team gained a net fifty-two yards by air. Though the battle was like war, only three penalties were assessed.

Back home, Notre Dame thrashed Northwestern, 27–0, in the rain.

Then in New Orleans, the Irish encountered the first Tulane team coached by Henry Frnka, former wizard at Tulsa. Notre Dame scored six touchdowns, all via rushes, on marches of seventy-three, eighty-one, ninety-one, fifty-one, eighty-five, and eighty yards. Jimmy Mello and young Ernie Zalejski each contributed a pair; Terry Brennan and Coy McGee scored the others. Fred Earley kicked five extra points. Tulane had only one scoring opportunity while absorbing the 41–0 defeat, and that was abruptly halted as Terry Brennan intercepted at the ND 5.

With Frank Leahy ailing, Ed "Moose" Krause was in charge for the season-ending visit by Southern California. Moose was worked up emotionally when the Irish returned to the locker room following warmup, and as kickoff time approached, ordered his athletes out, only to be reminded he hadn't named the starting lineup. "Who'll start?" gasped the excited Krause. "Why, we'll all start." Notre Dame dealt the Trojans a 26–6 defeat on touchdowns

by Coy McGee (two), Gerry Cowhig, and Leon Hart. The Southern Cal touchdown was only the fourth given up by Notre Dame all season.

Criticism that Leahy was operating a football factory, some of it from disgruntled losers, was shot down by the Rev. John J. Cavanaugh, who had succeeded to the university presidency. Said Father Cavanaugh: "When we in American sports hold the winner under suspicion merely because he is a winner, we discredit many of the fine qualities that have made football inspiring—the will to win, extraordinary school spirit and devotion, heroic observance of training rules, indefatigable application on the part of coaches and players to the details of the game. Then we come perilously close to the kind of dismal thinking that stigmatizes with suspicion the man who achieves success."

On December 30, 1946, there was announcement that the Army-Notre Dame series, an annual feature since 1913, would be terminated—at least for some years—after the 1947 game. But the 1947 final would mark Army's first gridiron appearance on the Notre Dame campus.

The Irish whirlwind swept on in 1947 to Notre Dame's first unbeaten, untied campaign since 1930. A bonus was the third Irish national championship under Coach Frank Leahy, although potent, unconquered Michigan was given a No. 1 rating after the Wolverines

routed Southern California in the Rose Bowl 49–0, in a pool arranged by the Associated Press as a vehicle for controversy. Coach Leahy's comment was it was a disappointment to fans everywhere that these great Irish and Wolverines could not have met on the gridiron.

Season competition began at Pittsburgh, where the Panthers opened stubbornly and were behind by only 7–6 before Johnny Lujack engineered a march putting Notre Dame in front, 13–6, just twelve seconds before intermission. Notre Dame's six-touchdown parade featured scores by Terry Brennan, who registered the first, Lancaster Smith, Coy McGee, and three ends—Leon Hart, Jim Martin, and Doug Waybright—who were on the receiving end of TD aerials from Lujack. The Irish hit Pitt for twenty points in the last quarter, moving the victory margin to 40–6.

John Lujack again was superb at Purdue, which played doggedly and moved into a 7–7 tie after ND opened with Lujack's twenty-one-yard scoring pass to Terry Brennan. Lujack, back to pass from the Purdue 31 in the same first quarter, found no receivers open and finally ran into the end zone. Steve Oracko's conversion was blocked, but Steve made amends with a second-period field goal that left Notre Dame with a 16–7 halftime advantage. The final was 22–7, Floyd Simmons tallying a TD in the third quarter.

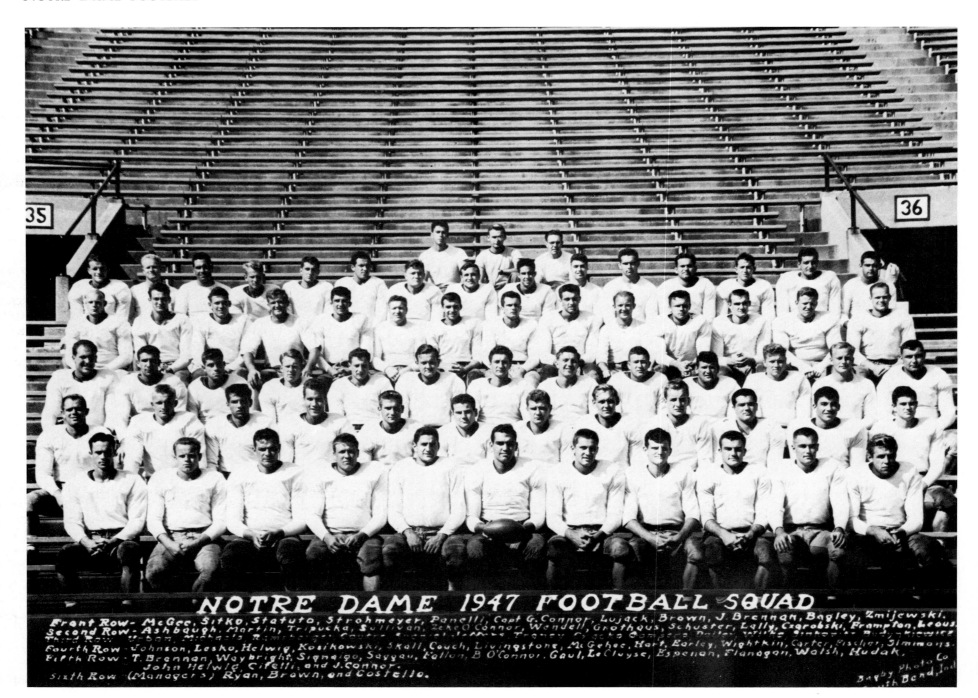

NOTRE DAME 1947 FOOTBALL SQUAD

Front Row— McGee, Sitko, Statuto, Strohmeyer, Panelli, Capt G. Connor, Lujack, Brown, J. Brennan, Bagley, Zmijewski.
Second Row— Ashbaugh, Martin, Tripucka, Sullivan, Zeke O'Connor, Wendell, Grothaus, Schuster, Lally, Czarobski, Frampton, Leous.
Third Row— Urban, Michaels, Ramsberger, Coutre, Spaniel, Mello, Tracey, Checke, O'Malley, Dallas, Wilke, Sitko, Przybycki, Zukowski.
Fourth Row— Johnson, Lesko, Helwig, Kosikowski, Skall, Couch, Livingstone, McGehee, Hart, Earley, Wightkin, Carter, Fischer, Simmons.
Fifth Row— T. Brennan, Waybright, Signaigo, Saggau, Fallon, B. O'Connor, Gaul, LeCluyse, Espenan, Flanagan, Walsh, Hudak.
John Helwig, Cifelli, and J. Connor.
Sixth Row— (Managers) Ryan, Brown, and Costello.

by Photo Co
South Bend, Ind.

Some regulars were used sparingly in the 31–0 victory over guest Nebraska.

Iowa was next in Notre Dame Stadium and fell 21–0. Bill Walsh recovered a Hawkeye fumble at the Iowa 29, on the game's sixth scrimmage play. On Notre Dame's sixth scrimmage play, Terry Brennan bolted three yards for the first TD. Fred Earley, three-for-three all afternoon, kicked point. Terry Brennan ran for a first down at Iowa's 14, closing the initial period. Again Brennan scored the touchdown, this on a ten-yard foray through Iowa's left guard. The Hawkeyes went on the prowl but were frustrated by Lancaster Smith's interception at the ND 6. Iowa attacked again starting the third quarter, operating from the old Notre Dame shift, and the Irish goal was in jeopardy following Emlen Tunnell's sixty-four-yard run, terminated when he was forced out by Lujack at the ND 10. Iowa was halted, two yards from the end zone, on fourth down. Larry Coutre went one yard for the concluding touchdown two plays into the final quarter.

Navy sank at Cleveland, 27–0, Johnny Lujack threw a twenty-nine-yard scoring aerial to Terry Brennan, Frank Tripucka passed thirty-one yards to Leon Hart for a touchdown, and Brennan also had a one-yard run over the TD stripe. The other touchdown also was also due to a larceny—Bob Livingstone intercepted a Navy pass and galloped forty-two yards

for his scoring contribution. Army had thirteen scouts watching the Navy game in preparation for the next Saturday's showdown at South Bend.

Army's opening kickoff by Jack Mackmull was out of bounds. On the repeat kickoff, Terry Brennan clutched the football between the Notre Dame 3 and 5 yard lines and blitzed through a swarm of tacklers—with key blocks by Connor, Fischer, and Martin—and found an almost clear route to touchdown territory. Terry sped up to outdistance Army's Bill Gustafson, who had cut across the field, at the Army 35. Fred Earley kicked Notre Dame's edge to 7–0. And outside the stadium, Terry's father, Martin, had been delayed while holding tickets for late-arriving friends. Martin heard oceanic cheering, and asked what had happened. "That kid Brennan just ran the kickoff back for a touchdown," Pop Brennan was told. Brennan climaxed the second drive, paced by his running, good gains by Emil Sitko and Mike Swistowicz, and Lujack-to-Hart pass, to tally on a three-yard run for a standup touchdown giving Notre Dame a 13–0 edge. Earley missed point.

Earley did add the conversion after Livingstone's six-yard TD run, inside his right tackle, in the third quarter. Army was knocking at the ND 24 as that period ended, and cut the Irish edge to 20–7 on Rip Rowan's one-yard touchdown plunge and Capt. Joe Steffey's

extra point. That touchdown—the first and only one an Army team coached by Col. Earl Blaik registered in five duels with ND elevens coached by Frank Leahy—inspired the Notre Dame athletes. They put the ball in play on their own 20 following Army's end zone kickoff and scored in eleven plays. Coutre, finding traffic tight as he tried to go through his right tackle, slid to the outside and ran twelve yards for the TD that wound up the point-gathering in Notre Dame's 27–7 victory. On the last play Terry's brother, Jim, intercepted an Army pass. The teams would not meet again until 1957.

Northwestern's plucky Wildcats, playing in their Dyche Stadium, trailed only 20–12 going into the last quarter, and fought on before being subdued, 26–19, in the rain. No other team, through the 1946 and 1947 campaigns, scored more than seven points against the Fighting Irish.

Coach Leahy was off scouting the Southern California Trojans when Tulane invaded ND. As temporary coach Ed "Moose" Krause watched, Emil Sitko and Terry Brennan each scored two touchdowns, with others added by Bill Gompers, John Panelli, Bob Livingstone, Cornie Clatt, and Jimmy Brennan, in the 59–6 triumph.

Notre Dame found a cocky bunch of Trojans on arrival in Los Angeles. Southern Cal, unbeaten but tied by Rice, was Rose Bowl bound. The Trojan line was no

match for the Irish forwards, and its rushers gained only one hundred eighteen yards compared to the three hundred ninety-seven piled up by the ND ground game. Notre Dame moved ahead on Fred Earley's field goal, the first time it gained possession courtesy of Capt. George Connor's fumble recovery. Emil Sitko's one-yard TD plunge, followed by Fred Earley's conversion, left Notre Dame guarding a 10–7 lead at the half. Southern California's touchdown resulted from a forty-four-yard advance following interception on Lujack. Sitko raced seventy-six yards to score on the first scrimmage play of the third period. Earley added the point, and subsequently kicked the score to 24–7 after Panelli's touchdown. The Irish pulled off exciting plays in the fourth quarter. They stopped the Trojans at the ND 8, from where Bob Livingstone shook loose on a ninety-two yard touchdown run. Earley added point. Al Zmijewski, a tackle deep on the reserve list, intercepted a Southern Cal lateral and struggled thirty yards for the final touchdown. Earley again converted.

Lujack won the Heisman. Notre Dame was ranked No. 1 nationally, ahead of awesome Michigan, in the final Associated Press poll at the season's end. When Michigan romped over Southern Cal in the Rose Bowl (a 49–0 conquest against Notre Dame's 38–7 rout of the Trojans) a supplementary poll placed the Wolverines first. Michigan fans pointed out that besides USC, their Wolverines and the Irish had met two other foes in common: Notre Dame beat Pitt, 40–6; Michigan licked the Panthers 69–0; and Michigan's margin over Northwestern, which fell by only 26–19 against Notre Dame, was 49–21. The debates were innumerable and Wilfrid Smith, famous *Chicago Tribune* football expert, frequently was asked whether Notre Dame or Michigan was the superior team. To each questioner, Smith responded: "Tell me if you're Catholic or Protestant before I answer." No matter. Notre Dame, for the third time under Leahy, was given the official Dr. Henry L. Williams national championship award, put up by Minnesota after the Golden Gophers retired the Knute Rockne national championship award in 1941. Since the 1947 Irish had retired the Williams trophy, Notre Dame put up the J. Hugh O'Donnell national championship trophy.

Purdue Coach Stuart Holcomb, now fielding the talent that would turn the Boilermaker-Irish rivalry into a spectacular collegiate gridiron series, long had been gunning for the 1948 encounter.

A newspaper account from Notre Dame that day stated: "Few games have been more replete with thrills—long passes, clever runs, unusual plays, and errors. No game could be closer. In the final analysis, the Irish were victors because they followed the ball more carefully and, in particular,

took advantage of Purdue's mediocre punting." That was all true.

The Irish opened up a 12–0 lead on Emil Sitko's first and second-quarter touchdown rushes of eighteen inches and one yard. Outplayed in the first twenty minutes, Purdue finally threatened the ND goal line. Frank Spaniel intercepted a Boilermaker pass in the end zone and made the error of trying to run out instead of taking the touchback. He was stopped at the ND 2. On third down, a Frank Tripucka pass was intercepted at the Irish 35. Purdue needed only three plays to produce the points that would leave Notre Dame with only a 12–7 edge at the half, getting the touchdown on an eighteen-yard pass from Bob DeMoss to Norbert Adams. Rudy Trbovich kicked point.

Purdue established a 13–12 lead as Bob Agnew plunged two yards for a touchdown that climaxed an attack the Boilermakers unleashed in taking the second-half kickoff. The Irish responded with John Panelli's seventy-yard TD return of a punt partially blocked by Jim Martin. Steve Oracko missed his third consecutive extra point attempt, leaving Notre Dame's advantage at 18–13. Again Purdue surged into the lead, 20–18, with a one-yard scoring thrust by DeMoss and Trbovich's conversion.

Early in the fourth period DeMoss passed from his end zone, Mike Swistowicz intercepting and returning to the Purdue 20. Gaining only four yards in three tries,

Notre Dame sent in Oracko to try the field goal. Leahy often remembered that at this moment he could clearly hear Notre Dame's president, Father John J. Cavanaugh, shout: "Good heavens, no, Frank. Not Oracko." Yet Oracko, under pressure, hit the bull's-eye with his three-point kick after the ball was snapped from the ND 16. Now Notre Dame led, 21—20. Assistant coach Joe McArdle, assigned to watch the game from an end-zone scoreboard, had stepped outside the door to see the field goal attempt more clearly. As the ball cleared the crossbar, "Captain Bligh" McArdle shouted in his booming voice, "God bless you, Steve Oracko!" That night two elderly priests, who had been in end zone pews, said that they had heard the voice of Rockne shouting from heaven: "God bless you, Steve Oracko!"

Purdue mounted another attack in the see-saw struggle but Leon Hart deflected DeMoss's lateral, the ball retrieved in mid-air by tackle Al Zmijewski, who ambled eight yards for his TD. Oracko's point made it 28—20. Three minutes

Leon Hart, Heisman Trophy-winner and All-American.

remained. Purdue turned its passing over to Bob Hartman and Ken Gorgal. Gorgal soon hurled twenty-four yards to Bob Grant and the ball was on the ND 1. Offsides cost Purdue five yards. DeMoss again took charge of the air offense and passed to Harley Jeffery for a Purdue touchdown on the last play of the game. Trbovich's successful kick narrowed the Irish victory margin to 28—27.

Six Irish scored touchdowns, and Steve Oracko kicked four points, in the 40—0 conquest at Pittsburgh. This brought up the start of the modern series against Michigan State, at Notre Dame.

The Irish turned back the Spartans, 26—7, after yielding a one touchdown lead, and rushed for three hundred ninety-eight yards to MSU's one hundred fifty-two. Emil Sitko averaged almost nine yards in twenty-four carries; Bill Gay averaged seven yards per thrust. Terry Brennan gained seventy-four yards; John Panelli fifty-five. Yet there were defensive lapses not expected of a Notre Dame team.

Despite twenty penalties costing one hundred seventy yards, the Irish scored in every period at Lincoln to rout Nebraska, 44—13. At Iowa, John Panelli scored two touchdowns, with two more added by Bill Gay and Larry Coutre, in Notre Dame's 27—12 triumph. Notre Dame's passing attack was braked while the Hawkeyes rolled up impressive yardage by air delivery. Iowa still was battling at

the end, controlling the ball at the Irish 13. Navy proved no contest in Baltimore, falling 41—7 before the Irish machine. Steve Oracko was six-for-six in extra point kicks in the 42—6 success at Indiana. Jack Landry nicked the Hoosiers for two touchdowns; Emil Sitko, John Panelli, Bill Wightkin, and Bill Gay each collected one TD.

Back at Notre Dame, Northwestern again was troublesome. The Wildcats, following recovery of a ND fumble, made an early advance to the Irish 9, with only a foot needed for first down. There Frank Aschenbrenner was stopped cold, Notre Dame taking over. Terry Brennan reeled off runs of nine, eight, five, twenty-two and six yards during an advance to Northwestern's 31, where the Irish confronted a fourth-and-three situation. John Panelli rushed all the way to the NU 11 and three plays later probed for the touchdown that established a 6—0 Notre Dame lead. It stood that way until early in the third quarter, when Art Murakowski's interception turned things around. Frank Tripucka, taking the snap at the NU 9, tried a cross-field throw. Murakowski grabbed it at the 10 and took off. With one Notre Dame player blocked out, only Tripucka remained to trouble Murakowski, and Art swerved from reach to continue the touchdown trip. Jim Farrar kicked Northwestern into a 7—6 lead. Late in this same third quarter Billy Gay returned a punt to the Notre Dame 37. Landry and

Gay continued to carry until Northwestern's 1-yard line was reached. Gay dived for the touchdown putting Notre Dame ahead, 12—7, at 5:20 into the final period. Steve Oracko was called for the extra point, but this wasn't Oracko's day—his on-target kick after Notre Dame's opening touchdown had been nullified by penalty, and Steve failed the subsequent attempt, and his two field goal tries had been futile. Now, seeking to mount Notre Dame's advantage to six points, Oracko failed again. The Irish hung on to win by that 12—7.

Notre Dame's 1948 unit now had won all of its eight assignments to date and some recalled that prior to the season coach Leahy had cautioned: "We may lose one or two and maybe get a tie somewhere along the line. Frank Tripucka must develop at quarterback. He's a long way from being an Angelo Bertelli or Johnny Lujack. Tripucka can pass and kick, but he can't run with the ball, and he isn't anything like Lujack on defense."

Yet the Irish charged on, hitting visiting Washington with twenty-five points in the first quarter. Washington was victim No. 9 in falling 46—0, with Leon Hart scoring two touchdowns to complement single TDs by John Panelli, Terry Brennan, Bill Wightkin, Bill Gay, and Jack Landry, and Oracko's four conversions.

So Notre Dame's unbeaten, untied streak—starting after the

scoreless classic with Army in 1946—stood at twenty-one going into the 1948 finale at Southern California. The Trojans were three-touchdown underdogs, an unrealistic margin considering the fury of the intersectional rivalry. Though a three-game loser through the season, Southern California was so ready for this one that Notre Dame nearly suffered a disaster, instead of a semi-disaster. The Trojans grabbed the football from Notre Dame seven times; on six fumble recoveries and an interception.

Notre Dame was on its own 48 when the scoreless first period concluded. Three plays advanced to the USC 45. Frank Tripucka passed over the middle to Leon Hart at the 40. Big Leon momentarily lost balance when hit by a Trojan, then swerved to his right and ran for the TD giving Notre Dame a 7—0 edge at halftime. Tripucka suffered severe back injuries and a broken rib on the play before intermission. This put Bob Williams, eighteen, at quarterback through the final half. Late in the third period Trojan Jack Kirby intercepted a Williams aerial and returned to the ND 42. The aroused Trojans were at the ND 15 as the last quarter began. Four plays later Bill Martin plunged over from the 1, and Dill's extra point made it 7—7. Now 100,571 fans were roaring in the Coliseum, and the crescendo was to increase. Time had become precious when the Trojans, starting from ND's

42, went ahead—14—7—on Martin's three-yard TD thrust and Dill's conversion. Tension mounted in the press box.

Halfback Billy Gay inquired how much official time was left. Referee James Cain told him two-and-one-half minutes. "That's time enough," snapped Gay, moving into position to accept Charley Peterson's kickoff at the ND 1. Gay turned toward his right sideline and picked up an army of blue-jerseyed blockers. He was hauled down only thirteen yards short of the goal. An eighty-six-yard run! With ninety seconds to play, Williams finally sneaked to the 8. Gay couldn't grab a Williams pass to the end zone. They tried it again, and USC's Gene Beck was called for interference. This left ND at the 3. John Panelli crashed for two. Emil Sitko smashed across for the TD and, with thirty-five seconds on the clock, Steve Oracko's extra point tied it. Notre Dame, though, wasn't quite ready for a 14—14 standoff. The on-side kick was recovered by ND and, on the final play, Williams was stopped at the USC 34 after a fourteen-yard run. The winning streak was ended, but still Coach Leahy's post-war Irish had not been defeated in twenty-eight games. The deadlock did cost Leahy a fourth consecutive national championship (his 1943-46-47 teams had set the groundwork) and unbeaten Michigan, voted No. 1 ahead of the Irish in the Associated Poll, was the first to win the J. Hugh O'Donnell

trophy. Bill Fischer, Leon Hart, Emil Sitko, and Marty Wendell earned first-team berths on one or more All-American teams.

Many factors, including graduation and a concentration on more specialized offensive and defensive units, caused some realignments for 1949. Terry Brennan, Frank Tripucka, John Panelli, Bill Fischer, Bill Walsh, and Marty Wendell were among the departed, and their absence forced Coach Frank Leahy to predict some dire happenings.

Fans who shared Leahy's concern that the unbeaten string might be approaching an end felt better after the 49—6 whipping of Indiana in the opener at Notre Dame. Emil Sitko, a doubtful starter, proved his injuries were not too severe by scoring three touchdowns. Billy Gay, Larry Coutre, Mike Swistowicz, and Bill Wightkin added other touchdowns. Steve Oracko kicked five points, and the Irish picked up a pair on automatic safety.

At Washington, Notre Dame was assessed ten major penalties and one of five yards. The Huskies recovered an early Irish fumble by Larry Coutre and immediately scored on a fifty-five-yard pass-play, Don Heinrich hurling to Roland Kirby, who evaded defender Billy Gay and went afoot the final thirty yards to produce a 7—0 Washington lead. Williams' three-yard TD pass to Leon Hart, and

Steve Oracko's extra point, tied it. Notre Dame assumed command on Leon Hart's six-yard, end-around touchdown thrust, Oracko missing the point. This opportunity was made possible by Bill Flynn's recovery at the Huskie 14 after Leon Hart had blocked a punt. John Helwig recovered a fumble on Washington's 36 to establish the opportunity for Larry Coutre's thirty-yard scoring romp. Oracko converted. Oracko also added point following the final touchdown, a two-yard slash by Jack Landry that concluded a drive from the Washington 18, where Flynn had seized a Huskie bobble. ND blocking was shoddy except on Coutre's long-distance dash, yet the Irish amassed four hundred and one yards by rushing and passing. Coach Leahy blasted the officiating: "How could it be a good game when we had to play four extra men?"

At Purdue, the Boilermakers came nowhere close to being the spoilers they almost were in 1948. Starting from their 4-yard line, the Irish needed only two plays to take a 7—0 edge. Frank Spaniel's opening rush of fifty-five yards was immediately followed by Emil Sitko's forty-one-yard scoring scoot. It was the first of Emil's three consecutive touchdowns. With Billy Gay and Bill Barrett also scoring TDs, and Steve Oracko five-for-five in the extra-point department, Notre Dame owned a 35—0 lead by the third period's end. Purdue picked up a consolation fourteen

NOTRE DAME
NATIONAL 1949 CHAMPIONS
1st Row- Cifelli,   Helwig,   Groom,   Toneff,   Mutscheller.
2nd Row- McGehee, Lally, Hart, Martin, Grothaus, Wallner, Wightkin
3rd Row- Johnson, Sociel Centre, Williams, Sitko, Zaleiski, Swistowicz, Petitbon

Bagby Photo.

points to avert a blanking, 35–14.

Coach Henry Frnka's first strong Tulane team came to Notre Dame with a No. 4 national ranking (behind ND, Army, and Oklahoma) and seemed to have brought along half of Dixie. The rebels chanted that this would be the game earning Tulane the national championship. Coach Leahy, nodding, cautioned: "Tulane may be the best team in the country." The Irish used fifty-three players, the most outstanding being Larry Coutre, who personally won Civil War No. 2 in the first period. Coutre scored three consecutive touchdowns on runs of fourteen, eighty-one, and two yards, the short TD smash arranged by Bob Williams' pass to Bill Wightkin for fifty-plus yards. Still in the first quarter, Leon Hart recovered a Green Wave fumble at the ND 49. Three plays afterwards, despite a major penalty, the Irish were at the Tulane 34. From there, Williams tossed to Frank Spaniel for a TD and at the quarter's conclusion the Gold and Blue led the Green Wave, 27–0. Six more Notre Dame points were added before halftime on a TD aerial from Williams to Hart.

They were barely back from the intermission before Tulane made its only points, Bill Bonar passing to George Kinek, who scatted unpursued the final seventy-six yards. Euel Davis converted.

Those seven points were matched by Spaniel's second TD, a twelve-yard run, followed by Oracko's fourth extra point. Billy

Barrett's fourth-quarter sprint of fifty-nine yards, with assistance from John Petitbon's blocking, tallied the final six points in a 46–7 Notre Dame rout. "What can you say after you're run over like that?" gasped Tulane coach Frnka.

Navy again was encountered at Baltimore and the Middies were less effective than in the previous season's drubbing. A great day for the Irish and Ernie Zalejski. Ernie started the 40–0 Navy scuttling by taking an aerial from Bob Williams, the TD play covering forty-eight yards. Next, Larry Coutre chased ninety-one yards to the Middie end zone. Emil Sitko powered fourteen yards for the third TD. Touchdown No. 4 resulted from another Williams to Zalejski pass-play, this covering twenty-eight yards. John Landry continued the touchdown parade with an eighteen-yard end run, and Zalejski wound it up flying seventy-six yards for his third score. Notre Dame did not throw a pass in the second half, and once Leahy had three reserve quarterbacks operating in the same backfield unit.

Invading Michigan State, the Irish established a 14–7 intermission margin, then added three more touchdowns before the Spartans' air bombardment produced the pair of TDs to cut Notre Dame's winning edge to 34–21. Bob Williams threw sixteen times, for thirteen completions and one hundred seventy-eight yards, since the Spartans' seven and eight man

lines left the air lanes vulnerable. Soon after the scoreless opening stanza, Billy Gay returned Al Dorow's punt twenty-five yards to MSU's 24. Sizing up the eight-man defensive line on third down, Williams passed to Ernie Zalejski, streaking at the goal line. Steve Oracko's extra point established Notre Dame's 7–0 lead. Minutes later Williams butter-fingered a handoff to Larry Coutre, Michigan State recovering five yards from the ND goal line. Sonny Grandelius scored in two thrusts, George Smith's conversion leaving it 7–7. Notre Dame received and soon, due to penalty, was backed up to its 5-yard line. Williams carried for ten and reached Leon Hart with a pass at ND's 34. The drive seemed stymied at the Spartan 45, where the Irish confronted fourth down and short yardage. Williams passed to Bill Wightkin at the MSU 22, sustaining the attack. The Spartans dug in. Coutre failed a third down smashed from the one, but scored on his next carry as Williams opened the massed defense by sending wide a decoy flanker. Oracko's extra point put Notre Dame in charge, 14–7.

Coutre returned the second-half kickoff to the Irish 21. The attack advanced to MSU's 40. Williams called for what practically was a Split-T play and slid to position to hit outside defensive left tackle, eluded a defending back, and completed the forty-yard route to the end zone. The ND advantage stayed at 20–7 when the conversion

failed because of a high snap from center. The score reached 27–7 early in the last period, thanks to Sitko's sixteen-yard scoring dash and Oracko's extra point. The Spartans received, and failed a fourth down gamble, ND taking over on the MSU 36. The probe reached the 12 in seven plays, inspiring Williams to loft a TD pass to Hart. After Oracko's extra point, Notre Dame was safe with a 34–7 bulge and hardly disturbed in the late Spartan counterassault producing fourteen points.

North Carolina made its first appearance against the Irish in a game at New York's Yankee Stadium. Notre Dame delighted subway alumni with a 42–6 conquest.

ND's opening touchdown drive against the guest Iowa Hawkeyes started with Bill Gay's fumble recovery at the Iowa 33. It concluded on Bob Williams' twenty-yard TD pass to Frank Spaniel, Steve Oracko adding point. Iowa evened things in the second quarter, capitalizing on recovery of a Williams fumble, but by intermission was back in arrears by 14–7. Notre Dame's second touchdown opportunity came as Leon Hart partially blocked a punt that went out on the Hawkeye 23. Barrett's seven-yard run ultimately produced the TD, Oracko converting. Notre Dame finished a 28–7 victor, and Oracko finished the day four-for-four by adding points capping two second-half touchdowns.

Southern California gained only

seventeen yards on the Irish lawn while Notre Dame was running its unbeaten streak to thirty-seven straight on a 32–0 decision.

Though Southern California had a thirty-six-yard edge in the passing statistics, there were no hobbles on Notre Dame's offense as five different Irish scored touchdowns complemented by Steve Oracko's pair of conversions. As important as the offensive stars were such defensive standouts as Leon Hart, who alternated between end and fullback, Bill Wightkin, Jim Martin, Bob Lally, John Helwig, Jerry Groom, Bob Toneff, and Paul Burns.

Southern Cal started out capturing Larry Coutre's fumble and probed to the ND 12. Here Hart crashed hard on the Trojan passer, who dropped the football. Notre Dame's Jim Mutscheller retrieved. Southern Cal, on next possession, gambled at its 40 with a fourth-down pass that failed. Moments later Hart took Williams' long pass on the SC 10 and raced for the opening TD. On their first play after the kickoff, the Trojans went to the air. John Petitbon intercepted and sped forty-three yards for a standup TD without feeling a Trojan touch. SC was contained on the ND 19 early in the second period, losing a yard to Jim Martin's tackle on fourth-and-one. The quarter was winding up as SC dropped a Williams punt, Notre Dame's Bill Barrett seizing it at the Trojan 24. Three plays later, Emil Sitko jaunted five yards for

The stadium, Oct. 27, 1956. ND vs. Oklahoma; 60,128 attending.

the TD establishing Notre Dame's 19—0 intermission lead. It would have been more had not Trojan sentinels stifled another immediate Irish bid at the SC 8 by batting down three consecutive Williams passes. Frank Spaniel's two-yard touchdown burst rolled the margin to 25—0 in the third period. The last quarter found Barrett smashing through center to score from the SC 1. Leahy pinpointed the turning point as Hart's catch of Williams' thirty-nine-yard pass for the opening touchdown. A California reporter noted that a year earlier Leahy had said he might retire. What was the situation? "I'm not thinking of quitting—now," said the ND coach. Why should he be? His 1949 Irish were 9—0 awaiting the finale against Southern Methodist in Dallas. Secretly, though, Leahy was having serious thoughts. He also was to have headaches with SMU.

One headache seemed removed when the storied All-American and Mr. Southern Methodist, Doak Walker, was unable to play. Yet ND was due for a migraine in the form of Southern Methodist's Kyle Rote, who passed, ran, and caught while the Texans stood up to the potent Irish for sixty minutes. Rote rushed twenty-four times from the SMU single wing to amass one hundred fifteen yards. Kyle clicked on ten of twenty-four aerials for an additional one hundred forty-six. A Rote pass reception gained fifteen yards. He scored all Southern Methodist touchdowns.

Bill Wightkin got behind the defending Rote, taking Bob Williams' pass on the SMU 12 and going on for the touchdown, that, with Steve Oracko's conversion, provided Notre Dame's 7—0 lead. It was 13—0 at halftime on Williams' long scoring pass to Ernie Zalejski, who outmaneuvered three defending backs to make the end-zone catch. Not that the Mustangs didn't cause some anxious moments in the first two periods: Jerry Groom intercepted a Fred Benners aerial to end one Mustang threat. Later, SMU had third down on the ND 1. Groom halted Rote twelve inches from a touchdown. Rote carried again on fourth and was stopped by Petitbon. And Billy Gay had intercepted a Mustang pass on the ND 48.

Notre Dame surged again in the third period, but the Mustangs recovered Ernie Zalejski's fumble on the SMU 13. The Irish came knocking again, only to lose another Zalejski fumble. Rote soon scored his first touchdown, Bill Sullivan's conversion cutting the Irish edge to 13—7. Notre Dame built its margin soon after Jim Mutscheller's pass interception at the SMU 22, Bill Barrett scoring on a three-yard TD burst. Oracko kicked Notre Dame's lead to 20—7. The Mustangs caught fire entering the last period, Rote's touchdown and Sullivan's point narrowing their deficit to 20—14. Return of a punt to the ND 14 set up Rote's final touchdown, a short third-down foray. With the score 20–20, Sullivan tried the conversion that could give Southern Methodist a single-point lead. Groom crashed in to block the attempt. Ten minutes remained.

Spaniel returned the kickoff to his 43. Emil Sitko subsequently was run out on the SMU 20 but Notre Dame, hurt by penalty, soon was back at the Mustang 49. And soon it was back at the 20 and touchdown-bound. The score went to the final 27–20 on Bill Barrett's six-yard TD sneak around his left end and Oracko's conversion.

Southern Methodist struck back to the Notre Dame 3, where Groom and Lally collaborated to intercept on Rote.

Coach Leahy temporarily barred visitors from the dressing room and told his athletes: "You are the greatest football team I even coached [an opinion revised after the 1953 final against SMU] . . . . as soon as we are dressed all of us are going to visit the cathedral to offer up a prayer of thanksgiving. Before you do any celebrating send a telegram to your father and mother thanking them for the privilege of letting you play for Notre Dame."

Notre Dame now was unbeaten through four post-war seasons. This was Leahy's second unbeaten, untied campaign with the Irish, and, overall, his fourth national championship. None of his ND elevens ever had gone 10–0

before. Leon Hart was his third Heisman trophy winner.

Arch Ward wrote: "Many followers of Notre Dame football rate this year's team the best in the university's brilliant history. Red Grange and more than a few others regard it as the greatest gridiron unit they ever have seen."

Yet Leahy knew the future was bleak, and was discouraged. Because his recruiting had been curtailed, and there seemed a trend toward de-emphasis, Leahy hoped to resign, and confided this to some players. "I was going to leave, too," he told me, later, "but one incident changed my mind." He related that after he gave the news to the players, Jerry Groom—slated to be the 1950 captain—came to him and said:

"Coach, remember what you promised my parents when I enrolled to Notre Dame— that you would be my coach for all four years? Well, I have another year to go." Groom changed Leahy's mind, and the coach continued.

The doom that Coach Leahy had feared became a reality in 1950. For the first time since 1940, Notre Dame wasn't ranked in the Top Ten. For the first time since the 1945 rout at Great Lakes (39–7), the Irish lost after going unbeaten, but twice tied, through thirty-nine games. The shocker was applied by the Purdue Boilermakers, who last had triumphed in the intrastate rivalry in 1933. Losses to

Indiana (20–7), Michigan State (36–33), and Southern California (9–7) were to follow. There was the 14–14 tie at Iowa. Victories were scored over North Carolina, 14–7, in the opener; at Tulane (13–9), against Navy (19–10) in Cleveland, and Pittsburgh (18–7). The final 4–4–1 record was the closest Leahy ever came to a losing season in his head coaching career.

Purdue was the season's second foe, and when the Boilermakers appeared, they were reminded that Notre Dame had won twenty-eight in a row on home turf after that 32–20 defeat by Michigan in '42. Purdue fans promised that Dale Samuels, their sophomore quarterback from Lindblom High School, Chicago, would astonish the Irish, who hadn't been very impressed with the outstanding prep record of the 5-feet 10-inch Samuels.

On the third scrimmage play, Purdue's Neil Schmidt raced eighty-six yards to cross the goal. But officials said Schmidt had stepped out on his own 26. Purdue still charged on and its first drive was halted a yard short of the goal.

The Boilermakers scored when the next opportunity was set up with officials ruling Samuels' thirty-yard pass to Schmidt complete at the ND 1 because of interference by Irish defender Dave Flood. John Kerestes plunged for the TD and Samuels kicked the extra point.

Purdue threatened again early in the second quarter as Dick

Schnaible ran forty-five yards to the ND 15 after his pass interception on Bob Williams. The Irish braced at their 4, pushed the Boilermakers back to the 12, and Capt. Jerry Groom ended this danger by batting down a Samuels pass in the end zone. But Purdue was getting ready to put some dents in a defense that seemed to be keeping ND in the game.

A thirty-five-yard Samuels-to-Schmidt aerial carried to the Irish 6. Kerestes reached the goal in two thrusts. Samuels kicked the score to 14–0, and was ready to add to that as soon as Notre Dame surrendered possession on the Purdue 44 because an ineligible Irish receiver had grabbed Williams' fourth-down pass. Six plays later Samuels pitched thirty yards to Schmidt for the TD, then again kicked the point.

Half-time: Purdue 21, Notre Dame, 0! Only the most fervent diehards now believed the unbeaten streak could be preserved, but the Irish came back fighting after the intermission, and for more than twenty minutes it appeared that at least a tie might be salvaged. Or even that victory might be snatched by another patent Notre Dame rally. The Irish kicked off and Purdue was downed deep in its territory. An offside penalty pushed the Boilermakers deeper. Then Phil Klezek's fumble was recovered at the Purdue 10 by Notre Dame's Dick Cotter. Billy Gay turned right end for seven yards. John Landry failed to gain.

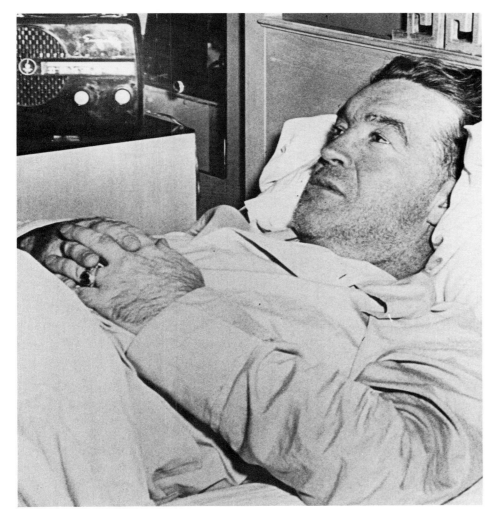

Leahy listens to the game in December, 1950.

Notre Dame, after an exchange of punts, began rolling from its 43.

Bill Barrett sprinted for twenty. Consecutive thrusts by John Petitbon, Landry, and Barrett carried to the Purdue 10. Petitbon ran to his right and scored on the first play of the final quarter. Again Caprara kicked the point. Purdue, 21; Notre Dame, 14, and plenty of time left! Unfortunately, time for Purdue to tally again on a march from its 41. Mike Maccioli, after dropping two Samuels passes from the ND 43, hung on to the third successive aerial, for Purdue's fourth touchdown. Almost automatically, Samuels kicked the point. Dale Samuels—a great athlete—had paced a football team to one of those rare occasions in Notre Dame stadium: a victory by the visitors. There were tears in Irish eyes that historical Saturday, and by the season's end the tears would be a flood. Notre Dame, voted Team of the Year in 1949, was to be named Disappointment of the Year in the Associated Press poll at the conclusion of 1950.

With Frank Leahy kept home by the flu, Assistant Bernie Crimmins took the squad to Southern California. Irish spirits were high for the traditional finale; they did not sense that they were about to become the fourth eleven in ND history to lose four games. If ND's year had been dismal, Southern Cal's had been worse. Coming into the intersectional classic, the 1950 Trojans had lost five, tied two, and won a single. Alumni were hollering for the hide of Coach Jeff Cravath, the Trojan center and captain when the rivalry began in 1926.

Notre Dame took a 7–0 lead on a fifty-four-yard drive in the second period. Williams, who with Capt. Jerry Groom, was to be named to some first-team All-Americans in this disappointing season, hit Petitbon with a pass that seemed a cinch to be a score. Petitbon skidded on his head to within a foot of the TD, and was removed with a mild concussion. Williams sneaked across the goal. Vince Meschievitz's extra point put the Irish ahead, 7–0.

It was all square, though, seconds after the ensuing kickoff, which Trojan Jim Sears ran back for ninety-four yards and a touchdown. Frank Gifford kicked the tying point. The Trojans put it away early in the third period. Trojan guard Paul McMurtry blocked a Williams punt from the ND 7, and the football bounded outside the end zone for the automatic safety points, providing Southern Cal's 9–7 victory.

Williams was injured in the fourth period and hospitalized, leaving John Mazur to quarterback a final Irish effort to escape defeat. Mazur's long distance pass was deflected from Meschievitz's arms at the goal line. Finally Meschievitz was far off target in a thirty-six-yard field goal attempt.

Southern California made only one first down, while the Irish garnered thirteen, and completed

Williams passed to Jim Mutscheller for Notre Dame's first touchdown. Joe Caprara's extra-point kick narrowed Purdue's margin to 21–7. The Boilermakers fired back to attempt to regain their twenty-one-point margin, and fell only a foot short on Samuels' fourth down sneak from the ND 1. The third quarter was winding up when

one of two passes while Notre Dame was making good on twelve of thirty attempts. Southern California did give the Irish a physical workout and the Notre Dame wounded, besides Williams and Petitbon, included Dave Flood, Bill Barrett, Bill Whiteside, Murray Johnson, Fred Wallner, Bill Flynn, and Jerry Groom.

The rebuilding began in 1951 and Indiana, opening guest at Notre Dame, was first to sample the results. The Irish entered the second period with a 7–0 lead, then hit for thirty-five points—including all of Neil Worden's four touchdowns—for a 42–0 halftime advantage and the ultimate 48–6 conquest. Bill Barrett, John Lattner, and Del Gander also scored Irish touchdowns. Minnie Mavraides kicked six conversions.

The following Friday night found Notre Dame at Detroit. John Petitbon seized the opening kickoff on his 15, chased to midfield, slanted to a sideline and with Neil Worden supplying a key block, completed his eighty-five-yard jaunt. Minnie Mavraides added point. Notre Dame was in charge with nineteen seconds elapsed. Coach Dutch Clark's Detroiters contained the next two Irish possessions but were in trouble in punting to Bill Barrett, who retreated seven yards before handing to Petitbon. Petitbon tucked himself behind a wave of blue-jerseyed blockers and sauntered eighty yards for a TD. Again Mavraides converted.

Detroit received, soon fumbling to Notre Dame at midfield. The Irish disdained a fourth down punt, and Worden crashed to first down at Detroit's 39. Petitbon took a lateral from quarterback John Mazur, turned defensive left end, and sped to his third touchdown of the period, which ended 20–0. Capt. Jim Mutscheller's crew rolled on to their second victory march of the young season, 40–6.

Southern Methodist brought a great passing star to Notre Dame, Fred Benners. Benners threw twenty-five passes, thirteen completed, on the Mustangs' first twenty-five plays. He tried to get off number twenty-six but was sacked by Notre Dame's chargers. Benners passed for all four SMU touchdowns, all to different receivers, while completing twenty-two of forty-two efforts and gaining three hundred, thirty-eight yards, to spark Southern Methodist to a 27–20 upset triumph. SMU was off to a 7–0 lead and never trailed. The Irish touchdowns were posted by Paul Reynolds, Chet Ostrowski, and John Lattner.

Notre Dame bounced back at Pittsburgh, 33–0. The licking could have been worse had not the Panthers dug in on seven other ND threats.

Purdue's Dale Samuels, passing hero of the 1950 Boilermaker triumph that marked ND's first defeat since 1945, again was at the helm as the 1951 elevens squared off at Notre Dame. This time

Samuels and Purdue associates finished on the short end, 30–9, but not before Irish partisans had been worried. Notre Dame carried a 7–0 lead into the intermission. That evaporated, due to two Irish fumbles, in less than four minutes of the third quarter. One Purdue fumble recovery set up Jim Reichert's fifty-one-yard field goal to register the Boilermakers' first points. Notre Dame received, fumbling again on the second scrimmage play, Purdue recovering at the Irish 43. Samuels immediately passed to Darrel Brewster, who had sneaked behind Irish safety John Petitbon to make the catch and continue across the goal. Purdue led, 9–7, but Samuels failed to increase it with his extra point attempt. This setback inspired Notre Dame to take off. ND received, and settled for the Minnie Mavraides' twenty-six-yard field goal pushing them ahead by a point. The next time the Irish had possession, John Lattner delivered a forty-yard touchdown dash, Mavraides converting. The reeling Boilermakers gave up thirteen more points in the last quarter.

The silver anniversary game of the Navy series was in Baltimore, where the turf was slippery and sloppy from a three-day rain. Neil Worden's thirty-six-yard touchdown run, without a Middie touching him, came in the second quarter to touch off the eventual 19–0 Irish conquest. Navy subsequently fumbled a kickoff, Dan

Shannon and Dave Flood recovering on the Middies' 23. John Mazur collected those twenty-three yards on a TD burst through his left tackle, Minnie Mavraides adding his only extra point of the day. In the last quarter Bill Barrett appeared trapped fielding a punt on his twenty-five. Shannon sprung the trap with a crunching block, enabling Barrett to chug seventy-five yards to the final touchdown.

Michigan State was a disaster, the worst defeat ever inflicted on a team coached by Frank Leahy. On the Spartans' first play from scrimmage, Dick Panin's eighty-eight-yard run provided the first six points of Michigan State's 35–0 conquest in East Lansing. Notre Dame did not penetrate MSU territory until the fourth period, with John Lattner reaching the Spartan 36 on a pass from Ralph Guglielmi. Michigan State finished second to Tennessee in the national championship derby.

Notre Dame's 400th football victory was posted at North Carolina. The Irish varied their offense against the determined Tar Heels, frequently lining up in the I-formation and shifting into the old Rockne "box" instead of Leahy's favored T, and sometimes ran off plays without shifting. The Irish second period touchdown assault that produced their 6–0 intermission lead was masterminded by freshman quarterback Tom Carey. It started with Paul Reynolds bolting twelve yards from the ND 45. It ended with Reynolds leaping one yard, over a pile of bodies, across the goal. Mavraides missed a field goal before the half concluded. Freshman Ralph Guglielmi was quarterback during the attack leading to Neil Worden's third period, six-yard touchdown dash mounting it to 12–0. The aroused Tar Heels tallied a touchdown as soon as they downed Notre Dame's kickoff. Connie Gravitte's aerial, and receiver Jack Cooke's run, covered sixty-three yards. Abie Williams kicked goal, leaving Carolina only five points behind and trying. A Tar Heel advance to the ND 7 ended with Gene Carrabine deflecting a fourth-down pass. John Lattner's interception frustrated the final Tar Heel assault, preserving Notre Dame's 12–7 victory.

In the next game, the Irish trailed visiting Iowa, 20–6, entering the last period. Lattner ran five yards for a touchdown (Neil Worden had registered in the second quarter) and Bob Joseph kicked point to narrow the Hawkeye edge to 20–13. It came to where only a minute stood between Notre Dame, making a magnificent

Ralph Guglielmi, 1954 All-American.

rallying drive, and defeat. But a pass interference penalty on Iowa had advanced the football to a yard from the goal. With 0:55 to go, Lattner twisted across, Joseph kicking the point accounting for the windup dead-heat, 20–20.

Another star was born in tinseled Southern California on Dec. 1, but it wasn't a Hollywood star. It was a Notre Dame football star: freshman quarterback Ralph Guglielmi. The young man from Columbus, Ohio, replaced John Mazur, the senior starter, entering the second quarter of the game against the Southern Cal Trojans.

By this time USC already was ahead, 6–0, on Frank Gifford's eight-yard run when Frank outmaneuvered Irish defender Bill Gaudreau. Notre Dame, on the ensuing kickoff, put the ball in play on its 23. Chet Ostrowski gained sixteen yards on a jump pass from Guglielmi. After some penalties, Guglielmi passed to Paul Reynolds for a first down on the ND 35. Guglielmi passed to John Petitbon, ND 48. Guglielmi long-distanced a pass to Chet Ostrowski at the Trojan 16. Lattner charged to the 3 and then scored on two smashes. Bob Joseph's extra point kick was blocked by Dan Zimmerman.

With the great Gifford running and passing, the Californians moved to a first down at the ND 23 but failed to score. So the halftime score stood at 6–6.

Dick Nunis intercepted a Guglielmi pass on the ND 33, soon after the intermission. The Trojans had been employing the single wing, but went into a T-formation play that caught ND defenders flat-footed as Jim Sears took a twenty-five-yard pass to the ND 5. Sears on the next play turned his right end and followed a cadre of blockers into the end zone. Gifford again failed the extra point attempt—Southern California, in front, 12—6, was finished scoring for the afternoon, though the Trojans subsequently had two notions about a third touchdown. The first was smashed when ND's Gene Carrabine intercepted a Sears pass on the Irish 27. From here, Notre Dame needed only eight plays to again deadlock the game.

Keeping to the ground and running Lattner, Joe Heap, and Worden, inside the tackles, Guglielmi generaled the Irish to USC's 39. Guglielmi here decided it was time to repay the Trojan trickery and sent two flankers to the right. He sent Worden spinning to the left with the football, and no Trojan touched the fullback on his route to the goal. Joseph again missed the extra point.

For the second time, USC had notions about third touchdown, and jaunted to a first down at the Irish 8. Flood stopped Sears at center, so Sears went to the air. Dan Shannon intercepted in the end zone.

Notre Dame moved from its 39 for the winning touchdown in the last quarter. The start saw Lattner taking a Guglielmi pass at the USC 30. Staying inside, Notre Dame carved out a first down at the 7.

Again freshman Guglielmi fooled the Trojans, sending Petitbon wide around right end to score. Joseph's extra point gave Notre Dame its final 19—12 edge.

The seven won, two lost, one tied season did not leave Notre Dame in the Top Ten, but the Irish were getting there. Bob Toneff and Jim Mutscheller were given some All-American credentials.

A 7-2-1 record in 1952 was good enough to place the Fighting Irish third in both final national rankings. Notre Dame triumphed over Texas, which finished tenth in the Associated Press balloting; over Oklahoma, number four in both final ratings; and against Southern Cal, which ended in a fourth place tie with Oklahoma in one ranking, and number five in the year-end ratings by Associated Press. The Irish tussled with Michigan State, unanimous national champion, before losing. It was a great season, though not starting spectacularly at Pennsylvania.

The Quakers were as much fighters as were the Irish. Notre Dame's only score came in the first quarter, when quarterbacks Tom Carey and Ralph Guglielmi generaled the Irish to the touchdown John Lattner scored on two thrusts from the Penn 3. Minnie Mavraides kicked the extra point for the 7—0 lead that was maintained until the third quarter, when Penn asked for a fair catch on its 35. On first down the

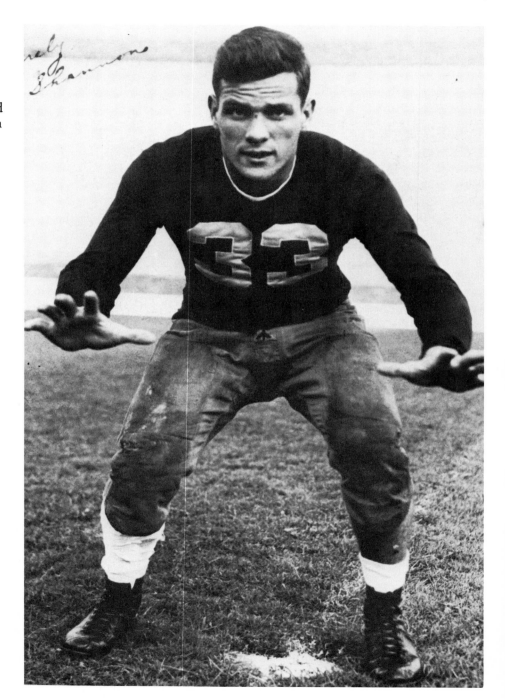

Quakers' Bud Adams threw to Ed Bell, over Dan Shannon's head, and Bell made fast tracks over the twenty-five yards between him and the touchdown stripe. Carl Sempler's conversion kick produced a 7–7 standoff, and that's the way it ended.

At Texas, the Irish spotted the touted Longhorns a 3–0 halftime lead. By the game's end, Notre Dame had registered touchdowns by Lattner, who plunged across from the Texas 1, where the ball had been placed following Joe Heap's surprise pass to Lattner, and Heap's fourth-quarter two-yard thrust. Minnie Mavraides kicked both conversions. Lattner's touchdown climaxed a seventy-four-yard advance, despite two fifteen-yard penalties, after the second half kickoff. Dan "Mr. Everywhere" Shannon set up the Heap TD. Shannon's tackle jarred the ball loose and ND recovered on the Longhorn 2. Offensive tackles Joe Bush and Fred Poehler opened necessary holes in the Texas line. Capt. Alessandrini stood out in the realigned second-half defense, one of the reasons

Dan Shannon, 1951-54.

Texas failed to post a touchdown for the first time in fifty-seven games. Intermission ceremonies were dedicated to Jack Chevigny, former Notre Dame assistant coach, and later Texas head coach, who died at Iwo Jima. Subsequently, Coach Frank Leahy recalled some amusing gamesmanship. Anticipating the ninety-degree weather and noting that Notre Dame's bench was positioned in the fierce sunshine, Leahy asked Texas officials if the Irish could sit on the same side of the field as the Longhorns. "Texas is a heavy favorite, and if we're fatigued by heat the thousands who paid to see this game will see only a rout," was the way Leahy argued. The Texans assented. Leahy also arranged for ice and sun shields.

Leahy wasn't laughing after Pittsburgh clobbered Notre Dame in a 22–19 upset. Pitt's 13–0 first-quarter lead stood at the half, the opening touchdown a seventy-eight-yard dash by Panther Bill Reynolds. Neil Worden returned Pitt's third-period kickoff to his 22. Lattner's sixteen-yard run, coupled with two Ralph Guglielmi passes to Joe Heap and one to Worden, carried to the Pitt 12. Worden went through the middle to score, Mavraides missing the conversion. Pitt prowled back for the TD that, with the conversion, established a 20–6 lead. Notre Dame drove seventy-three yards following kickoff. Guglielmi mixed his passes with running plays, a final aerial going to Art Hunter

one foot from Pitt's end zone. Guglielmi sneaked through for the TD, Mavraides adding point, and with the fourth quarter only ten seconds away, Pitt's lead had dwindled to 20–13. An interception stymied the next Irish drive. Then Heap, on a punt return, flew ninety-two yards for a touchdown. Mavraides kicked the point that would have made it 20–20; the Irish were penalized fifteen yards for holding. A premature center snap frustrated Minnie's second kick. Pitt mounted its winning margin to 22–19 by tackling Guglielmi for a safety.

North Carolina came to Notre Dame and it was 7–7 within four minutes, Notre Dame's Neil Worden posting the first touchdown. It was still tied after twenty-five minutes, when the Irish, travelling principally by air, began from their own 21. With halftime a half-minute away, Art Hunter collected Ralph Guglielmi's eleven-yard touchdown aerial. The second of Bob Arrix's four conversions sent the Irish to the lecture hall with a 14–7 bulge. Two second-half touchdowns were provided by Tom McHugh, one by Joe Heap on his eighty-four-yard kickoff return starting the third period. Final, Notre Dame 34, North Carolina 14.

Neil Worden scored both touchdowns, and Bob Arrix posted a field goal as Navy was scuttled in Cleveland, 17–6. Time now for the first match ever, between those gridiron powerhouses, Oklahoma and Notre Dame.

Oklahoma, unbeaten, was a twelve-point favorite taking the Irish turf. The odds seemed justified. Whereas Notre Dame had conquered Texas by eleven points, the Sooners had tromped the Longhorns, 49–20. Oklahoma also owned a 49–20 decision over the Pitt team that had beaten Notre Dame.

Three times Billy Vessels put the Sooners ahead—with touchdown bursts of twenty yards after a first-period pass from Eddie Crowder; sixty-two yards, and forty-seven yards. Buddy Leake kicked extra point on each Oklahoma touchdown. But the Sooners were playing the Fighting Irish.

A holding penalty set Notre Dame back to its 1 in the first quarter. Johnny Lattner's punt bounded backwards, dead on the Irish 28. Vessels took Crowder's eight-yard aerial and was touchdown bound for a 7–0 lead. Crowder's second-period fumble was retrieved at the Irish 41 by Notre Dame's Bob O'Neil. Guglielmi passed to Heap for fifteen. Guglielmi turned to the ground attack, Neil Worden, Francis Paterra, and Guglielmi himself toting. Guglielmi again passed to Heap, who caught on the 3 and fell into the end zone. Bob Arrix kicked point for a 7–7 deadlock.

Vessels' sixty-two-yard scoring blitz, through Notre Dame's eight-man line, gave the Sooners their second lead, leaving it 14–7 at halftime. Lattner fumbled to end

Notre Dame's march to Oklahoma's 6 following the second-half kick-off. Lattner made amends by intercepting a Crowder pass and returning to the Sooner 8. Offsides cost Oklahoma five yards. On third down, Worden smashed a yard for the TD. Arrix converted and it was a 14–14 stalemate, though only the third play following Notre Dame's kickoff. Then the Vessels lightning struck again. That forty-seven-yard TD bolt established Oklahoma's third lead, 21–14. Yet it was to be a long time before Oklahoma again ran a play from scrimmage.

Paterra took the Sooner kickoff from his end zone to the Irish 25. Four plays gained sixteen yards. Guglielmi came off the bench to lateral to Joe Heap, who fired a pass to Lattner at Oklahoma's 27. A penalty cost the Sooners five yards. With the ball at the 22, Carey returned to quarterback and sent Worden crashing the line on seven consecutive plays. The seventh Worden probe was for three yards and a fourth-quarter touchdown. A 21–21 deadlock ensued on the Arrix extra point.

Larry Grigg took Mavraides' kickoff on the Oklahoma 6 and charged up field. ND's mighty Dan Shannon charged downfield to meet Grigg. They met at the 20 and produced what became known as "the tackle heard around the world." Fans shuddered at the impact. Shannon was knocked out. Grigg was missing the football, recovered by Notre Dame's Al

Kohanowich at Oklahoma's 24. Lattner soon sledged inside Oklahoma's left tackle galloping to Oklahoma's 7. Quarterback Tom Carey came in to call Notre Dame's first shift of the afternoon. This maneuver pulled the Sooners offside, the five-yard penalty moving the football to two yards from the goal. It was a foot away following Worden's line smash. Carey then sneaked it over for the touchdown and a memorable 27–21 Notre Dame victory.

The Irish upset specialists went to East Lansing to encounter the Goliaths, Michigan State's Spartans. They took the lead on the eventual national champs with a third-quarter, sixteen-yard field goal by Bob Arrix. But the aroused Spartans rebounded to win, 21–3.

Leahy was ill, with Joe McArdle in charge, when the Irish won at Iowa, 27–0, with Lattner's eighty-six-yard touchdown punt return the feature.

Southern California's unbeaten Trojans came to Notre Dame in frostbite weather but found things too hot. John Lattner scored a second-period touchdown, Bob Arrix kicked a third-period field goal, in Notre Dame's 9–0 windup victory. Looking back, Leahy and his Irish could savor victories over Southern Cal's Pacific champions, the Southwest Conference champions of Texas, Oklahoma's Big Seven kings, and Purdue, which shared the Western Conference crown with Wisconsin (Michigan State still was not

involved in official Western Conference—Big Ten play), and that opening tie against Penn, the Ivy League rulers.

John Lattner was unanimous All-American; Art Hunter made some first team All-American selections; Don Penza received mentions.

"In my opinion, this is the greatest football team Notre Dame ever has had. It succeeded against a terrific schedule. This season thrills me. It is not often a football team faces a schedule like ours and escapes defeat. I am fortunate to have the finest aides in football."
                    —Frank Leahy

The 1953 season marked the return of one-platoon football. The Fighting Irish opened at Oklahoma, which hadn't been beaten on its home field in twenty-four games and was fired up to avenge the 1952 upset at South Bend. No matter that this time Notre Dame was almost an eighteen-point favorite. John Lattner juggled the opening kick-off at the 2, putting ND immediately in the hole. The Irish worked out to the 23, when Oklahoma recovered Neil Worden's fumble. The Sooners drove to a 7–0 lead. Now came Oklahoma's turn to fumble, Jim Schrader recovering Max Boydston's bobble at the Sooner 15. Four plays later Ralph Guglielmi passed to Joe Heap for the touchdown and Minnie

Mavraides' first of four extra-point kicks created a 7–7 deadlock. (Mavraides missed a field goal attempt set up by Capt. Don Penza's fumble recovery in this opening period.) Oklahoma marched eighty yards, highlighted by Buddy Leake's sixty-two-yard pass to Carl Allison, and went ahead 14–7 on Jack Ging's five-yard scoring thrust over center and Leake's conversion. Penza knocked down an Oklahoma pass, then blocked a punt and recovered the ball on the Sooners 9 with less than two minutes until halftime. Guglielmi crossed in two carries. Again a deadlock, 14–14. Notre Dame took command, 21–14, in the third quarter, as Heap took Guglielmi's thirty-six-yard aerial in the end zone the first play after Guglielmi had intercepted on Leake. Penza popped up again to recover a Leake bobble near mid-field, Worden subsequently scoring on a nine-yard thrust and boosting the ND edge to 28–14. Oklahoma's consolation touchdown came in the game's closing moments when Merrill Green, behind the key blocking of Leake and Larry Grigg, raced sixty yards with a Lattner punt.

On to Purdue, and how much had Oklahoma taken out of the Irish? Not a thing. The Irish scored thirty-seven points in forty-one minutes, then coasted to a 37–7 decision. The ground offense ripped every Boilermaker defensive alignment. Guglielmi completed seven of nine passes, Carey was zero for two. Notre Dame recovered four of Purdue's six fumbles; Purdue captured three of ND's six. Every man on the travelling squad saw action.

Pittsburgh fell, 23–14. Then Georgia Tech's unbeaten Yellow-jackets buzzed into South Bend with intent to sting the Irish.

Georgia Tech, returning to the schedule for the first time since 1945, was unbeaten in thirty-one games, including five this season, and defending Southeastern Conference champion. Notre Dame, counting on power to overcome Tech's superior speed, ranked first nationally. The Irish power showed as they drove from the opening kickoff to score in ten plays. Neil Worden ran seven yards for the touchdown and Minnie Mavraides' kick provided a 7–0 bulge that stood at the intermission. Coach Leahy, who had been complaining of difficulty breathing, staggered to the Irish locker room and collapsed. Complaining of chest and stomach pains, he rested in a chair in an anteroom. Capt. Don Penza went

Guglielmi with ball, against North Carolina, 1954.

to check and, finding his coach receiving emergency medical aid (the last rites were soon to be administered), returned in tears to the locker room. "We didn't know if Leahy was dying or not," reported assistant Bill Earley. "None of us did. All the players cried like babies."

Oxygen was being administered to the stricken coach as the players took the field. Reporters who noticed Leahy's absence on the bench—Joe McArdle and Earley were directing the team—raced to the dressing room. They arrived to see a stretcher transporting the pale coach to an ambulance headed for St. Joseph Hospital. President Theodore Hesburgh and Bonnie Rockne also headed for the hospital.

Georgia Tech tied it, 7—7, on Ward Mitchell's one-yard TD thrust. Johnny Lattner subsequently explained: "We were really worried. So confused we let Georgia Tech get that touchdown. But when Tech tied it, we just got mad. Every chance we got we talked about Coach Leahy."

Joe Heap returned the ensuing kickoff thirty-five yards to launch an attack climaxed by Guglielmi's nine-yard scoring pass to Heap. With 4:05 to play in the third quarter, Mavraides' kick provided ND a 14—7 cushion. Georgia Tech had to punt from its 13 and Jim Carlen had a bad pass from center Jimmy Morris. Carlen made two futile attempts to recover in the end zone, but Notre Dame's Art Hunter made the recovery for an ND touchdown. Down 21—7, Georgia Tech fought back and narrowed the advantage to seven points with a fifty-three-yard touchdown pass in the fourth quarter. Heap's twenty-eight-yard punt return touched up the clinching Irish drive, with Lattner scoring from the 1. Final, 28—14.

Leahy's brother, Tom, came to the winner's locker room, grabbed Capt. Penza, and said: "Frank asked me to congratulate the team on its wonderful showing." Tom reported that preliminary examinations ruled out a heart attack and that the diagnosis was virus enteritis. Later it was discovered that coach Leahy had an attack of pancreatitis, which sometimes is fatal. Three days later he was watching practices via closed-circuit television and advising assistants by telephone.

Leahy reported he must watch the Navy game on TV at his home in Long Beach, Ind., and that McArdle would direct the team with assists from Earley and Bob McBride, with Johnny Lujack on the press-box phones and freshman coach Terry Brennan watching from a scoreboard vantage point at one end of Notre Dame stadium. Notre Dame beat Navy, 38—7. Leahy was back at the helm to go to Pennsylvania for a 28—20 Irish conquest and to North Carolina, where a 34—14 win ran Notre Dame's 1953 streak to seven, all impressive. Next, Iowa's Hawkeyes, which had tied ND in 1951, appeared at South Bend.

The Hawkeyes intended to be spoilers, and almost were. A pass interception torched a seventy-one-yard scoring drive, pushing Iowa to a 7—0 lead in the first quarter. Late in the second period Lattner returned a punt twenty-five yards and Notre Dame was marching. By the time the Irish reached Iowa's 12, they had exhausted their time-outs and the clock seemed destined to end the half before another play. Frank Varrichione, utilizing a trick almost as old as football, sank to the turf, apparently injured. Officials called time and Varrichione was taken from the field. The Irish huddled and play was resumed with two seconds to go. Guglielmi fired a tying touchdown pass to Dan Shannon in the end zone, making it 7—7.

Iowa intercepted a Guglielmi pass on the ND 48 late in the fourth quarter, advancing to a 14—7 bulge when Frank Gilliam caught a four-yard TD pass. Once more Notre Dame had to chase the clock. The unbeaten season seemed doomed.

They took to the air following Worden's twenty-one-yard kickoff return. Lattner caught three consecutive passes as the drive reached Iowa's 9. After Guglielmi missed two consecutive passes to Heap, there was time for one more play. Six seconds remained as Guglielmi, running to his left, passed far to the right to again hit Shannon in the end zone. That left it up to sophomore Don Schaefer, who had kicked the first extra point. Again Schaefer made good, achieving a 14—14 tie. The game ended on Notre Dame's kickoff.

Because it was Notre Dame, Varrichione was criticized for the first-half ploy which so many other teams had employed without causing any adverse comment. Reporters asked Lattner about the injury, pointing out that Varrichione was back for the second half. "Pretty smart thinking, wasn't it?" asked Johnny. In the press box, one old-timer commented, "I saw a Big Ten team in that situation once, and all eleven of their men dropped down with injuries at the same time."

Tied, yes. But still unbeaten and off to Southern California, where an earthquake named Lattner rocked the Trojans. Lattner scored four touchdowns—the first player ever to tally that many against USC—in the 48—14 rout. One Lattner scoring jaunt was fifty yards. He averaged 9.25 yards in seventeen carries. Heap rocked ND to a 6—0 lead on a ninety-four-yard punt return. Other Notre Dame touchdowns were contributed by Worden and Pat Bisceglia, also heralded for his outstanding line play. Worden scored on a two-yard thrust immediately following his fifty-five-yard run. Bisceglia recovered a fumbled Trojan end zone lateral. Among the non-scoring standouts were Ray Lemek ("there was no greater player in the game"), Art Hunter, Jack Lee, Jim Schrader, Dan Shannon, and Capt. Don Penza. And then it was home to take on Southern Methodist and see if Coach Leahy would have his first unbeaten season since 1949. He would.

Southern Methodist was pummeled, 40–14. Worden scored three touchdowns, running his career total to twenty-nine. Lattner added two, and Varrichione was credited with a touchdown for recovering the end-zone fumble after Paul Matz's hard tackle on the Mustangs passer. Wilfrid Smith of *The Chicago Tribune* wrote: "Notre Dame proved to a crowd of 55,522 and millions of television viewers it has one of the great offensive football teams in collegiate history."

At the game's end, the blue-jerseyed Irish put Leahy on their shoulders and carried him to the western stands, where he waved and blew kisses to his wife, Florence. The press was kept waiting as Leahy thanked his squad, praised them as "the greatest," and asked that all go to Dillon Hall chapel for prayers of thanksgiving as soon as they were dressed. Only after that did Leahy have time for the writers in the anteroom. He came in, accompanied by his friend, Arch Ward, who had witnessed the dressingroom scenes. Leahy told writers he believed this was Notre Dame's greatest team, ever. He looked haggard, but continued his high praise, on and on.

Outside, joyous students were chanting that they didn't care a fig for the whole state of Maryland, whose unbeaten Terps were destined to be voted national champions—ahead of the second-place Irish—due to the ND tie with Iowa. Lattner, who soon would be named Leahy's fourth Heisman trophy winner and repeat winner of the Maxwell Award, stood near a dressing room sign that read: "Through these portals pass the national champions of 1953." John studied the sign, smiled, and said: "I don't know if we're America's best team, but we've got America's best coach."

Less than two months later, the coach announced his retirement. To all except insiders, the question always will be, "Did he jump, or was he pushed?"

"You [students] are the difference in a coach's success. You are the spirit of Notre Dame. In Terry Brennan you have a truly All-American coach."—Frank Leahy

The Rev. Theodore Hesburgh, already nationally renowned in his short tenure as university president, made two announcements at the Notre Dame Club of Chicago dinner early in March of 1953: 1. Notre Dame, maintaining its policy against post-season competition, had declined a five-year contract to play in the Orange Bowl game; 2. Terry Brennan would leave Chicago's Mount Carmel High School to become freshman coach at his alma mater. Father Hesburgh said "the university has

Father Hesburgh and Athletic Director Moose Krause enjoying a 1955 game against SMU.

considered Terry as a prospective member of its athletic staff since his undergraduate days." Not quite eleven months later, at 10 P.M. on a Friday in January, 1954, Father Hesburgh summoned Terry to the campus to tell him that Frank Leahy was resigning. The head job could be Terry's if he felt he was experienced enough to handle it. As Terry accepted, Father Hesburgh offered some advice: because he was a relatively young man when he became president, Hesburgh said, he surrounded himself with mature, experienced aides. He suggested Terry do the same. Years later the president was to remind Terry that this suggestion had not been totally followed. The story soon leaked out that Leahy had resigned because physicians advised "withdrawal from the emotional and physical strain of football coaching." Speculation was that Leahy's successor would come from the staff: Veteran Joe McArdle, Bob McBride (a Leahy favorite), Johnny Lujack, Bill Earley, John Druze, Wally Ziemba, or Brennan, age twenty-five. Brennan's appointment was made official on February 1.

Terence Patrick Brennan! If anyone ever had a name fitting an Irish football coach, TPB had it. The signing of St. Patrick could not have been more popular.

The new coach had been christened Terence Aloysius Brennan, though one record showed him as Terence Michael

Brennan. He solved this at confirmation when he chose to be Terence Patrick Brennan. Even as a youngster, Terry was a headstrong Irishman. Terry was football captain at Milwaukee's Marquette High School, an honor previously held by his brother, Jimmy. Jimmy played for Notre Dame in 1944 and his raves convinced Terry to attend ND. A knee injury in Terry's senior high school year necessitated surgery. Subsequent injury to the other knee, at Notre Dame, influenced Terry to forsake professional overtures from the Philadelphia Eagles and Chicago Hornets. He was a better winner all four years as a Notre Dame back, starting twenty-nine games and scoring twenty-one touchdowns. He had eleven touchdowns in 1947, including the legendary ninety-seven yard kickoff return against Army, to lead the Irish in scoring. Ironically, Terry received scant consideration for All-American honors.

After graduation he enrolled in De Paul University's law school and earned his degree. He also became coach at Chicago's Mount Carmel High in 1949, succeeding Bob McBride, who was moving on to Notre Dame. His 1950-51-52 Carmel Caravan elevens each won the All-Chicago championship. Meanwhile, Notre Dame and Father Hesburgh were clocking Terry's progress, and this led to an ultimate changing of the guard.

President Hesburgh observed the change by saying: "We have

been richly blessed . . . . In Frank Leahy we had a man of whom the university never had to be ashamed—a good father, a good husband, a good Christian gentleman. We are not saying goodbye to Frank Leahy. He will live in the memory and history of Notre Dame for years and years."

Father Hesburgh then turned to Brennan: "This has been a very easy change, indeed. If I say Frank Leahy was a good Christian gentleman, I know this young man is the same thing. I think we could have looked far and wide and never found a better man to carry on the traditions." Leahy said: "Terry borders almost on the genius as a coach." Brennan observed: "A great man is leaving Notre Dame. There is going to be a tremendous void." He said he did not desire a mammoth coaching staff. When he came to select it, Terry retained two Leahy aides, Johnny Druze and Bill Earley. The other assistants would be Bill Fischer, George Dickson, and Francis Johnston. If Father Hesburgh took note that none of those three had previous college coaching experience, he held his counsel.

Moving up after a season's apprenticeship, Brennan was aware of the talent available. First, there was the freshman Golden Boy from Louisville, Paul Hornung, whom Leahy had predicted would be "one of Notre Dame's greatest stars." Guglielmi and Heap, suspended from school for breaking curfew after the '53 SMU windup, were

back for spring practice, set to anchor the backfield. Dan Shannon and Paul Matz, co-captains and starting ends, had played for Terry at Mount Carmel. So had Tom Carey, Guglielmi's perennial understudy and a first-string quarterback almost anywhere else. Three other ex-Carmel players also were on hand. Sam Palumbo would move up to regular left tackle, replacing Frank Varrichione, who went to right side. Ray Lemek again would be the first stringer at left guard, and with Minnie Mavraides gone, the regular right guard position was inherited by Jack Lee. Dick Szymanski moved up at center to succeed departed Jim Schrader. The graduation of John Lattner and Neil Worden had taken heavy artillery out of the backfield; they would be ably replaced by Jim Morse and Don Schaefer, the latter moving to fullback from reserve quarterback. Hornung would see action both at quarter and full. Paul Reynolds, a back who missed the great 1953 campaign because of injury, was set to go.

Texas came to Notre Dame for the opener. Old timers cautioned Brennan that twenty years earlier the Longhorns, coached by Jack Chevigny, scored a 7—6 triumph in South Bend to spoil Elmer Layden's debut as Irish chieftain. Their worries were groundless. Notre Dame vanquished the Texans, 21—0, in the first game under Brennan. Visions of an unbeaten season? They were shattered the next Saturday in South Bend as Len Dawson passed for four touchdowns to pace Purdue's 27–14 upset victory. But Notre Dame rebounded at Pittsburgh, 33–0.

Michigan State was an underdog coming to Notre Dame with dreams of a fourth consecutive victory over the Irish. The battle, over soggy turf in cold and drizzle, proved again that there is never any underdog in the storied MSU-ND duels. The weather made Notre Dame elect to kick off, and MSU took a 7–0 lead on a sixty-one-yard charge climaxed by Clarence Peaks' TD and a conversion by Jerry Planutis. Ralph Guglielmi's fumble was pounced on by the Spartans and they quickly scored a second touchdown on a long-distance pass play, Earl Morrall to John Lewis. Joe Heap's touchdown run, the eleventh play of a sixty-nine-yard foray, and Don Schaefer's extra point, pared Michigan State's advantage to 13–7 in the second period.

The Spartans received following intermission and Johnny Matsock's fifty-eight-yard break-away run advanced them close to another tally. Heap's fumble recovery halted this. Next time the Spartans sought to boost their lead, a Morrall pass was intercepted by Dick Szymanski and the Irish were marching. Heap's one-yard touchdown burst was nullified by a holding penalty. Heap immediately retaliated with a sixteen-yard

St. Mary's College girls, rooting for ND. Purdue won.

scoring run, and the Schaefer extra point gave ND its first advantage, 14–13. Morrall was short with a field goal attempt after MSU had blasted to the Irish 11 late in the third quarter. Early in the fourth, Planutis also failed a field goal.

With about six minutes to play, Notre Dame went into business from its 36. Paul Reynolds produced the touchdown by running eight yards around defensive right end. Schaefer missed the con-

version that would have given ND a commanding eight-point bulge. The Spartans had 150 seconds to rally. They needed only eight-five.

What a windup! Morrall's forty-four-yard aerial to Lewis set up Bert Zagers' fourteen-yard touchdown blast. Notre Dame, 20; MSU 19. Morrall knelt to hold for the Planutis extra-point kick that could tie things up. The Planutis attempt went wide. No one in the press box could be certain, but Notre Dame players—while cele-

brating the 20–19 victory—said Pat Bisceglia had slightly deflected the kick.

The following Saturday the Irish were in Baltimore to squeeze out a 6–0 decision over a Navy squad that their coach, Eddie Erdelatz, was to call "A Team Named Desire" when the Middies finished fifth nationally and won the Sugar Bowl championship in New Orleans.

After Navy, the Irish conquered Pennsylvania (42–7), North Carolina (42–13), and Iowa (34–18), prior to a visit from Southern California. The Trojan game proved a great day, but not until the total sixty minutes had elapsed. Rain left the ND turf slick and soft, a disadvantage for the fleet Irish backs against a burly Trojan defense. Notre Dame lost four of nine fumbles, two recovered by USC center Marv Goux. USC received and punted after one first down. Joe Heap slipped attempting the return and was out on the ND 14. Goux snared Don Schaefer's fumble. Five plays later Joe Contratto sneaked one foot for a TD. Following conversion, USC led, 7–0. In the second quarter the Trojans took over on the ND 19 as Heap was rushed on his punt from the 4. The Irish held, the Trojans failing a thirty-five-yard field goal attempt. Tom Carey, at quarterback, ran and passed in the eighty-yard Irish drive to tie. Facing third down at the Trojan 12, Carey lateraled to Heap, who aimed a running pass to Jim Morse. Morse made the catch a step from the goal. Schaefer kicked point, 7–7.

A third-quarter, thirty-four-yard field goal put SC in command, 10–7. Schaefer scored with a two-yard touchdown thrust, kicked point, and Notre Dame led, 14–10, four plays into the final period. The Trojans unleashed the horses. Chuck Griffith scored in taking Contratto's pass. With the conversion, the lead was back with USC, 17–14. Schaefer lugged the kickoff to the ND 40. Heap fumbled, the Trojans recovered but had to punt out on the ND 21 as the Irish defense refused to bend. Heap ran for three and Schaefer, who played sixty minutes, added four. Third down. Ralph Guglielmi faked on a split-T option. He lateraled to Morse, set to turn defensive right end. Morse had good early blocking, broke Contratto's attempted tackle at the SC 47, and completed his seventy-two-yard TD jaunt as regrouped Irish blockers cut off pursuit. Schaefer converted, 21–17. The Trojans subsequently checked ND only fourteen yards from another touchdown. On SC's first play after that blockade, Frank Clayton received a bad snap from center. The ball bounced into the end zone, leading to the safety accounting for the 23–17 final with 1:10 remaining. Brennan's Irish were 8–1, with only Southern Methodist left.

Notre Dame was the overwhelming favorite at Dallas because the star Mustang quarter-

back, Duane Nutt, was out. Notre Dame's Ray Lemek was injured and the ailing Szymanski missed his final opportunity to wear the Irish uniform.

Notre Dame was penalized 175 yards, not including a fifteen-yard assessment that SMU declined, and times when infractions were nullified by offsetting violations. Two last-period Notre Dame touchdowns were voided by penalty. It was the last ND game for Dan Shannon, Paul Matz, Sam Palumbo, Frank Varrichione, Jack Lee, Ralph Guglielmi, Joe Heap, and Tom Carey. Guglielmi completed nine passes. Don Schaefer and Heap gained two hundred sixty-four yards in their thirty-seven rushes; thirteen more rushes than were made by the entire SMU backfield.

Morse returned the opening kickoff to the ND 41. Nine plays later Heap tallied from the SMU 4. Schaefer's extra-point kick was wide, and a few minutes later that failure looked expensive. John Roach of SMU recovered a Heap fumble at the Mustang 47. The Mustangs pounded until Roach scored on a ten-yard burst through Notre Dame's defensive left tackle. Ed Barnet's extra point put SMU in front, 7–6.

Then Guglielmi scored on the option from three yards out. Schaefer converted to make it 15–7, in the second period. SMU could not advance following the kickoff. Bob Scannell, an end, blocked Roach's punt, scooped up the ball

on the SMU 20, and raced across the goal stripe. Larry Cooke's conversion attempt failed, leaving it 19–7, Notre Dame, at halftime. The opening ND attack in the third period sputtered at the SMU 5. Another was terminated by Schaefer's fumble. Next time Notre Dame moved from its 10, with Schaefer gaining a yard. Heap took the ball from Guglielmi, went into high gear after swinging around defensive right end, and eluded four tacklers on a eighty-nine-yard TD sprint. Schaefer's extra point left it 26–7 at the end of three. The Mustangs produced a consolation seven points in the last period when two Irish scores were nullified by penalty, and saw Paul Reynolds' thirty-four-yard run whistled back because officials ruled that Carey had been stopped before giving the football to Reynolds.

Terry Brennan's first Notre Dame team finished 9–1 and ranked fourth in final polls. Guglielmi was unanimous All-American; Varrichione and Shannon also received All-American mention.

After closing 1954 against Southern Methodist, the Irish opened against the invading Mustangs in 1955 and romped, 17–0. Indiana fell, 14–0. This brought up the first encounter with a new intersectional foe, University of Miami, a Friday night game in Florida's Orange Bowl. The Hurricanes had been pointing for this since it had

been scheduled. There were 75,685 present, at that time "a record southern collegiate crowd," to watch the Notre Dame warriors engage the "new gridiron Titans of Dixie." ND took the lead, 7–0, forty seconds into the second quarter as Gene Kapish grabbed Paul Hornung's eleven-yard TD pass and Don Schaefer made good the conversion. Aubrey Lewis sneaked behind Miami defender Mario Bonifiglio to snare Hornung's third-quarter, thirty-two-yard aerial, and jump the single yard to the goal line. Schaefer's point accounted for the 14–0 final. Miami, though, gave the Irish anxious moments, only to be frustrated by an ND defense that was "never better."

So Notre Dame now had registered its third shutout of the season and had won eleven consecutive games under Brennan since the 1954 loss to Purdue. Ahead, though, was Michigan State, which would rank second behind Oklahoma in the season's final polls. The host Spartans were eager to avenge the previous year's one-point loss at Notre Dame, and Gerry Planutis, Michigan State's "goat" in that defeat, was most vengeful. The Spartans mounted a late first-quarter drive from their 48 and it climaxed with Clarence Peaks' three-yard TD smash early in the next period. Planutis converted for a 7–0 Spartan lead.

Yet, before intermission, Paul Hornung engineered a 7–7 deadlock with the extra-point kick that followed his spectacular TD pass to Jimmy Morse. Hornung was in the grasp of a tackler, behind the Spartan 40, when he lofted the ball to Morse, who had maneuvered behind MSU defenders Gary Lowe and Jim Wulff at the 7. Morse made the catch and hastened into touchdown territory. Michigan State went ahead in the third quarter with an eighty-yard advance following Hornung's punt into the end zone. Planutis and Walt Kowalczyk were the workhorses as MSU stayed on the ground. Planutis scored on a two-yard plunge and added point. The Spartans, ahead 14–7, were determined to stay there while Notre Dame was probing to the MSU 29. Here the Irish faced fourth-and-two. Hornung was stopped inches short of first down on perhaps the key play of the afternoon. The early fourth quarter found Notre Dame starting from its 1 after a punt. Hornung carried first in a drive to give the Irish some breathing room. A penalty set ND back to its 9. Hornung was rushed getting off a pass and Spartan Embry Robinson intercepted at the ND 14. Kowalczyk

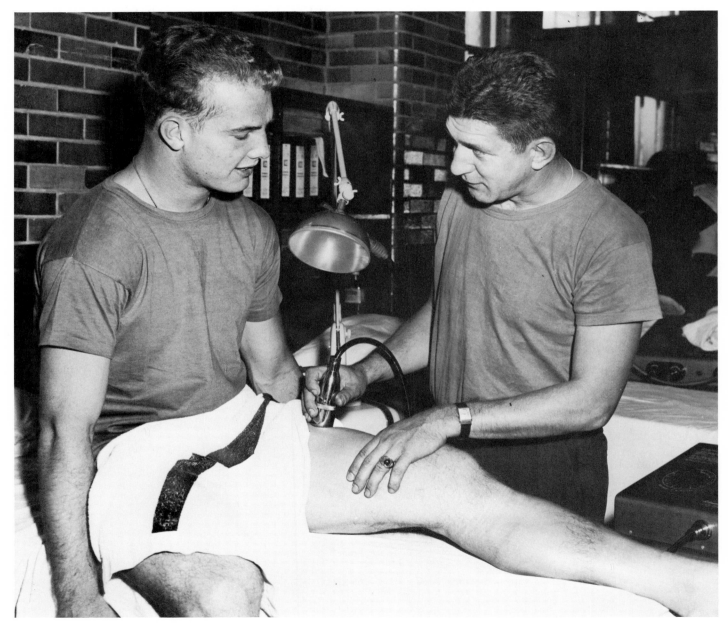

Paul Hornung, All-American and Heisman winner, with trainer Gene Paszkiet in 1955.

fumbled when tackled by Hornung and ND's Dean Studer recovered at the 9. But Planutis recovered Don Schaefer's second-down fumble at the ND 16. This time the Spartans would not be denied the clinching touchdown, Earl Morrall ultimately accounting for it by a half-yard sneak. Planutis kicked the MSU margin to 21–7 and thought, "How sweet it is!" When Brennan congratulated the winning coach, Duffy Daugherty, Duffy said: "You know you're in the big leagues when you take one from Notre Dame."

The Irish stopped Purdue (22–7), Navy (21–7), Pennsylvania (46–14), and rallied in the waning minutes to topple spirited North Carolina, 21–14, before Iowa's Hawkeyes checked in at South Bend. Starting with its 10–7 upset in 1921, Knute Rockne's only loss in three consecutive seasons, Iowa had a reputation as Notre Dame's Jonah. Would Iowa be up to it this November 19, 1955?

It was scoreless in the second period when Dick Prendergast recovered a Hawkeye fumble by Bill Happel at the Iowa 44. This led to Dean Studer's one-yard touchdown plunge, Paul Hornung's extra point, and a 7–0 Notre Dame lead. Iowa moved into a tie in the third quarter on a two-yard touchdown by Fred Harris and Jim Freeman's extra point. Notre Dame checked the Hawkeyes six inches from the lead touchdown early in the last quarter. The respite was momentary. After Notre Dame's punt, Iowa again began to roam and went ahead on Jerry Reichow's tumbling end-zone catch of Don Dobrino's pass. Freeman missed the extra point, but gained a second chance because Notre Dame was offside. Freeman booted Iowa ahead, 14–7.

Hornung ignited things by returning the kickoff to Notre Dame's 38. Soon Iowa was defending on its 15. Hornung chased back fifteen yards before seeing Jimmy Morse alone in the end zone. Morse made the TD catch and there remained 7:37 of playing time as Hornung's conversion created the 14–14 deadlock. Still time to shake down the thunder. The Irish put the Hawkeyes in the hole as the ensuing kickoff left Iowa on its 2. After the Iowa punt, Notre Dame rolled from the Hawkeye 43, and found itself with fourth down coming up only three yards from goal. Morse was to hold for Hornung's field goal attempt, but what's this? Notre Dame was penalized fifteen yards for unsportsmanlike conduct; "coaching from the sidelines" because some Notre Damer had tossed a kicking tee onto the field. Undaunted at the 18-yard line, Hornung mechanically hit the bull's-eye with his three-point attempt. Two minutes, fifteen seconds remained on the clock. The Irish preserved the 17–14 victory, happy that they had stifled three

Action against SMU in 1955.

Hawkeye scoring chances in the opening half. This left Notre Dame 8–1, and the favorites, heading to Southern California. The Trojans had lost four games, but no matter—they were playing Notre Dame.

Ellsworth Kissinger's one-yard touchdown smash sparked USC to a 7–0 lead as they advanced sixty-eight yards from the opening kick-off. Notre Dame used sixteen scrimmage plays, after receiving, to even up at 7–7. Paul Hornung, unable to find an open receiver, made an eight-yard run for the ND touchdown. Seven seconds into the second quarter, the Trojans had a 14–7 bulge, courtesy of a fifteen-yard touchdown sprint by C. R. Roberts. Within three minutes, the Irish again were in trouble. USC was at the ND 17, fourth down and long yardage needed. The Trojans sent in a sub, ostensibly with a trick play. It was. Bob Isaacson lined up for a field goal, Kissinger to hold. Kissinger leaped to accept the snap and passed to Jon Arnett for first down at the 10. On second down, Arnett hiked ten yards around his right end, and Isaacson's extra point left the Irish 21–7 in arrears. Two minutes before intermission, Hornung dropped back from the ND 22 and gave Jim Morse time to get clear. Morse took the throw in full stride near the Trojan 45 and went on to Touchdownville. Hornung's kick was wide. Between halves a ceremony honored the two coaches who started this fabled intersectional rivalry in 1926, Notre Dame's Knute Rockne and Southern Cal's Howard Jones.

Notre Dame was at the Trojan 3 when the scoreless third period concluded. Don Schaefer fumbled and SC's Ron Brown recovered. The Californians quick-kicked to the ND 34. Immediately a Hornung-to-Morse aerial had Notre Dame at the Trojan 6. Hornung scored on a fourth-down, one-yard plunge, and his extra point narrowed the USC lead to 21–20. Then the roof fell in. Southern California broke loose for twenty-one points. Jim Contratto passed to Arnett and Don McFarland for touchdowns. Dick Fitzgerald's fumble at the Notre Dame 21 set up Arnett's concluding seven-yard TD burst. Counting touchdowns and extra points, Arnett scored more points than the entire Notre Dame team. With its 42–20 conquest, USC had scored the most points against Notre Dame since Army's 48–0 decision ten years earlier. Notre

Frank Leahy watched a 1954 game after retiring.

Dame (8–2) was ranked eighth and ninth in the wire service polls. Michigan State was their only opponent to finish in either Top Ten. All-American recognition went to Hornung, Schaefer, and Pat Bisceglia. But the Irish were in for their worst disaster since the potato famine.

A small shakeup in the coaching staff marked early preparations for 1956. Johnny Druze, who arrived at Notre Dame with Frank Leahy in 1941, left to become head coach at Marquette. He was replaced by Jack Zilly, an end in the early Leahy era. Jim Finks, a Tulsa graduate and much later a top executive with National Football League clubs, retired as Pittsburgh Steeler quarterback to join Brennan's braintrust. Finks' priority was Golden Boy himself—Paul Hornung. Hornung was practically a one-man gang, and the brilliance of the blond bombshell from Louisville was one bright spot in a season darkened by eight losses. The 40–0 defeat by Oklahoma, and a 48–8 loss to Iowa, were the worst whippings ever suffered by a Terry Brennan squad. As a junior, Hornung had led the Irish in scoring, passing, and pass interceptions. In this senior season Hornung was to pace Notre Dame in scoring (fifty-six points), rushing (four hundred twenty yards), passing (completing fifty-nine of one hundred eleven aerials for nine hundred and seventeen yards), and kickoff returns (Hornung returned sixteen for four hundred ninety-six

yards, breaking the Irish return record of four hundred ninety yards set by Paul Castner in 1922). Hornung was destined to become Notre Dame's fourth Heisman trophy winner, and also to be the key figure in a season-end feud between Coach Brennan and ex-coach Leahy.

The first game, a night duel with Southern Methodist in Dallas, was an omen. The Mustangs grabbed a 6–0 lead in the first quarter on Charlie Arnold's thirty-one-yard pass to Bob Waggoner. SMU surged fifty-four yards in the second period, Arnold scoring on a one-yard sneak, to leave it 13–0 at intermission. But the Irish were not going to roll over and play dead. Hornung unleashed a pass from the ND 45 in the third quarter, and Capt. Jim Morse, gathering the ball at the SMU 35, streaked for a touchdown. Hornung kicked point, paring the Southern Methodist advantage to 13–7. Hornung sprinted fifty-seven yards for a touchdown in the fourth quarter, but missed the kick, leaving a 13–13 deadlock. Once more the Irish were threatening to shake down the thunder. They didn't. Southern Methodist did.

Arnold, a daring quarterback from Dallas Jesuit High School, paced the Methodists' winning assault. Coming up to fourth down at his own 23, with a yard needed, Arnold took a gamble. He handed off to Lon Slaughter, who made first down by bare inches. SMU again faced a fourth-and-one situ-

ation on its 33, and again Arnold dared, sending a Mustang back into the massed Irish defense. Once more the risk paid off by scant inches. But when SMU came up to fourth down on the Mustang 40, the needed distance was judged too great to justify another bold play and SMU elected to punt. Notre Dame was holding on the kick and SMU found new life on first down by penalty. Arnold passed to Slaughter at the ND 14 and the Cotton Bowl stadium was in an uproar. Only 1:50 was left to play as Slaughter, taking the ball from Arnold on a trick maneuver, went fourteen yards for the touchdown, sealing a 19–13 SMU victory. With one hundred ten seconds remaining, Notre Dame lined up to receive. A touchdown would tie; a touchdown and extra point would win for Notre Dame.

This was one of those back-to-the-wall situations savored by all Fighting Irish teams. Yet this night they were not quite up to it, though almost. Notre Dame had a first down on the Southern Methodist 7 as the game ended. The Irish had reached that point when Morse grabbed Hornung's forty-six-yard pass, only to be hit by a swarm of Mustangs at the 7.

Indiana invaded Notre Dame and came closer than would be indicated by the 20–6 verdict for the Irish. Notre Dame led, 7–0, within less than six minutes, Hornung getting the TD on two plunges from the Hoosier 5. Notre Dame was in front at the half, 13–6, after

Hornung's twelve-yard touchdown pass to Aubrey Lewis. Indiana came within a foot of the ND goal in the third period, when Notre Dame wound up the scoring with a ninety-eight-yard drive culminated by Lewis's nine-yard touchdown sweep.

Now it was disaster time. Purdue won, 28–14. Michigan State overcame Notre Dame's stubborn first half play to ease to a 47–14 conquest. Losses to Oklahoma, Navy (33–7), and Pittsburgh (26–13) followed. North Carolina came in for Hornung's last game in Notre Dame Stadium. It was Paul's big day: he scored all the points in a 21–14 ND triumph. He set up the first Irish touchdown with a long pass to Morse, then carried over from a foot out, to make it 7–0 in the second quarter. Moments later Co-Capt. Ed Sullivan intercepted a North Carolina pass at the ND 22. Aubrey Lewis scooted seventy-eight yards to get within the shadow of the Tarheel goal posts. Hornung's plunge through defensive left tackle put the Irish up, 14–0.

1956 action at East Lansing. MSU 47; ND 14.

A North Carolina touchdown via the air lanes narrowed this to 14—7 before intermission. The Tarheels began the third period as they had ended the second, going sixty-three yards to score and effect a 14—14 stalemate. North Carolina quickly came knocking again, determined to take the lead. Another pass interception by Sullivan stymied that drive. The deadlock obtained until seventy-six seconds remained, when Hornung plunged one foot for his third touchdown. He scored his third extra point with some help from fate. A high pass from center forced Paul to try to run on the conversion attempt, and he was inundated by North Carolina tacklers. An offside on the Tarheels gave Hornung another chance, and this time Paul made the kick. At the gun, one would have thought the Irish had won the Rose Bowl. The jubilance ended the next Saturday with the humiliating loss at Iowa. And then, the windup at Southern California.

The Fighting Irish started fighting among themselves after they arrived at Los Angeles. Ex-coach Leahy declared that the 1956 Notre Dame team was letting down. "This is the first Notre Dame team without fight," said Leahy. "What has happened to the old Notre Dame spirit, those great fourth-quarter finishes, that old try right down to the final whistle even if there were no chance of winning?"

Immediately former Coach Elmer Layden agreed to a request

to respond: "Leahy's statements were in poor taste. Leahy's publicity-crazy. He's trying to keep his name in the newspapers. When I was at Notre Dame, I coached under an eight semester rule. So does Brennan. But due to the war, some of Leahy's best players were seven years older when they graduated than when they enrolled. Being able to coach men, instead of boys, is nice if you can get it."

Brennan told me he would not comment on Leahy's remarks until after the Trojan game, when he would have a blistering answer. He briefed me on how the situation would be explained: "It's vindictiveness. Frank is mad because I will not let Hornung appear on his television show. I tried to reason with Coach, pointing out that when he was at Notre Dame he took strong precautions against the players being distracted prior to a big game."

Minutes later I sought comment from a high official at Notre Dame and was told: "Brennan is not going to make any statement." I said, "But he already has made it to me, and I feel free to print it after the game." In that event, I was told, Brennan could lose his job immediately. And the Notre Dame official reminded me that ex-Notre Damer Arch Ward, my predecessor as *The Chicago Tribune's* columnist, "never would print such a story about Notre Dame." Maybe so, I agreed, "but *The Tribune's* column has changed hands." Though it was

contrary to all my feelings as a newspaperman, I deferred to Brennan's job and never printed his side of the brouhaha.

Bob Williams was quarterback against the Trojans. Hornung, suffering injured thumbs, played left half and carried only nine times. He completed one of two passes, returned two punts for forty-five yards, and made four tackles. Southern California took a 7–0 lead. Williams went six yards for a matching touchdown but Hornung missed the extra-point kick. Notre Dame kicked off and Southern Cal drove back to boost its margin to 14–6. Bob Wetoska scored on a ten-yard pass from Williams, with Hornung kicking the point, and the Trojans' halftime lead was a skimpy 14–13. That was boosted to 21–13 with touchdown late in the third quarter, yet lasted only as long as it took Hornung to seize the ensuing kickoff on the ND 5 and run ninety-five yards to the goal. Paul had straight-armed himself into the clear by the time he passed the Irish 35 and had open sailing. He kicked the point and again the Irish trailed by only one. The Trojans clinched things, 28–20, with a final TD and conversion. As Hornung walked off the field afterwards, he was besieged and cheered by admiring Southern California players.

And Frank Leahy said: "They played like a real Notre Dame team. I'm proud of them."

Memories of 1956's two-victory, eight-defeat campaign—up to this

time the most disappointing in ND history—were still fresh and rankling early in January of 1957 when the Rev. Theodore Hesburgh, the university president, announced: "Coach Terry Brennan was engaged in 1954 on a verbal agreement for three years. Upon recommendation of the faculty board of athletics we are now reengaging him for next year." So began a rebuilding that, considering the departure of Paul Hornung, the Heisman trophy winner, and Capt. Jim Morse, left Brennan with an unenviable challenge.

The opener was at Purdue. The Irish drove seventy-six yards to a touchdown the second time they had the ball. A key play was halfback Dick Lynch's running pass to Aubrey Lewis for a first down at Purdue's 37. Later, only twelve yards from the goal, quarterback Bob Williams faked a handoff to Lewis and passed to Lynch. Lynch evaded Purdue's Tom Fletcher and Nick Mumley to cross the goal. Lewis missed the extra-point kick. Late in the game, Williams passed fifty-nine yards to Bob Wetoska, who was tackled by Leonard Wilson on the Purdue 8. Chuck Lima ran for two yards to set up Williams's six-yard TD pass to Frank Reynolds, running the score to the final 12–0 with sixty-one seconds left. Despite some fierce Purdue line play, ND clearly was superior.

Indiana fell, 26–0. Next came Army, absent from the schedule for ten years. A crowd of 95,000 in Philadelphia saw the Irish win, 23–

21, on Monty Stickles' field goal. After a 13–7 conquest of Pittsburgh, the born-again Irish were four-and-zero. But immediately ahead were Navy, to be ranked fifth in the final Associated Press ratings poll, and Michigan State, which would wind up third in the AP year-end poll. Navy won, 20–6, in the rain at Notre Dame. Michigan State triumphed (34–6) for the third consecutive season.

So some doubts about the team had arisen when the Irish embarked for Oklahoma for a game that will stir memories as long as football is played. Oklahoma hadn't lost in forty-seven games; not since that 28–21 defeat by Leahy's Notre Damers in 1953. The Sooners had not been shut out of the scoring column in one hundred twenty-two games and were at least three-touchdown favorites. Many predicted the outcome would be as dire as the previous year, when Oklahoma invaded Notre Dame for a 40–0 decision. Oklahoma was a powerhouse that would finish fourth in the final rankings. And here's why the Sooners didn't wind up in a more lofty niche:

This day Notre Dame's men indeed were the *Fighting* Irish. In the second quarter, Nick Pietrosante recovered a fumble on the Oklahoma 49. The Irish probed deep and eventually were a foot short of the Sooner goal, with two downs left. The Sooners were also fighting and their defense won the battle of inches. ND came back later to threaten from the Oklahoma 5. Frank Reynolds aimed a running pass at Monty Stickles. Oklahoma's Dave Baker intercepted in the end zone. The hands of the clock were washing away the precious closing minutes as the Irish began their eighty-yard payoff jaunt. They truly scrapped and struggled to a first down at Oklahoma's 8. Never did eight yards look so long. Lynch was stopped flat before Pietrosante gained four. Williams could pick up only one. Fourth down, three yards to go. Lynch took a pitchout from Williams, turned defensive left end, and zoomed across the goal. Stickles' extra point made it the winning 7–0. The Oklahomans were stunned by the upset, even more shocked at being held scoreless. The shutout was a tribute to magnificent defensive play paced by Lynch, Reynolds, Jim Schaaf, and All-American Al Ecuyer.

So looming now on the suicide schedule was Iowa, then a Big Ten dreadnought slated to wind up sixth nationally. The Hawkeyes won, 21–13, at Notre Dame. The next Saturday brought in Southern California, and the men of Troy took a 40–12 drubbing. The Irish scoring avalanche was triggered with Bob Williams intercepting a pass and running back to the SC 29. Ron Toth made the touchdown with a three-yard plunge through the Trojans' eight-man line. Southern California fumbled three plays after the next kickoff, with Notre Dame tackle Chuck Puntillo claiming the ball on the SC 27. This op-

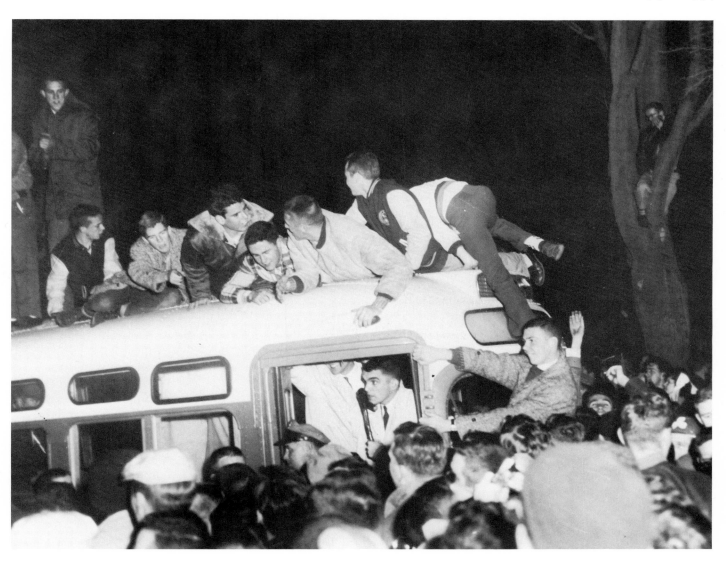

1957 homecoming madness, after beating Oklahoma 7-0 and ending Oklahoma's 47-game winning streak.

portunity was cashed on Williams' seventeen-yard pass to Stickles, who then kicked point to mount the ND edge to 13—0. Southern California moved back in the game by recovering a Williams fumble at ND's 22. Though set back by one offside penalty, SC scored in five plays; the climax was Rex Johnston's ten-yard TD thrust. The Trojan revival lasted only thirteen seconds from the ensuing kickoff, returned ninety-two yards by Pat Doyle. Doyle headed up the middle of the field, behind excellent blocking, until near the 50. He veered towards the west sideline and enroute to the end zone outdistanced the last two pursuers. Jim Crotty's two-yard scoring slash, on a quick handoff, concluded a sixty-six-yard Irish drive starting the third period. The Trojans, now opposing Notre Dame's third-string backfield and second-team line, retaliated with a sixty-seven-yard touchdown blitz. The Irish piled up two more touchdowns on passes. Bob Williams again hit Monty Stickles, this time for seven yards, on the same pass play that provided the tandem's early TD. George Izo's eight-yard aerial was nabbed by Dick Prendergast to end the scoring.

The windup in Dallas was an awesome 54—21 conquest of Southern Methodist and the brilliant Mustang passer, Don Meredith. Meredith completed seven of fifteen attempts, including touchdown tosses of forty-eight and eight yards to Lon Slaughter. The

long-distance Meredith-to-Slaughter relay pushed SMU to a 7—0 lead. Before the first quarter ended, Chuck Lima's touchdown, from inside the 3, squared it at 7—7. Three of the Irish each contributed a pair of touchdowns: Pat Doyle on runs of forty-five and eighteen yards, Bob Williams on runs of five and three yards, and Norm Odyniec on two rushes from close in. Ron Toth's touchdown was set up by Dick Crotty's seventy-yard kickoff return. The ever alert Irish capitalized on four intercepted passes and two fumble recoveries.

The Rev. Theodore Hesburgh illustriously completed his six-year term as Notre Dame president during 1958, but, breaking a long precedent, the Holy Cross order kept him in the post. The 7—3 season of 1957, meanwhile, earned Terry Brennan another term as head football coach. Father Hesburgh had a more binding agreement than Brennan.

Bill "Red" Mack made his varsity debut, scoring Notre Dame's first touchdown of 1958, as the Irish started with an 18—0 success against Indiana. A week later, in Dallas, Mack again scored the first touchdown to spark ND over Southern Methodist, 14—6. Mack ran forty-one yards, late in the second period, with Monty Stickles kicking point, to establish a 7—0 lead, although SMU was at the ND 18 as the half ended. The Mustangs rebounded in the third period, Tirey Wilemon scooting forty-four yards to the end zone. The extra

point attempt failed, SMU still in arrears, now 7—6. A seventy-two-yard assault in the last period, climaxed by Bob Williams' one-foot sneak for an Irish TD on the sixteenth play, followed by Stickles' conversion, insured the victory.

Now Army, to wind up third nationally, made its second appearance, ever, at Notre Dame. This was the last time Col. Earl "Red" Blaik would send a team against the Irish; also the last meeting between the ancient rivals until 1965. For this dramatic game Notre Dame brought back from Kansas the aging Jesse Harper, who had coached the Irish to a 35—13 upset conquest when the storied series opened at the plains of West Point in 1913 on an afternoon that saw a Cadet tackle named Dwight David Eisenhower watching from the sidelines because of a broken leg. The 1958 match-up between Army speed and Irish defense was to bring no joy to Harper. The speed prevailed.

Brennan, in the post-mortem, said: "There's no question about Army being No. 1 in the country." Col. Blaik noted: "We are happy to have beaten a Notre Dame team that played exceedingly well. This is a strong Notre Dame team."

Army's first thrust was thwarted when Bob Williams intercepted on Pete Dawkins, a left-handed passer who captained the Cadets, at the Notre Dame 4. The reprieve was brief. Army came back knocking, from the ND 21, due to Bob Novo-

gratz's recovery of a fumble by Jim Just, who had not been able to control the handoff. Three plays later Cadet quarterback Joe Caldwell passed sixteen yards to Jack Morrison in the end zone. Jim Kennedy missed the point. The 6—0 lead obtained into the third quarter. Notre Dame, back from the intermission with determination, pushed Army back to its 1 (with assistance of two penalties) and Caldwell elected to punt on third down. The pass from center was high and wide. Caldwell tried to run from the end zone. Monty Stickles grabbed his arm, inspiring Caldwell to cock for a desperation pass. Myron Pottios halted Caldwell for the safety and Notre Dame's only two points.

Army kicked off, Just returning to the Cadet 48 to torch a drive on to Army's 19. Three passes failed after a holding penalty had cost fifteen yards, and on fourth down Williams, unable to spot a receiver, was tackled at the Cadet 44. With less than three minutes remaining in the third period, the Irish mounted an assault that chained together five first downs. Twice the Irish made required yardage on fourth down; the second gamble resulted in Norm Odyniec's lengthy sprint to Army's 21. Norm, who had switched backfield positions in mid-week, was an Irish standout.

Nick Pietrosante plowed two yards to the 17. Williams missed two passes and George Izo came in to quarterback the fourth down.

Izo pulled back too quickly from center at the snap, bobbled the ball, and that threat was over. Next time, ND was contained at the Cadet 34.

Only two seconds were left when Dawkins, polishing off a fourteen-play assault, swept defensive right end for six yards and a TD. Dawkins pushed it to the ultimate 14—2, passing to Bob Anderson for a two-point conversion. Ironically, the Army drive that cinched the decision was almost turned into a Notre Dame victory. Knowing that a 6—2 lead against the Fighting Irish was anything but sufficient, the Cadets took chances. Caldwell risked a flat pass to Dawkins on the Army 44, practically inviting disaster. Notre Dame's Williams streaked between passer and receiver and, going full speed, grabbed at the football but dropped it. An interception would have meant a touchdown, probably a close decision for the Irish, because there was no one between the speeding Williams and Army's goal.

Duke came to Notre Dame, which took the lead within eight minutes as Monty Stickles grabbed an eight-yard TD pass from Bob Williams. A pass for a two-point conversion failed, making it possible for Duke to quickly establish a 7—6 edge. Stickles' twenty-three-yard field goal in the third quarter accounted for Notre Dame's 9—7 triumph.

The Irish lost to Purdue, 29—22, and defeated Navy, 40—20, prior to dropping a squeaker at Pittsburgh. The Panthers opened a two touch-down lead, following some scoreless skirmishing, by capitalizing on a fumble recovery and pass interception. Notre Dame rallied and was guarding a lead as Pitt faced fourth down, at the ND 5, and the contest's final half-minute ticking away. Bill Kaliden, reserve Pittsburgh quarterback, ran diagonally to his right and into the end zone for a heart-breaker touchdown as the clock reached 0:11. Notre Dame received and attempted a miracle play. George Izo hit Red Mack with a forty-seven-yard pass. Mack was not to keep his balance for a possible jaunt into the end zone. As Mack fell, so did hearts of ND fans. Great play. Tough defeat, 29—26.

North Carolina appeared for what was to be Terry Brennan's last coaching assignment in the Notre Dame arena where he had made so much history. The Tar Heels, after losing the season's first two, had posted six consecutive successes. North Carolina recovered a Monty Stickles fumble and quickly took over, 6—0, on its first possession. Notre Dame retorted with a three-touchdown avalanche (Nick Pietrosante's two short plunges and Red Mack's seven-yard run) and three extra-point kicks by Stickles, for a 21—6 lead. North Carolina, which failed all extra-point attempts, responded with its own three-touchdown salvo, firing the first when Wade Smith, gathering in a thirty-yard pass against defending Bob Scarpitto at the ND 3, continued into the end zone with 1:59 still to go in the first half.

The Tar Heels continued to chop at Notre Dame's 21—12 lead from the third quarter's outset. A pair of touchdown plunges by Kolchak, two and three yards, put North Carolina ahead, 24—21. Following kickoff, the Irish were goal-line bound. Magnificent Jim Crotty broke for runs of thirty-one, ten, and ten yards during the assault climaxed by Red Mack's TD run from the NC 15. Mack lugged Tar Heel Wade Smith across the goal. With Stickles' extra point, ND was in charge 28-24 but temporarily frustrated in efforts to boost the margin. In Notre Dame's final series of the third period, Norm Odyniec ran fifty-six yards to the NC 13. A subsequent fifteen-yard holding penalty on Notre Dame recharged the Tar Heels, who ultimately held for downs at their 9. Yet they only had postponed a fifth Irish touchdown. George Izo got that with a three-yard run, Stickles missing the point. Final: Notre Dame, 34; North Carolina, 24. Now to invade the lair of Iowa's Hawkeyes, the Big Ten champions destined to finish No. 2 (behind Louisiana State) in both final ranking polls.

The Hawkeyes never trailed, though they had only a 13—7 edge at the half and a 19—14 margin early in the fourth quarter. The fleet Hawkeyes opened it up to insurmountable 31—14, holding on for their 31—21 victory. Notre Dame scored on Monty Stickles' ten-yard romp into the end zone, after collecting George Izo's fifty-nine-yard aerial; Bob Scarpitto's twenty-eight-yard jaunt with an air mail delivery from Izo; and Izo's three-yard sweep. Stickles kicked all points. Hawkeye coach Forest Evashevski said: "I think Terry Brennan has done a real swell job with this Notre Dame team."

Notre Dame won at Southern California, 20—13, to finish with a 6—4 season record and No. 17 national ranking, garnished by some All-American rankings for Nick Pietrosante, Al Ecuyer, and Monty Stickles. The victory was not easy, though ND went ahead, 6—0, on Nick Pietrosante's one-yard plunge. The Trojans took control, 7—6, on the extra point following Don Buford's forty-one-yard scoring pass to Hillard Hill. Buford, later a major league baseball performer, was all over. He returned two kick-offs for sixty-eight yards, made the only Trojan punt return, caught a pass, gained thirty-four yards rushing, and came up from safety to four times tackle ND carriers.

Southern Cal increased its lead to 13—6. Bob Williams, who had lost the No. 1 quarterback job to George Izo during the season, was reinstalled after the Trojans began picking off Izo passes, and scored the second ND touchdown by smashing six yards. Stickles, who missed the first extra point, did not have a chance this time because of a bad center snap,

Williams downing the ball.

Southern California, leading 13–12, kicked to start the third quarter. Frank Reynolds returned to the ND 37. Norm Odyniec was the workhorse while the Irish ground to the SC 21 before Williams tried a pass. The aerial was taken on the nine by Bob Wetoska, who carried two Trojans with him into the end zone. Williams passed to Jim Crotty for a two-point conversion. Notre Dame's 20–13 lead was the victory margin after a scoreless final quarter that saw the Irish dig in to stymie an SC counterattack only a yard short of touchdown.

After mass on Sunday, I interviewed Brennan for a *Chicago Tribune* column. Some of Terry's quotes printed were: " .... I knew if we didn't get the breaks—

ND vs. Syracuse in 1961. A thrilling 17-15 victory, in which Joe Perkowski kicked the winning 41-yard field goal with three seconds to go.

and we didn't—we would do well to equal last season's seven won, three lost mark."

"Unfortunately, some always judge Notre Dame by the football material we had immediately after World War II. Many schools had fine football material immediately after World War II, but the situation was not a normal one."

Among other things, I quoted Brennan as expressing confidence in his assistants. I had some admiration for the man who had found the odds great, not small.

Returning home, Chicago writers heard increasing rumbles that Brennan was to be dismissed. They increased as time passed, so early one week I telephoned the Rev. Edmund P. Joyce, executive vice-president and chairman of the faculty board in control of athletics. After what I interpreted to be reassurances from Father Joyce, I told The Tribune's editors: "Nothing to it." The following Saturday I had a lengthy dinner with James Mullen, then sports editor of the Chicago Sun-Times and a rabid Irish fan who also had made the trip to Los Angeles. We spent the evening guaranteeing each other that there was no way Terry Brennan would not return for 1959. How was I to know that my sports editor, Wilfrid Smith, already had responded to an inside tip, made a hasty flight to South Bend, and returned with the exclusive story that Brennan was out? The first I knew was Sunday afternoon, reading the first edition of Mon-

day's Tribune. Smith's story pointed out that Brennan had amassed thirty-two victories, against eighteen defeats, and in his first season (9–1) had earned designation "as coach of the year."

Brennan and Notre Dame immediately confirmed Smith's story. Brennan said he had been discharged. Father Hesburgh said that the coach's release had been recommended by the faculty board, and that, as president, he had accepted the recommendation "with reluctance." Father Hesburgh had met with Brennan—reportedly in the same offices where Terry had been tendered the job—to deliver the news.

The day following revelation of Brennan's firing, the university announced its new coach would be Joseph Kuharich, who was leaving the Washington Redskins to return to the university where he had starred as guard for Elmer Layden's teams. The following day, two days before Christmas, Kuharich was on campus and asking for unity. Kuharich was more than an alumnus; he was a South Bend native.

But events were to prove that a woman scorned hath no fury like friends of a dismissed popular coach and his popular assistants. "Some Christmas present!" summarized the chant in much of the nation's press.

Early in 1959, Father Hesburgh telephoned that he would be in Chicago and wanted to have a private dinner with me at the Black-

stone Hotel. Over dinner, he detailed the hiring and dismissal of Terry Brennan. Father Hesburgh said that he originally had advised Terry to surround himself with older, experienced aides, and had on occasion, repeated the counsel. However, said Father Hesburgh, Terry was inclined to make his own choices and be loyal to them. The main reason for the visit, however, added the Notre Dame president, was to explain why Father Joyce had not confirmed that Brennan's job was in jeopardy because the faculty board had recommended dismissal.

"Father Joyce could not tell you about the recommendation," said Father Hesburgh, "because he hadn't even informed me. I was away at the time, but on return had a conference with Father Joyce, who was extremely fair in Brennan's behalf. He first gave me all the reasons for retaining Terry; then he presented all the evidence indicating that the board's recommendation be accepted. One of the strongest indictments was the attitude Terry displayed in the interview you printed from Los Angeles." Winding up, Father Hesburgh noted, "I don't know where we would have turned had Joe Kuharich not been available."

Joseph Kuharich, son of immigrants from Yugoslavia, was born practically within the shadows of the Golden Dome. With other youngsters, Kuharich took to sneaking into old Cartier Field to watch Knute Rockne direct prac-

tices. Often, Kuharich told me, Rock gave him a friendly smack on the trousers when he found Joe eying drills. Joe wanted to be a part of Notre Dame football and applied for a scholarship after graduating from South Bend Riley High School. Elmer Layden, then coach, noted that Joe weighed only 148 pounds, and tabled the application. Eugene "Scrapiron" Young, the Notre Dame trainer, pleaded the little man's case, and Joe was enrolled. As a sophomore in 1935, he was a benchwarmer watching that melodramatic rally to beat Ohio State, 18–13, and his weight had reached 188 pounds. The next two seasons Joe, eventually to play at 193, was regular right guard. He participated in another victory over Ohio State, and two over Minnesota's Golden Gophers.

Coach Layden said: "Joe Kuharich not only is one of the best and most spirited football players I've ever known, but he's one of the smartest." Layden hired Kuharich as a graduate assistant for the 1938 season; in 1939 Joe coached at Vincentian Institute, Albany, N.Y. The Brooklyn team had National Football League rights to Joe's services, but traded them to the Chicago Cardinals when Joe vetoed Brooklyn. Joe played in the Cardinal line in 1940 and 1941, sometimes calling Cardinal signals from his guard position. Service interrupted, and Kuharich was a navy lieutenant when he returned to help the Cardinals complete

Coach Joe Kuharich wincing in 1962. Behind him, assistant Bill Daddio. ND 43; Pitt 22.

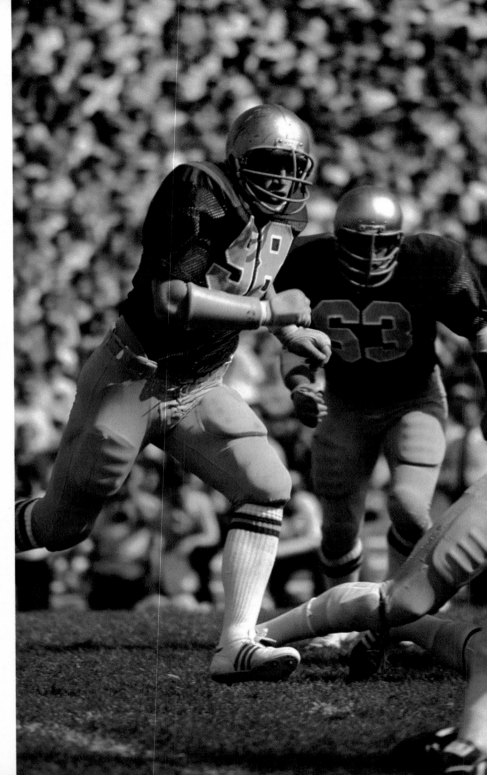

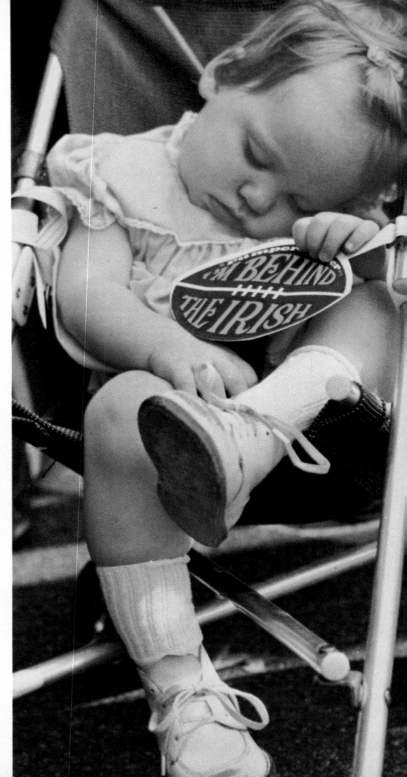

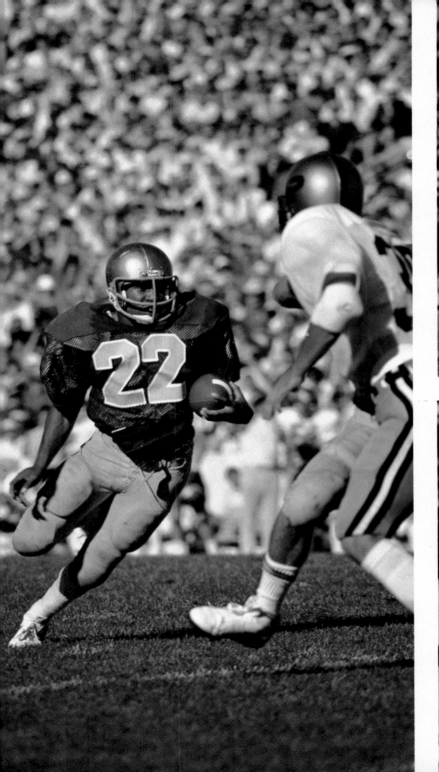
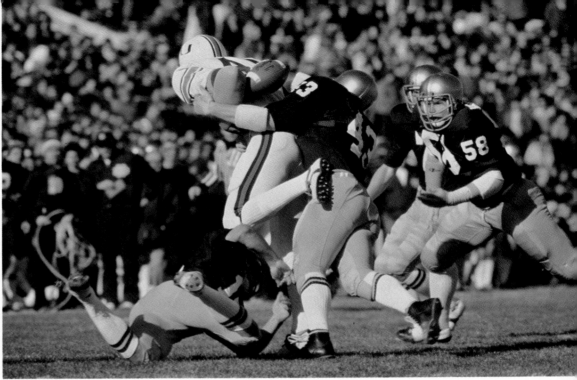

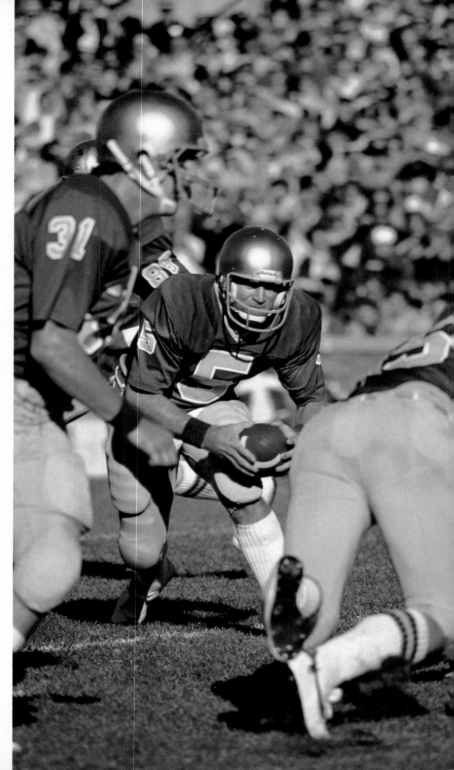

their 1945 campaign. Former Notre Dame coach Ed McKeever, leaving Cornell to become head coach at University of San Francisco, hired Kuharich as assistant. One year later, McKeever left to lead Chicago's entry in the All-America conference, and Kuharich became Numero Uno with the Dons.

Kuharich's 1951 San Francisco Dons were unbeaten and might have been national championship calibre although they were ignored in the national Top Ten rankings and when bowl invitations were issued. More than a dozen of Kuharich's 1951 Dons, including Ollie Matson, Ed Brown, and Gino Marchetti, had outstanding professional careers. Kuharich resigned from San Francisco—which subsequently gave up football—after 1951 and surfaced as coach of the Cardinals, who had considered him two years before when the job finally went to Curly Lambeau, the Notre Damer who ultimately put Green Bay on the pro football map. Kuharich's Cardinals started fast, then folded. Cardinal management and Joe hassled about two assistants, Mike Nixon and Bill Daddio. The staunch Kuharich said if the aides had to go, he also would walk. He walked and became an assistant under Lambeau with the Washington Redskins in 1954. Lambeau and Washington owner George Preston Marshall agreed to disagree and Lambeau walked, Kuharich moving up. After a good Redskins

season in 1955, Marshall signed Joe to a three-year Redskins contract, but asked: "Suppose Notre Dame . . . ?" Kuharich smiled and said: "George, you know how I feel about Notre Dame." Early in 1958, Marshall gave Kuharich a five-year Redskin contract. In December, Joe received a message from South Bend: "Show us a letter saying you'll be released from the Redskin contract, and then we can talk business." Marshall, with misgivings, signed the letter.

The North Carolina Tar Heels were well-seasoned and hoped to end their long string of losses to the Irish as they invaded South Bend for Kuharich's opener. Rain fell hard in the first quarter, when Bob Scarpitto's touchdown and Monty Stickles' extra point sent Notre Dame off to the lead, 7–0. Early in the second period Ray Ratkowski returned a punt to the Tar Heel 29. Don White's pass bounced off Stickles' fingers in the end zone. Ratkowski and Jim Crotty gained ten yards in a pair of thrusts. Crotty took a pitchout from White and, as blockers cleared the route, ran across the goal. Stickles kicked it to 14–0. Nearing the half, Les Traver blocked a punt by North Carolina's Jack Cummings. Cummings recovered on the visitors' 11-yard line. He punted again, out of bounds at the Tar Heel 30. George Sefcik ran for twelve. Three plays later Sefcik took a White aerial at the 3. White was thrown for a yard loss. Crotty plunged for the

touchdown. No matter that Stickles missed the conversion—Notre Dame had a 20–0 lead at intermission, with much thanks to the defensive play of end Pat Heenan.

North Carolina was shut out until twenty-seven seconds remained, when it got on the board with a touchdown and a pass for a two-point conversion. Notre Dame previously had added eight second-half points, so Kuharich began with a 28–8 victory.

A 28–8 defeat at Purdue was followed by a 28–6 triumph at California. Michigan State administered Kuharich's Irish a 19–0 spanking, followed by a 30–24 defeat courtesy of Ara Parseghian's Northwestern Wildcats. A 25–22 decision over Navy, engineered with thirty-two seconds left in the game, thrilled fans in Notre Dame stadium. They were not so thrilled the following week when visiting Georgia Tech sealed its 14–10 conquest with the closing heroics. A trip to Pittsburgh brought another defeat, 28–13. With Iowa and Southern California remaining, Kuharich's first Irish team had won three and lost five.

Iowa's opening lead was matched, 7–7, when Monty Stickles kicked the conversion after taking a touchdown pass from George Izo on a twenty-nine-yard play. The Hawkeyes added two second-quarter touchdowns, failing a kick and a run for conversions, to lead by twelve. Izo, who had been plagued with a knee injury since early September and had hurled only three

touchdown passes prior to this contest, rallied the Irish before intermission with another scoring aerial (total forty-four yards), this taken by Pat Heenan, and George wasn't yet through. Iowa was, though the Hawkeyes went into the last quarter guarding a 19–13 lead. That advantage still stood with 3:34 to play, when an Iowa punt rolled to its 44. Izo's first-down pass was taken by George Sefcik, who raced twenty yards goalward and tied the score. Stickles kicked the big extra point in a 20–19 Irish conquest.

Southern California arrived at Notre Dame as a strong favorite though beaten the previous week by UCLA after winning eight in succession. The injured Myron Pottios and Red Mack watched from the press box as Irish fullback Gerry Gray had himself a day. Gray scored two touchdowns, setting up the first with a thirty-six-yard run to the SC two. He got those two TD yards on the next play. Later, Gray tallied on a one-yard run. He also tackled a Trojan runner for a safety, so with the pair of conversion kicks by Monty Stickles, the Irish had a 16–0 bulge in the third quarter and eased to their 16–6 decision for a five won, five lost Kuharich debut season. Somewhat as a benediction, the Rev. Edmund P. Joyce said: "The team began the season as a young, inexperienced squad. It was plagued with serious injuries to an unusually large number of key personnel. As the season progressed, however, it demonstrated qualities which we like to see in every Notre Dame team—continued improvement, refusal to become discouraged by defeats, and an indomitable spirit to win over the best opposition." Oh, if Father Joyce could have envisioned what 1960 had in store!

Kuharich's 1960 Irish opened with a bang, and closed with another success. In between, frustration and desperation. George Haffner was ND quarterback starting at California. Notre Dame couldn't cash a first scoring opportunity gained on Les Traver's fumble recovery. They made good on the next break, Joe Carollo's recovery of a Cal fumble at the Golden Bears 24, with Bob Scarpitto's subsequent eight-yard TD run pushing the Irish to a 7—0 edge. Cal scrapped back to 7—7 before second quarter's end. The Irish solved this after intermission. Scarpitto's second touchdown jaunt was for thirty-three yards. Now the Golden Bears outsmarted themselves. Having fooled Notre Dame with one quick-kick, Cal tried another. ND guard Nick De-Pola snatched the ball virtually off kicker Jerry Scattini's toe and continued eight yards to cross the goal. Joe Perkowski's three conversion kicks contributed to the 21—7 success.

Notre Dame made a contest out of it only in the first quarter against Purdue's invading Boilermakers, who engineered a 51—19 triumph. Compounding the misery,

injuries sidelined Red Mack and end John Powers for the year. Mack, hurt in early practice, saw only limited action prior to the costly reinjury against Purdue.

North Carolina, after losing ten previous encounters with the Fighting Irish, finally took one, 12-7. All Carolina counters came before halftime. Late in the contest Max Burnell smashed into the Tar Heel backfield, forced a fumble, and recovered on the Carolina 25. Bob Scarpitto wound up this sole ND scoring drive by smashing across in two thrusts from the 3-yard line. Joe Perkowski kicked point. There was time for one more attempt for ND to rally. The rally ended with interception of George Haffner's pass intended for Leo Caito, and bells began to peal across the North Carolina campus.

The Irish never were inside Michigan State's 25-yard line in losing to the Spartans, 21—0. That was the fifth consecutive defeat absorbed from a Michigan State team coached by Duffy Daugherty.

First use of Leprechaun, during the 1960 California game. He's Terry Crawford.

In Evanston, a record Dyche Stadium crowd saw Northwestern post a 7—0 first quarter lead on Al Kimbrough's touchdown and Mike Stock's extra point. George Haffner threw twenty-five yards to Jim Sherlock for the TD putting Notre Dame on the board in the third quarter. The Irish debated the conversion; try a kick, or go for a two-point conversion and the lead? They opted for a Joe Perkowski kick that failed, leaving the Wildcats 7—6 victors. Later Coach Joe Kuharich explained: "Joe is a reliable kicker. We were beginning to move and thought there would be time to get down there again—at least to try a field goal."

At Philadelphia, potent Navy led, 7—0, after a quarter. Angelo Dabiero's three-yard scoring run and Joe Perkowski's extra point made it 7—7 before intermission. Strong winds were a factor in Perkowski missing two third-quarter field goal attempts to put the Irish in charge. Navy broke the deadlock in the last period and won, 14—7, following an interception on George Haffner, with a touchdown (Joe Bellino) and extra point.

The Irish invited Bill Shakespeare, Wayne Millner, Andy Pilney, and other heroes of the 1935 classic upset of Ohio State, to Notre Dame to see the Pittsburgh clash. Pitt rolled up a 20—0 lead before ND came to life in the third period. Daryle Lamonica, at quarterback, engineered his mates to the Pitt 10. Angelo Dabiero picked up a yard, then cut for nine more

and the touchdown. Bill Henneghan kicked point. George Haffner was at quarterback when the Irish gained possession at mid-field in the fourth quarter. Haffner passed sixteen yards to Max Burnell, to Les Traver for another sixteen, and then to Bob Scarpitto at the Pitt 4. The Panthers dropped Scarpitto for a seven-yard loss. Haffner missed one aerial but reached Burnell for a touchdown on the next. Henneghan's point kick went wide, leaving the Irish 20—13 in arrears. Notre Dame charged again, reaching Pitt's 39 before being assessed a fifteen-yard penalty. Still the Irish scented a triumph or tie. Haffner passed, only to see Pitt intercept with twenty seconds to go.

At Miami, touchdowns by Mike Lind, Bill Ahern, and Daryle Lamonica, all on short plunges, left Notre Dame even at 21—21 after three periods. Miami, which had never trailed, broke the deadlock on Jim Vollenweider's four-yard scoring run and Al Dangel's fourth extra point. The 28—21 loss was Notre Dame's seventh in a row and an eighth was on tap as Iowa appeared in South Bend. The Hawkeyes made their final game for Coach Forest Evashevski a memorable one for him in ripping the Irish 28—0. Iowa finished second in the final United Press rankings, and third—a niche ahead of Navy —in Associated Press balloting.

Now only victory at Southern California could prevent a 1—9 or 1—8—1 record that would have been

the worst ever. But Daryle Lamonica, the soph quarterback, came of age amidst the mud and rain in Los Angeles, and when it was over Notre Dame, if nothing else, was football champion of California (having won the season opener against Cal), and the 2—8 record no worse than Brennan's mark in 1956. With Lamonica directing the attack, the Irish rushed for 288 yards to seventy-four amassed by the weightier Trojans. ND ran seventy-two plays from scrimmage; USC only twenty-three. Southern Cal didn't register a first down until after Notre Dame had scored all the points in its 17—0 conquest.

Notre Dame's official response to the dismal 1960 campaign was to extend Kuharich's contract, which had two years to run, until February 1, 1966. Kuharich said: "Next season [1961] we'll have primarily a junior and senior team. We'll depend on experience, including Nick Buoniconti and Norb Roy, two guards who have just been elected co-captains."

Oklahoma's Sooners showed up at Notre Dame for the 1961 opener on a gusty afternoon. Senior Angelo Dabiero's fifty-one-yard touchdown run nudged the Irish into a 6—0 first quarter lead after Buoniconti blocked a Sooner field-goal attempt, Dabiero recovering the loose ball to set the stage for his almost immediate TD jaunt. Joe Perkowski missed the extra point, but Oklahoma's kicker also failed after the visitors made it

6—6 in the second quarter. Notre Dame stopped Oklahoma's next bid, triggered by interception on Frank Budka, at the Irish 26.

Taking possession, Notre Dame sent Mike Lind on a lengthy scamper. Dabiero added spice to this attack with a twenty-one-yard run. The payoff came after reaching Oklahoma's 22, where Lind found opening over defensive left tackle and continued on to the Sooner goal. Perkowski kicked the point. Notre Dame's maintained its 13—6 edge into the fourth quarter before icing the decision with a final touchdown drive. Dabiero touched the fuse by running for twenty-two, and soon again was off for thirty, in pacing this march. The conclusion came with Lind carrying two yards into the end zone. Perkowski's kick missed, the Irish ending up as 19—6 winners.

On to Purdue, which had administered that 51—9 drubbing the previous year. The Boilermakers started as though they meant business, advancing seventy-four yards in nine plays to score a touchdown (by Ron DeGravio) and extra point on their first possession. It was 7—7 in less than five minutes. Notre Dame posted three first downs in nine plays. Gerry Gray dashed for twenty-seven, finding the route clear after wedging through Purdue's massed eight-man line, for a touchdown. It was a fourth-down play, with Gray actually assigned to pick up the one yard needed to sustain possession. Purdue's stacking to stop the first down made things easy for Gray once he reached the secondary. Perkowski kicked the conversion.

Purdue throttled from its own 31 to the ND 4 in the remainder of the opening quarter. Roy Walker picked up those four yards and a touchdown, Skip Ohl again kicking the extra point. Purdue moved from a 14–7 lead to 17–7 on Ohl's field goal from the ND 26. Jim Snowden, following a twenty-six-yard Daryle Lamonica to Jim Kelly, plowed two yards for the second Irish TD. Perkowski's kick was blocked. There were still fifty seconds in the half, time enough for

Ohl to kick the forty-yard field goal sending Purdue's lead to 20–13. The Boilermakers were scoreless in the second half that produced an Irish victory. With a first down at Purdue's 5 in the third quarter, the Irish were expected to run. Lamonica surprised the Boilermakers by lofting a touchdown pass to Jim Kelly. Now behind only a point, Notre Dame disdained a kick conversion that would tie it. The Irish envisioned going ahead, 21-20, with a two-point conversion, Lamonica electing to pass. The aerial missed and Purdue retained its slim lead. Notre Dame kicked off, next forcing the Boilermakers

to punt out of bounds on the ND 42. Rally time, lads. Denny Phillips scooted for three. A penalty delayed the rally. Jim Snowden's ten-yard charge was the response, and Paul Costa carried on to Purdue's 47. Costa added another twenty-nine after accepting a deep lateral. Two thrusts by Snowden and one by Costa left Notre Dame short of first down. Lamonica held the ball for Perkowski's field goal projecting Notre Dame to the 22–20 victory.

Southern California, which had decided that its visits to the Midwest should be made in Indian Summer weather instead of late in the season, loomed next. The Trojans were held to a minus four yards rushing. Angelo Dabiero was the first Notre Dame player to get his hands on the ball, returning an SC punt for fifty yards and apparent touchdown. There was a clipping infraction en route, so the Irish started anew from their 45. They quickly amassed a 7–0 lead on Daryle Lamonica's twelve-yard touchdown run around his right end (Perkowski kick) and moved to 14–0 the next time they controlled the football, Perkowski again adding point following Lamonica's nineteen-yard toss to Jim Kelly in the SC end zone. The conversion effort failed after Ed Rutkowski scored from six yards out in the second quarter. Lamonica ran a yard for a touchdown in the third period, Perkowski converting. Perkowski kicked a forty-nine-yard field goal, Frank Budka holding, in

Action against Oklahoma in 1961. ND won. Buoniconti is 64; Dabiero, 44; Traver, 81; Perini, 84.

the last stanza, sending Notre Dame's winning margin to 30–0. After three games, Kuharich's 1961 team was one victory beyond the entire 1960 season.

Michigan State ended the party by winning, 17–7, in East Lansing. George Saimes ran for a pair of Spartan touchdowns, twenty-six and twenty-five yards, and Art Brandstatter kicked a twenty-yard field goal in MS's sixth consecutive triumph in the series. Notre Dame's 7–0 first-quarter lead, on Daryle Lamonica's two-yard touchdown run and Joe Perkowski's conversion, held until the Spartans took over following intermission. "We were on the ropes; we picked ourselves off the floor," said Michigan State coach Duffy Daugherty.

Mike Lind's early fourteen-yard touchdown run, coupled with Perkowski's extra point, sent the Irish ahead of the Northwestern Wildcats, 7–0. Northwestern's fifty-yard pass play produced a touchdown in the third period, but the Wildcats trailing 10–6 after Perkowski's thirty-six-yard three-pointer in the same quarter. Larry Benz, who tossed the first 'Cat TD aerial to Willie Stinson, clicked again in the last stanza with a scoring pass to Albert Kimbrough, rallying Northwestern to its 12–10 conquest. This was Joe Kuharich's third consecutive loss to the rival coach, Ara Parseghian.

Navy came to Notre Dame and was behind, 3–0, as quickly as Joe Perkowski toed home a forty-three-yard goal from field. Navy rallied with a touchdown, extra point, and a forty-two-yard field goal by the country's ace, Greg Mather, for a 10–3 halftime bulge. The Irish squared that on Dick Naab's short touchdown sledge, with Perkowski adding the point, in the third period. Daryle Lamonica's fourth-quarter fumble was claimed by the Middies, who seized the opportunity to move Mather into position to assure the 13–10 Navy victory with his twenty-two-yard three-point kick.

The Notre Damers reentered the winner's circle at Pittsburgh. They opened in the first quarter, Frank Budka and receiver Les Traver collaborating on a fifty-nine-yard scoring pass play, Joe Perkowski kicking it to 7–0. Pittsburgh countered with a forty-five-yard field goal prior to intermission. Pitt's Panthers surged in front by 10–7 as Fred Cox, the goal kicker, ran for a TD (two yards) and added the point. Dick Naab and George Sefcik ran for Irish touchdowns in the same third period, though both conversion attempts were failures, to establish a 19–10 bulge. Before the fourth quarter opened, Cox's fifty-two-yard field goal had pared the Irish margin by three points. Charlie O'Hara, from the Irish reserves, provided a forty-seven-yard touchdown dash in the fourth quarter, Perkowski kicking point to run Notre Dame's edge to 26–13. The Irish rode out a 26–20 victory.

Notre Dame has come from behind to win football games in strangely diverse manners and with seemingly miraculous maneuvers, but years later what happened against Syracuse still seemed unbelievable. At the end of one half it was Notre Dame, 7–0, thanks to a forty-one-yard Frank Budka to Angelo Dabiero scoring pass play and Joe Perkowski's conversion. Budka's twenty-five-yard pass collaboration with receiver Les Traver, and another Perkowski extra point, sent the Irish up by 14–0 in the third quarter. Notre Dame led, 14–8, at the conclusion of that period but Syracuse was on top, 15–14, as the clock hit 0:00 on what seemed the final play. Yet Notre Dame won, 17–15, and what a furore! Details of as wild-and-wooly concluding stampede as ever run off by the Irish cowboys:

Syracuse sought to kill out the closing seconds, so its fabulous Ernie Davis tried a fourth-down scamper. Ernie was stopped short, ND taking over at its 30. Seventy yards to go, seventeen seconds to play. The odds were never greater. Budka frantically hunted for a receiver, then in desperation raced just past the midfield stripe. Nine valuable seconds had been used. Budka quickly hurled to George Sefcik, who stopped time by stepping out on Syracuse's 39. Three seconds left—Sefcik knelt to hold for Perkowski's fifty-five-yard field-goal attempt. Sefcik was bumped by Walter Sweeney, Syracuse end, while placing the ball. The ball rolled to a stop on the turf after the clock had ticked to 0:00. But this wasn't the toll of midnight for a Cinderella Notre Dame team, and Syracuse had not emerged a 14–13 winner. The head linesman had dropped a flag on the Syracuse infraction. The rules, subsequently changed for clarification, were vague but specific that a game could not end on penalty. Syracuse was assessed fifteen yards. Perkowski gained another and better opportunity. This time Sefcik set the ball on the Orange 31 and Perkowski booted it home for the 17–15 conquest. The luck and fight o' the Irish had simultaneously reached their zenith, and thousands of fans swarmed on the turf.

Now 5–3 for the season, Notre Dame faced two concluding road games. The Irish hit the Hawkeyes for a TD in the final fifty-five seconds of the first half, but needed thirty-five points just to tie. At the half it was 35–7; at the end, 42–21.

At Duke, Angelo Dabiero ran fifty-four yards for a lightning-quick touchdown that, with Joe Perkowski's conversion, established a 7–0 lead. It was Notre Dame's only lead. Duke deadlocked the score in the opening period and went in front, 20–13, in the second period while Notre Dame's scoring was being concluded by the six points posted on Mike Lind's one-yard TD plunge. Final: Duke 37, Notre Dame, 13.

Mike Lind was 1962 captain, and the Irish suffered when the 200-pound fullback could see no more

A crushing tackle by Bill Pfeiffer stops Purdue in '62 at the 1 yard line.

than twenty-one minutes of action. The opener at Oklahoma once again proved the Sooner is not the better. Ed Rutkowski's seven-yard run, plus his extra-point kick, started the scoring. Oklahoma matched those points in the same first period and it remained 7—7 until the third quarter, when Bill Ahern's nine-yard touchdown trip accounted for the 13—7 final favoring Notre Dame. The waning moments found Oklahoma homecomers anticipating victory as the Sooners pulled to first down only three yards short of the ND goal. At fourth down, they remained a yard shy. ND's Frank Minik crashed in to grab a loose pitchout and, for a moment, that was that. Oklahoma had one more opportunity on recovery of Daryle Lamonica's fumble. Lamonica solved that by intercepting a Sooner pass and Notre Dame killed the clock.

Four Big Ten teams came up next, Notre Dame losing to all. Visiting Purdue grabbed a 24–0 lead before the Irish averted a shutout under leadership of Denis Szot, a young quarterback who set up the Boilermakers' last touchdown by fumbling at the Irish 21 after he replaced Daryle Lamonica. Szot responded to that bobble by engineering a sixty-four-yard scoring march that started with 7:56 to play. Jim Kelly climaxed the drive with his catch of Szot's seventeen-yard pass. The two-point conversion attempt failed. Bill Pfieffer recovered a Purdue fumble to send Szot back to work. Denis passed to Kelly for eighteen yards, missed an aerial, then reached Don Hogan in the end zone for an apparent TD. Penalty erased the score and this belated Irish rally fizzled. Yet Szot came back, taking ND to the Purdue 1 with a seventeen-yarder to Ron Bliey, as the contested ended, 24–6, Purdue.

A 17–8 defeat came at Wisconsin, which at year's end was to be rated No. 2 nationally. The Badgers went into the last period with a seventeen-point edge. Notre Dame finally scored, Don Hogan running three yards to goal with only 2:13 to go. Denis Szot, who completed passes of thirty-three and sixteen yards in the downfield drive, hurled to Jim Snowden to add two points by conversion.

Michigan State's captain,

George Saimes, the plague of Notre Dame in the Spartans' 1961 victory, was even tougher when Duffy Daugherty's 1962 crew invaded Notre Dame stadium. Saimes scored three touchdowns, starting with a fifty-four-yard burst on the game's fifth play. Saimes set up his second TD by intercepting a Daryle Lamonica pass. Michigan State already was in front in the first quarter, 12–0, before the Irish scored their only points on Joe Farrell's one-yard run and Ed Rutkowski's conversion. The 31–7 thrashing was Notre Dame's seventh consecutive defeat by the Spartans and Coach Daugherty.

Things were more brutal at Northwestern, Ara Parseghian directing his unbeaten Wildcats to a 35–6 decision before 55,752. Northwestern set up its first three touchdowns by a fumble recovery, pass interception, and a blocked punt. The last pair concluded marches of seventy-five and eighty yards. Notre Dame, down 29–0, produced its only points on Joe Farrell's three-yard run.

Big Ten opposition temporarily out of the way, the Irish went on a winning streak. At Philadelphia, freezing weather limited the Navy game crowd to 35,000, an excellent turnout considering that the inclement conditions kept attendances to sparse thousands at the day's other eastern contests. Daryle Lamonica's one-yard TD plunge, plus Ed Rutkowski's conversion, gave Notre Dame a 7–0 halftime lead. Navy went in front,

12–7, on third and fourth-period touchdowns, inspiring Lamonica to generate the winning rally. Daryle put ND in command by a point with a forty-five-yard aerial touchdown play that had Denny Phillips on the catching end. A subsequent Lamonica one-yard TD, with Rutkowski's extra-point kick, insured the 20–12 decision. Now three home games loomed. Daryle Lamonica threw four touchdown passes, three of them to Jim Kelly, in the 43–22 rout of Pittsburgh.

North Carolina went ahead in the first period, 7–0, and was scoreless thereafter while Notre Dame exploded for three running touchdowns (a pair by Joe Farrell and one by Daryle Lamonica) to win, 21–7.

The ensuing Saturday brought in Iowa's Hawkeyes, determined to give Big Ten Conference teams a sweep of their five encounters with the Irish. Notre Dame, owning only a 13–6 edge entering the last period, scored three consecutive touchdowns (Daryle Lamonica's twenty-seven-yard run; Lamonica's twenty-four-yard pass to Frank Minik; and Bill Ahern's eight-yard sprint) to put the game away prior to granting the Hawkeyes the consolation touchdown that pared the winning margin to 35–12.

The night before the Southern California game in Los Angeles, Daryle Lamonica predicted a three-touchdown Notre Dame conquest. Before kickoff the Irish received a "good luck" telegram,

bearing 11,000 signatures and requiring eleven hours to transmit. The Trojan horses ran roughshod to a 25–0 victory, completing their first unbeaten season since 1932, and winning the national championship in both polls. Coach Kuharich, who in four years had three five-won, five-lost seasons, and 1960's disastrous two-won, eight-lost campaign, said: "We were hurt by the loss of Frank Budka [broken leg in the second period], and Dennis Phillips' arm injury. Daryle Lamonica has had better days."

Though his contract called for two more years, Kuharich unexpectedly resigned on March 13, 1963, to become supervisor of officials for the National Football League. So, on short notice, the Fighting Irish again turned to Old Faithful, Hugh Devore.

Ara Parseghian's Golden Years

Bob Best

Introduction

The first time I drove up Notre Dame Avenue after being named head football coach, an enormous sense of responsibility overwhelmed me. The Notre Dame football program had been in a period of decline. It is hard to believe but Notre Dame had had several losing seasons in the previous years. Yet all of the elements for success were there. The great Notre Dame tradition of Rockne and Gipp, Leahy and Lujack was still alive, despite the eclipse. There were talented athletes ready and anxious to win. The primary task at hand was to restore confidence and belief in the Notre Dame spirit, in the winning attitude that had prevailed here for so many years.

I didn't realize the magnitude of Notre Dame until I actually came to the campus and began to be exposed to all it is and represents. There is a Notre Dame mystique that defies definition or description. It is something special in its combination of religion, education, and athletics. It is not only national, but international in scope. And there is a real tradition of achieving excellence whatever the odds. It was that tradition that we wanted to restore on the football field.

I had the good fortune of assembling a fine group of associate coaches. A team is no stronger than its weakest player on the field or the weakest coach on its staff. The coaches, like the team, need to work together, to channel energy in one direction, toward one goal. We did not necessarily look for coaches who had the deepest technical knowledge of football. What we wanted was quality people of integrity; people who could contribute knowledge and enthusiasm to our joint effort. We found them and they joined us.

Our first season was successful because the players and coaches wanted to win and believed that we could. People couldn't wait to come to practice. Their confidence and enthusiasm carried us to nine straight wins before a tough loss in our last game. It was an exciting beginning. Once begun, spirit, dedication and character have a way of building their own momentum. You could sense it in the way our people played and in the manner in which they conducted themselves, win or lose.

During eleven years at Notre Dame we regarded each and every game as a "big" game and we were able to win a large share of them. But the very success that requires and comes from intense and focused energy can also bring impossible expectations. Some writers seemed to think that the only "big" games we ever played were the ones we lost. Looking back now I have to say that the game that stands out most in my mind is the 1973 Sugar Bowl game against Alabama. Despite their great football traditions, Notre Dame and Alabama had never played each other before. It was a clash between two undefeated teams with the National Championship on the line. It was a potentially explosive situation with its North-South and religious undertones. What happened was not fights or violence by players or fans. Instead, two class teams met in an intense contest. After the game there was an enormous respect for each other and another great series in college football had begun.

My decision to leave coaching when I did was well thought out and I have never had reason to second-guess it. I can say in all honesty that the Notre Dame years were the greatest period in my life and my family's life. Our loyalty to and respect for Notre Dame will always be a part of us.

—Ara Parseghian

WHEN JOE KUHARICH left Notre Dame abruptly in the spring of 1963 to accept a fifteen-year contract to coach the Philadelphia Eagles, Fathers Ted Hesburgh and Ned Joyce knew exactly whom they wanted as his replacement. This man had been conspicuously successful as a head coach at two major universities—Arizona State and Missouri. The man was Dan Devine.

Naturally Devine was honored by the offer, but he actually had better prospects at Missouri. He had replaced Don Faurot as football coach and was eventually slated to take over for him as athletic director as well. When the Notre Dame offer came, Devine told the Missouri officials to *show me* and they decided to escalate the time-table for the additional role. So Devine chose to stay.

That left Fathers Hesburgh and Joyce with little time to find a new coach before the start of spring practice. They felt it best to look to Kuharich's assistant coaches, as a temporary measure at least, and settled on Hugh Devore. Devore had the deepest Notre Dame roots of all the candidates. He had previously filled in for Frank Leahy as head coach in 1945 while Leahy was serving in World War II. Devore directed that team to a 7–2–1 season.

Getting such a late start created an impossible situation for Devore, and Notre Dame's 2–7 record in 1963 really does not reflect the job he performed. The Irish made a

game out of all but two. They lost to Wisconsin 14–9 and Syracuse 14–7, with touchdowns scored against them in the closing minutes. They lost to Purdue 7–6, when the two point conversion failed. Their wins were against Southern California and UCLA.

Nonetheless, the decision had been made to seek another coach for the 1964 season. This time Hesburgh and Joyce were after a man whose record was not especially conspicuous. Not, that is, unless you consider where he established it. Here was a guy who had

an eight-year mark of 36–35–1 and one 0–9 season. But he also had conference title contenders, and fans at Northwestern University had not been used to that. This man was Ara Parseghian, and what impressed Hesburgh and Joyce was the way he had been able to beat their team the past four years. He did it at a university that was as demanding academically as Notre Dame.

Parseghian was their man, and after some last-minute soul-searching on his part, he became Notre Dame's twenty-second head

coach. The next eleven years would be filled with some of the greatest moments in Fighting Irish football history. They would also include some of the worst. Not in terms of record; for Parseghian's teams never lost more than two regular-season games. The bad times came with attitudinal changes in the players.

The changes were all positive in Parseghian's first season. Notre Dame had not won a national championship in fifteen years when Parseghian took over. The Irish had not even finished in the top ten

in seven years, quite a drought for Notre Dame. This 1964 team was ready for a change, and Parseghian turned out to be just the coach to give it to them. He pushed the right buttons with the players in his very first meeting with them.

"I've been around football nearly all my life, and I think I know what it takes to win," he told them. "It's like my fist. When I make a fist, it's strong, and you can't tear it apart. As long as there's unity, there's strength. We must become so close with the bonds of loyalty and sacrifice, so deep with the conviction of sole purpose, that no one, no group, no thing can ever tear us apart. If your loyalty begins to fade, it becomes a little easier to go out and have a beer, to slack off a little in practice, to listen to those who tell you you should be playing ahead of someone else. If that happens, this fist becomes a limp hand.

"Notre Dame has a great football tradition. That's probably a big reason you decided to come here. This team had a fire blazed to the sky in the past. Perhaps the flame has burned low of late, but it is not out. You guys could possibly be the first Notre Dame class ever to graduate without having a winning year. You don't want that, and neither do I. Within this room we have the makings of a great football team. We'll have to work. It's not going to be easy. But if you want it badly enough, we can do it."

Parseghian used the spring session to evaluate his personnel, and he was quick to shift people to new positions. Notre Dame may have had the biggest and slowest backfield of all time with halfbacks Paul Costa (240) and Jim Snowden (250) and fullback Pete Duranko (235). Parseghian moved Costa to defensive end, Snowden to offensive tackle, and Duranko to defensive tackle.

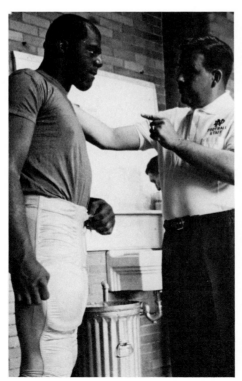

Parseghian in agony. USC just scored, late in the last game of 1964, to ruin ND's undefeated season.

All-American Alan Page picks up tips from defensive coordinator John Ray, 1964.

1966 pep rally, prior to Michigan State game.

But Parseghian's most pressing problem was to find a quarterback. His choices were seniors Sandy Bonvechio and John Huarte. They had been the backups in that order to the graduated Frank Budka. Parseghian saw promise in Huarte. Given this fresh start, Huarte's confidence increased daily and so did his completions. Unfortunately Huarte became one of the few casualties of spring practice. He damaged his shoulder in the final scrimmage before the Old Timers Game. Local opinion favored surgery, which almost certainly would have ruled him out for the 1964 season. Parseghian decided to send him to Chicago for further examination. There Huarte was advised not to have the operation but to rest the shoulder for six weeks. Huarte gladly complied, and his shoulder was fine by the time two-a-days started in the fall.

Huarte proved there was nothing wrong with his arm either in Notre Dame's first game of the 1964 season at Wisconsin. Ken Ivan put the Irish on top with a thirty-one-yard field goal late in the first quarter. Then Huarte spotted Jack Snow open thirty yards down field, and the speedy receiver took it all the way for a sixty-one-yard scoring play. Huarte was even more impressive in the second half, highlighted by a forty-two-yard touchdown pass to Snow. Notre Dame opened under Parseghian with a 31–7 victory.

Ara's first home game was just as rewarding, a 34–15 win against archrival Purdue. Then after solid victories over Air Force, UCLA, Stanford, and Navy, the nation started to take notice of Fighting Irish football once more. Huarte and Snow became instant sensations. The Irish, long the favorites of so many football fans around the country but forgotten of late, were quickly becoming the rags to riches team of 1964. *Life* did a feature story on Huarte and Snow. *Sports Illustrated* and *Time* both billed Notre Dame as the team to watch for the remainder of the year.

All that attention nearly took its toll. No one could blame these players for reading their press clippings. It had been many years since they had any they wanted to read. But the schedule doesn't stop with the presses, and Pittsburgh was next up. The team played flatly, but the defense was good enough to hold off the Panthers, 17–15.

This was a team that learned from its mistakes, and the Irish were sufficiently motivated in the next two games to beat the hated Michigan State Spartans, 34–7, and then, in 10° weather, the Iowa Hawkeyes, 28–0.

What Parseghian had done to get this team to 9–0 was one of the greatest coaching efforts of all time. In just his first year, Notre Dame fans were using the same adjectives to describe Parseghian as the likes of Rockne and Leahy. The Fighting Irish had forgotten

how to fight in much of the previous decade. They had lost touch with what it meant to play football for Notre Dame. Parseghian had never set foot on the Notre Dame campus except for the times he coached Northwestern in Notre Dame Stadium. Yet in the short time he had been head coach at this school, he studied the Notre Dame tradition and thrust himself, his staff, and his players into it.

That effort left the Irish one game away from the national championship. *All* that stood in their way was a meeting with the University of Southern California, a team that would haunt Parseghian throughout his career at Notre Dame.

The Irish got a break early. Don Gmitter recovered a fumble at the USC 46, and Huarte threw to Phil Sheridan and Nick Eddy to move the ball to the eight. Ken Ivan kicked a field goal from there. On the next possession Huarte threw to Snow in the end zone to cap a fifty-one-yard drive. Huarte directed one more drive before the half, this one seventy-two yards in eleven plays. That sent Notre Dame into the dressing room with a 17–0 lead.

But the Trojans were far from finished. They started the second half by driving sixty-eight yards in nine plays. Mike Garrett, USC's sensational tailback, scored the touchdown and gained thirty-six yards in the drive.

Notre Dame had two more excellent scoring threats but could not make them count. After moving from their 19 to the USC 9, Huarte and Bill Wolski missed connections on a pitchout, and USC recovered. Later with the ball on USC's six-inch line, second-and-goal, Joe Kantor dove over left guard for an apparent score. The six points were denied when Notre Dame was flagged for holding. That moved the ball to the 16-yard line, and in three attempts the Irish could not push it over.

Seeing Notre Dame fail inspired the Trojans. They moved the ball quickly down the field, and with 5:09 to play, quarterback Craig Fertig threw a touchdown pass to Fred Hill to leave USC trailing, 17–13.

Notre Dame could not maintain possession but seemed to be in good position when Jack Snow's punt put the ball on the USC 23. However, the Irish were again called for holding, and this time Mike Garrett

Nick Rassas celebrates his TD punt return.

All-American Joe Theismann in action against LSU, 1970.

Coley O'Brien at work.

returned the punt to the Notre Dame 40.

Fertig immediately passed twenty-three yards to Hill. The defense held the Trojans to two yards in the next three plays. With fourth-and-eight from the 15, Fertig dropped back to pass. Linebacker Ken Maglicic came within inches of tackling him. But Fertig managed to release the ball. Defensive back Tony Carey zeroed in, but in the scramble he fell, flanker Rod Sherman caught the pass and carried it into the end zone. With only 1:33 to play, USC took the lead, 20–17.

Desperation passes failed, and Notre Dame lost the game and all hope of achieving the impossible dream.

It was difficult to be a good teacher in such a despondent locker room, but Parseghian gave the team one more lecture on Notre Dame football following the game.

"I want all of you to realize one thing," he said. "What we do here and now will follow us for many years. There are thousands of things we could say. There are the officials and the calls we could blame. But when we won this year, we won as Notre Dame men—fair, hard, and with humility. To be less than that at this moment, to cry foul, to alibi, would undo much that this season has done. For the next ten minutes, no one will be allowed in here. If you've got to scream, if you want to cry, swear or punch a locker, do it now. I can understand all those sentiments. But after we open the doors, I want all of you to hold your tongues, to lift your heads high, and in the face of defeat be Notre Dame men. I've never been associated with a greater bunch than you guys. No one will ever forget the achievements you made this year."

Especially not the students, faculty and townspeople back in South Bend. On the day the team flew back, these supporters had lined the streets from the airport to campus, applauding their heroes in 9° temperatures. The team buses headed for the Old Fieldhouse where it seemed half the free world had assembled. The overflow stood outside in the snow.

The next thirty minutes were as emotional as any this university had ever generated. The crowd erupted when they saw the team enter. The players and coaches were escorted to their seats to a steadily building ovation. The applause and chants lasted for twenty minutes. This was to have been a spontaneous program. Still, Parseghian felt he should formally address these supporters.

"We wanted to bring you back the national championship," he began.

"You did, you did, you did . . ." they shouted.

Parseghian could not continue. The band played the "Victory March" and then the Alma Mater. No one, players and coaches alike, could hold back the tears.

The next week John Huarte was named the Heisman Trophy winner for 1964. Parseghian was selected co-coach of the year. These were awards both men richly deserved, but they were hollow consolation after such a crushing finish to the season. Given the choice, Parseghian would have traded his plaque for one less penalty against Southern Cal or one more year of eligibility for Huarte.

The 1965 team was built of good runners, blockers, and defenders, but no passers. In the spring there were three quarterbacks to choose from—sophomores Tom Schoen, John Pergine, and Dan Koenings. Schoen was the quickest, but his passing was erratic. Pergine was the largest, but though he had a strong arm he was inaccurate. Koenings was the best passer but did not have the agility of the other two. All three had drawbacks, so Parseghian looked elsewhere.

Bill Zloch had been recruited by Joe Kuharich as a quarterback, but Parseghian moved him to split end in 1964. Zloch had almost everything you could want in a quarterback—intelligence, quickness, leadership, and "moxie." But he too had one big drawback; he was not a good passer. Still, Zloch was a winner, and Parseghian picked him to be the starting quarterback.

Parseghian explained his plans to the team when they came back in the fall of 1965.

"We'll be a different styled team than last year," he said. "We'll play possession and position, relying on our kicking, defense, and ground attack. We're Notre Dame."

We can't win on past performances. We're coming along, but we've got a long way to go. I see some things that please me, but we've got to eliminate mistakes and penalties."

Notre Dame did not make many mistakes in the '65 opener at the University of California. Zloch even threw a twenty-four-yard touchdown pass. In reality, though, the Irish were able to beat Cal 48–6 with the things Parseghian had talked about. Notre Dame rushed for 381 yards thanks to Larry Conjar, Nick Eddy, and Bill Wolski. Nick Rassas intercepted two passes and returned a punt sixty-five yards for a touchdown. The defense played superbly.

Unfortunately, the same could not be said the next week against Purdue. The offense produced twenty-one points and with less than six minutes to play that was enough to lead the Boilermakers. But Bob Griese had an *amazing* afternoon and saved his best for the end. He directed Purdue on a four-play, sixty-seven-yard touchdown drive with passes of thirty-four, thirteen, and nineteen yards. Then his fullback carried the ball over for the score.

"I didn't have to see this stat sheet to know what happened today," Parseghian told the press after the game. "Bob Griese had a sensational game. He hit nineteen of twenty-two? That's hard to do in practice, much less in a game. Passing is a percentage thing, like shooting baskets. One day you hit a lot, the next not as much. But what

Griese did was unbelievable."

The next game would be Parseghian's first against his old team, Northwestern, and his former assistant coach, Alex Agase. The Wildcats picked off a Zloch pass and returned it for a touchdown, but that was the extent of their scoring. Nick Rassas had a ninety-two-yard interception return of his own and followed quickly with an eighty-five-yard punt return, both for touchdowns. Notre Dame won that one, 38–7, and beat Army the next week, 17–0.

Next up was "Grudge Week." Southern Cal was coming into Notre Dame Stadium—undefeated. All the holdovers from the 1964 team wanted this game badly. The students hung signs around campus, including on top of the Golden Dome. These banners carried a simple message, *Remember*.

Defensive back Tony Carey reflected the feelings of the players better than anyone. He shouted one last thought to his teammates as they were ready to take the field that day.

"Look guys," he said, "I've been living with this thing for one whole year. No one has ever blamed me, but I've lived just to pay these guys back."

Toot toot tootsie.

And so they did. The defense held the Heisman Trophy-winning Mike Garrett to forty-three yards rushing, his career low. Meanwhile, Larry Conjar gained 116 yards on the ground and scored four touchdowns. Conjar outgained the entire USC offense by forty-two yards. Nick Eddy added sixty-five rushing yards, Bill Wolski sixty-four, and Bill Zloch fifty. Notre Dame beat the Trojans, 28—7. And while the debt had not been fully repaid, it did ease the pain.

The Irish continued sailing along the next three weeks, beating Navy, Pittsburgh, and North Carolina by large margins. But then the offense ran out.

Michigan State had an outstanding squad in 1965, finishing first and second in the two major polls at season's end. The Spartans, while being talented, were also very intelligent. They seemed to know Notre Dame's weaknesses in 1965 better than any team the Irish had faced. Defense kept the Irish in the game until the Spartans took a 6—3 lead in the third quarter. Early in the closing period Zloch threw an interception which Michigan State recovered at the Notre Dame 19. On the next play MSU went up 12—3 on a Steve Juday touchdown pass.

Michigan State was then in the position to put extreme heat on Bill Zloch, and he had no way to combat it. The Spartans had eleven men within three yards of the line of scrimmage on nearly every play. They taunted Zloch and dared him

to throw. Notre Dame had just twelve net yards total offense that day.

In the finale, the yardage production was slightly better but the point total was even less. Notre Dame and Miami battled for 60 minutes without scoring, leaving the Irish with a 7—2—1 mark in 1965 and an eighth-place national ranking.

Parseghian knew his second Notre Dame team could have been a great one with a good passing attack. He agonized as he watched the performances of quarterbacks Coley O'Brien and Terry Hanratty on the 1965 freshman team, knowing that either could have made a big difference had freshmen been eligible for varsity play. But come the spring of 1966, Parseghian was licking his lips, trying to decide which of the two quarterbacks would start. Making the offensive prospects even brighter was the presence of sophomore-to-be receiver Jim Seymour.

Hanratty got the starting call in the 1966 season opener against Purdue. The nationally televised debut of the "Baby Bombers," as Hanratty and Seymour came to be known, was better than billed. After Purdue's Leroy Keyes carried a fumble ninety-five yards for a touchdown and Nick Eddy came right back with a ninety-seven-yard kickoff return, it was time for the Hanratty-Seymour combination to start its chapter in the Notre Dame football history book.

On the next offensive series, Hanratty was confronted by a third-and-fourteen situation from the Notre Dame 16 yard line. Seymour ran a deep pattern and broke free at the Purdue 30. In full stride Seymour pulled in Hanratty's pass and kept going for an eighty-four-yard touchdown play. The sophomores connected for a thirty-nine-yard touchdown to open the fourth quarter. And when Purdue got within six points of the Irish, Hanratty and Seymour held off Bob Griese and his Boilermakers with a seven-yard touchdown pass. That gave Notre Dame a 26–14 win.

The Bombers would never be better than they were in their first game. Hanratty completed sixteen of twenty-four passes for 304 yards, while Seymour caught thirteen of them for 276 yards. They were the focal point of Ara's postgame press conference.

"Both Terry Hanratty and Jim Seymour produced for us beyond my fondest hopes," he said. "Hanratty followed our game plan very well. I have been so high on these boys that I feared I might be a bit overconfident, afraid I might be overrating them. But they showed everyone today just how good they are."

The Irish had little trouble in their next three games, beating Northwestern, Army, and North Carolina handily. The next big test was against the Oklahoma Sooners, who entered the game 5–0 and ninth-ranked nationally. Notre Dame jumped off to a 17–0

half-time lead, but Seymour and linebacker Mike McGill were lost to injuries for the remainder of the game. That seemed to inspire their teammates, who went on to a 38–0 win. Notre Dame's impressive road victory convinced the pollsters to vote the Irish number one.

Notre Dame had little trouble hanging on to that ranking the next three weeks. Navy, Pittsburgh, and Duke all suffered lopsided defeats, setting up the most talked about college matchup of all time—Notre Dame versus Michigan State. Number 1 versus number 2. Michigan State had not lost a regular season game in two years. And since a Big 10 rule precluded them from repeating as Rose Bowl representatives, this game was the Spartans' chance to wrap up their second straight national championship.

The Irish were definitely not in the best possible physical shape. Several weeks earlier, they received the disappointing news that backup quarterback Coley O'Brien had developed diabetes. O'Brien had not been looking sharp in practice, and when he exhibited the signs of the disease, tests were taken and revealed the unfortunate fact. O'Brien tried to cope as best he could, but for the time being he did not have the endurance to be the quarterback he once was.

Premier running-back Nick Eddy had injured his shoulder against Pittsburgh and then aggravated it in the Duke game. His status was questionable for the Spartans

game. Eddy further strained the shoulder when he slipped getting off the train to East Lansing. He was then ruled out of the game.

Notre Dame's woes did not end there, however. On the second offensive series of the second quarter, Hanratty rolled out to pass, but a Michigan State blitz flushed him out. When he tried to run, middle-linebacker Charlie Thornhill got an arm on him, slowing him for the "kill" by Bubba Smith, MSU's massive defensive end. Smith's momentum drove Hanratty's shoulder into the ground. Hanratty was out for the rest of the game and the rest of the season with a separated shoulder.

O'Brien was forced into action at quarterback. He would take his snaps from inexperienced sophomore Tim Monty. On the next play, center George Goeddeke limped off the field with a sprained ankle that finished him for the day.

Michigan State scored ten points on the first two possessions of the second quarter. But O'Brien hung in there; the offensive line saw to that. On Notre Dame's next series, O'Brien directed a fifty-four-yard march in just four plays, all in the air. He completed passes of eleven and nine yards and then threw to Bob Gladieux thirty-four yards away on the goal line for a touchdown.

O'Brien started the second half with a hot hand. He took Notre Dame from its 20 to Michigan State's 30 with three long pass completions. Then running backs

Rocky Bleier, Larry Conjar, and Dave Haley moved the ball to the 10. Joe Azzaro opened the fourth quarter with a field goal that tied the game.

With half the period left to play, Tom Schoen made his second interception of the afternoon, giving the Irish possession at MSU's 18 yard line. O'Brien, playing longer and harder than someone in his condition could possibly be expected to, was noticeably fatigued by now. After the Irish lost six yards on the first two attempts, O'Brien tried to pass to Jim Seymour. It was well off the mark, and Azzaro was sent into the game for a pressure-packed forty-one-yard attempt. His kick had the distance and the elevation, but it was wide right by inches.

The Irish defense continued its strong showing and the Spartans elected to punt the ball back on fourth-and-four. Notre Dame took over on its 30 with three minutes left. Three rushes by O'Brien, Bleier, and Conjar set up a fourth-and-one situation. In a gutsy move, Parseghian signaled O'Brien to go for it. O'Brien rushed for two yards for the first down, but he was now "running on fumes."

With time for two more plays, Parseghian directed O'Brien to pass. The fatigued quarterback dropped back, but before he could release the ball Bubba Smith broke over center and tackled O'Brien for a seven yard loss.

That set up the play that would leave its mark on Notre Dame football and Ara Parseghian forever. It would create a whole new expression, "playing for a tie."

There was one play left. The wind was blowing into Notre Dame's face, and Michigan State was in a prevent defense. O'Brien was a totally drained quarterback. He was taking a snap from a novice. Two of the best backfield receivers, Nick Eddy and Bob Gladieux, were on the bench with injuries. Weighing all those factors, Parseghian called for a quarterback sneak, and the game ended.

Immediately, many of the fans started booing. A Michigan State coach and some of the players chastised the Irish for settling for a tie. Parseghian tried to put things in perspective for his players in the locker room after the game.

"Men, I'm proud of you," he said. "Get one thing straight, though. We did not lose. We were number one when we came here, we fell behind and had some tough things happen, but we overcame them. No one could have wanted to win this more than I. Some of the Michigan State people are hollering about the tie, trying to detract from our efforts. They're trying to make it come out a win for them. They

can't go anywhere. Time will prove everything that has happened here today. And you'll see that after the rabble rousers have had their say, cooler minds who understand the true odds will know that Notre Dame is a team of champions."

The media did not have the cooler minds Parseghian spoke of. They soon picked up on the "playing for a tie" angle. Parseghian explained his thinking frequently during the next several days, but it really did not do any good. It was excellent ammunition for Notre Dame critics. They conveniently ignored the injury factor Notre Dame was faced with. It did not matter to them that considering all the conditions one careless play could have jeopardized the remarkable comeback made by a group

Anthony Davis of USC scored six TDs against the Irish, and rubbed salt in with a little dance after each score in 1972.

consisting largely of reserves.

Those reserves would be called on one more time for the season finale against Southern California. Hanratty, Goeddeke, Bleier, and Gladieux were all sidelined. The game was as critical as the one in Los Angeles two years prior had been. Notre Dame was ranked no. 1 in one poll and 2 in the other. A win against the Trojans would surely capture the national championship.

The Irish not only won the game, they turned it into a rout. History would not repeat itself on this occasion. Notre Dame jumped off to a 27–0 halftime lead and increased that to 51–0 by game's end. As expected, the victory gave the Irish the national championship in the Associated Press and United Press International polls.

Though he would never publicly declare it, the 1966 team was undoubtedly the best Parseghian ever had. Eleven players—Nick Eddy, Jim Lynch, Tom Regner, Alan Page, Pete Duranko, Kevin Hardy, Jim Seymour, Paul Seiler, George Goeddeke, Tom Schoen and Larry Conjar—were named All-Americans, more than any Notre Dame squad ever produced. For offensive and defensive balance and depth, this Parseghian-coached team was unrivaled.

Enough of the same players returned in 1967 for Notre Dame to make a run at a repeat of the national title. However, the axiom that it is harder to stay on top than get to the top could not have been better illustrated than by the performance of this squad.

In the season opener the Irish appeared to be marching to the same cadence that made them number one the previous year. California came all the way to Notre Dame Stadium for a 41–8 pasting. Notre Dame's eleven-game streak without a loss would soon end, though.

The next week at Purdue the Irish faced a new Boilermaker quarterback. Bob Griese was gone, but his successor would pick up where he left off. Mike Phipps completed fourteen passes for 238 yards and two touchdowns. Terry Hanratty put the ball up sixty-three times and made good on twenty-nine of them for 366 yards and one touchdown. Unfortunately, four of his throws were intercepted. The final stats read Notre Dame 485 yards of total offense, Purdue 349. The final score read Purdue 28 points, Notre Dame 21.

The Irish have rarely played better than they did against Iowa. Gaining 242 yards rushing and another 200 passing, Notre Dame rolled to a 56–6 win. But this precision was again short-lived.

Southern Cal was next up. And even though the Trojans were ranked number one, Notre Dame was a twelve-point favorite. Evidently the oddsmakers had not yet heard of O. J. Simpson. The Irish took a 7–0 lead into the locker room, but the Trojans brought O.J. back out of theirs. Content to give the ball to Simpson on nearly every play, USC ground out a 24–7 win. John McKay did not have a good passing attack that season, and the Irish were quickly proving they did not either. Hanratty threw four more interceptions against USC.

Like many good passing combinations, Hanratty and Seymour had become too confident with one another. The tendency in such cases is for the quarterback to go to his favorite receiver whether he is covered or not. The quarterback develops the false sense that he can get the ball to the receiver no matter what and his man will catch it somehow.

Parseghian talked to Hanratty about the problem and designed the offense to take the pressure off Hanratty. That strategy helped Notre Dame beat Illinois, 47–7, but Hanratty still had four more inter-ceptions that game. However, he did not throw another one the remainder of the season.

The 1967 edition of Notre Dame-Michigan State was a drastic change from 1966, but beating the Spartans is always pleasureable for Notre Dame. The Irish moved ahead 17–0. MSU closed that to 17–12 before Notre Dame scored one more touchdown to wrap things up. Jeff Zimmerman gained 135 yards rushing that day.

Navy and Pittsburgh also fell prey, setting up a meeting with Georgia Tech that could give Notre Dame its 500th football victory of all time. The Yellow Jacket players did not offer much in the way of resistance, but their fans did not seem to care. They were too busy throwing debris and religious slurs at the Notre Dame bench, a scene that was becoming familiar in this series.

Notre Dame got away with a 36–3 victory, but the team suffered a loss nonetheless. Team captain Rocky Bleier tore ligaments in his knee and was finished for the season. He actually suffered the injury in the first half and scored two touchdowns after being hurt. It was not until the game was out of reach that he reported his discom-fort to the trainers.

Bleier had been a quiet inspiration for his teammates and would later become an inspiration for the entire nation. After leaving Notre Dame, he was drafted first by the Pittsburgh Steelers and second by Uncle Sam. Bleier accepted both calls and was seriously injured during his tour of duty in Vietnam. He refused to accept doctors' diagnoses that he would never walk right again, let alone play football. He worked harder than ever before and not only rejoined the Steelers but became a key member of their Super Bowl drives.

The Miami Hurricanes were the final opponents on the 1967 schedule. This was one of their better teams, having won their previous six games and allowing only fourteen points in their previous last four.

Miami took the early lead, 13–3, but Notre Dame cut that to 16–10 by the half. Jeff Zimmerman did most of the work on a third-quarter touchdown that finally put Notre Dame ahead. After John Pergine made an interception to give the ball back to the Irish at the Hurri-cane 38, Bob Gladieux needed only two plays to give Notre Dame an eight-point lead. Miami scored again with three minutes left, but Bob Olson broke up the two-point conversion attempt to clinch Notre Dame's 24–22 victory. That made it 8–2 for the season and a fourth-place ranking.

While passing accuracy hurt Notre Dame in 1967, pass defense was the shortcoming in 1968. Hanratty and his offensive team-mates scored enough points that year, but the opponents got their fair share too.

The season opened impressively enough. The Oklahoma Sooners brought a top-10 team to South Bend, and the Irish sent them home stunned, 45–21. Hanratty threw for 202 yards on 18 of 27 completions. Coach Chuck Fairbanks and his Sooners credited the Irish pass defense as a prime factor in the game.

So did the Purdue Boilermakers in reverse in their 37-22 walloping of the Irish the next week. Mike Phipps was able to complete 16 passes in 24 tries for one touch-down. Running back Leroy Keyes threw another one on a halfback option. The Notre Dame offense moved the ball 454 yards, but the defense could not hold Purdue.

The Big 10 opponents the next three weeks did not present the same threat as Purdue, and the Irish had little trouble with Iowa, Northwestern, and Illinois. But as they continued moving through that conference they eventually caught up with Michigan State. As usual this game was filled with intrigue.

Spartan coach Duffy Daugherty had told the media during the week that if Notre Dame won the toss and elected to receive, his team would try an onside kick. Par-seghian did not know whether to believe this or not, but he warned his players to be on the lookout for it anyway. Notre Dame did receive, Michigan State did try the onside kick, and thanks to a good bounce the Spartans recovered the ball. MSU capitalized on this opportu-nity, moving the ball forty-two yards in six plays for a touchdown. With less than two minutes to play, Notre Dame was still trying to come from behind, 21–17. The Irish had the ball on MSU's 3 on third down. Two previous rushing attempts had gone nowhere, so Parseghian sent in a pass play. The pass was intended for Jim Seymour, who had beaten his defender and was poised for the reception. The Irish undoubtedly would have had a touchdown if Seymour had not been knocked down. Interference was obvious, but the official responsible for calling it slipped and did not see the play. None of the other officials would rule on it.

Hanratty's rushing attempt on fourth down was stopped, and the Spartans ran out the clock for the victory. After the game, Parseghian's remarks to the media were uncommon.

"I'm deeply concerned about the third-down call they missed," he snapped. "Jim Seymour was tackled in the end zone, and nobody called it. Seymour beat his man to the outside. One official fell down on the play, but there were four others to make the call. It disturbs me that they missed an out-and-out violation. It influenced the outcome of the game. We would have had the ball at the one-foot line with first down. I don't plan to lodge an official complaint because nothing can be done about it. They can't change the call or game."

Navy bore the brunt of Notre Dame's anger the next week, 45–14. Parseghian was not pleased with his team's ability to get the ball into the end zone from inside the 20, and the week before meeting Pittsburgh he scheduled a rare contact drill. He wanted to work on goal-line situations but planned to control the action to protect his quarterback. That plan did not work.

On the very first play Hanratty took the snap, slipped, and recovered too late to fake to the fullback. He was also too late to pitch to the halfback, so Hanratty did the right thing and carried the ball himself. It turned out to be the wrong thing, however. Hanratty's leg got twisted as he was tackled, and his knee snapped. The injury was serious enough to require surgery and Hanratty's marvelous Notre Dame career, one that was highlighted by breaking George Gipp's total offense record, had been ended.

It did mean the beginning of a career for another record-setting quarterback, Joe Theismann. These young men both got things done, but they did so in different ways. Hanratty was accepted by all his teammates as a guy who had a good time during the week but knew what he was doing on Saturdays. He minded his own business and did not bark orders to the other players on offense. Theismann, meanwhile, was an operator. His every movement was planned. He was cocky, but he never made a promise he could not keep. If one of his teammates made a mistake, he let him know about it. They came to accept that because they discovered Theismann knew their play as well as his own. Both players were alike in one sense. More often than not they would find a way to beat you.

Pittsburgh and Georgia Tech found that out. With Theismann at quarterback, the Irish beat them, 56–7 and 34–6, respectively. Southern Cal also learned something about Theismann—he did not quit. On the first offensive play of this annual spectacle, Theismann looked for Seymour but threw instead to Sandy Durko, a USC defender, who ran it into the end zone to give the Trojans a 7–0 lead.

Theismann came right back and directed an eighty-six-yard touchdown drive in eighteen plays. Bob Gladieux broke loose for a fifty-seven-yard touchdown the next time Notre Dame got the ball. Then at the end of the half, Theismann proved his versatility. The crafty little quarterback handed off to Coley O'Brien, a halfback in 1968, while he slipped casually into the end zone. O'Brien then threw to Theismann to give Notre Dame a two-touchdown bulge at halftime.

The Irish defense did an outstanding job on O. J. Simpson in this game. They held one of the game's all-time greats to his all-time low, fifty-five net yards in twenty-one carries. As usual, though, the Trojans had other ways to score, and they did so to tie the game at twenty-one. Scott Hempel tried and missed field goals from forty-one and thirty-three yards out, and the Irish finished the season 7–2–1, good enough for fifth place in the polls.

The most memorable thing about the 1969 season took place before it even began. For years the post-season bowl committees and Notre Dame coaches had pleaded with the hierarchy to participate in bowl games. The argument against it was that it would give the players one more month of football and one month less to study for final exams. Until now, these tests had been given after the Christmas break.

Before the 1969–70 school year, the academic structure was changed, and the dreaded Saturday morning classes and January exams were things of the past. Now exams would be administered before Christmas vacation.

With that change made, with the lure of the financial rewards the bowls offered, with the continued petitions from the coaching staff to give the team a chance to participate in these attractive match-ups, permission was finally granted. Now the Irish would have to prove themselves worthy.

That appeared to be a major obstacle in the first quarter of the first game. Northwestern intercepted a pass for a touchdown and followed with a field goal for a 10–0 lead. The Irish stayed on the ground much of the remainder of the game and earned a 35–10 victory.

Mike Phipps stayed in the air most of the next week and for the third year in a row he had a hot hand against the Irish. He threw for 213 yards and made it a clean sweep against Notre Dame during his career, 28–14.

Theismann got Notre Dame going again with 294 yards on twenty completions versus Michigan State. His favorite target had become Tom Gatewood, who caught ten of his passes for 155 yards. It resulted in a 42–28 win.

The Irish tuned up against Army, 45–0, before hosting USC. O. J. Simpson was gone, and Clarence Davis had assumed the Trojan tailback throne. Notre Dame had its usual success against Southern Cal's speedsters, holding Davis to seventy-five yards in thirty carries. Quarterback Jimmy Jones provided USC's offense this day, throwing two touchdown passes.

Down 14–7, Theismann moved the Irish from their 22 to USC's 3. The drive was stymied when the Trojan defense sacked Theismann for a fifteen-yard loss on fourth down. That's when All-American defensive tackle Mike McCoy decided to take things into his own hands. The thing turned out to be Southern Cal's punt, and the Irish recovered on the 7. It took four tries, but halfback Denny Allan tied the score with 6:41 to play.

Notre Dame had one last shot at a win. With the wind behind him, Hempel tried a forty-eight-yard field goal. The ball was on line and had the distance but not quite enough elevation. It hit the cross

bar, bounced up and short of the mark.

The Irish won the next five games in style against Tulane, Navy, Pittsburgh, Georgia Tech, and Air Force. That was good enough for Cotton Bowl officials. They invited the Irish to attend their second bowl game ever and the first since the 1925 Rose Bowl. The opponent would be the no. 1 ranked Texas Longhorns.

President Richard Nixon had already proclaimed the Longhorns the national champions after their season-ending win over unbeaten Arkansas. They had a team worthy of that designation but for much of the afternoon they probably were wishing Notre Dame had not lifted the bowl ban.

The Irish jumped off to a 10–0 lead. Hempel kicked a twenty-six-yard field goal with nine minutes to

play in the first quarter. Shortly thereafter Notre Dame scored a fifty-four-yard touchdown. The whole offense did a superb job at faking a run to the split-end side. Tom Gatewood stayed in briefly to block and freeze the defensive backs, then broke free to look for Theismann's pass. The play worked to perfection.

Up to this point, Notre Dame's defense had stopped Texas' heralded Wishbone Offense better than anyone. It was a run-oriented offense that utilized a fullback, two halfbacks, *and* the quarterback as ball carriers. However, once Texas mixed in some short passes with the runs, Notre Dame bent. The Longhorns scored on a nine-play, seventy-four-yard drive early in the second quarter.

Notre Dame seemingly had another golden opportunity just before the half. With the ball on the Texas 12 and 1:56 to play, the defense cornered quarterback Jim Street and forced him to bobble the ball. The Irish recovered, but the officials claimed time out had been called by a player coming off the bench.

Neither team scored in the third quarter, but in the fourth quarter Texas took the lead with 10:13 to play. Theismann hung in and directed an eighty-yard drive in eight plays. He gained twenty-five yards by calling his own number twice. The scoring pass was twenty-four yards to Jim Yoder that put Notre Dame up, 17–14.

The Longhorns' next possession will be remembered as one of the most exciting drives in football history. There were close calls on every third-down play. And it all came down to fourth and two at the Notre Dame 10. Street threw a low pass in the direction of split end Cotton Speyrer. Speyrer was able to bend low enough to reach it just before it hit the ground. That made it first and two, and in three plays Texas took a 21–17 lead.

Theismann had one minute to do something. He completed a sixteen-yard pass to Denny Allan and a twenty-two-yarder to Dewey Poskon. That gave Notre Dame thirty-eight seconds to score from the Texas 39. Hope ran out when Theismann threw again for Poskon and defensive back Tom Campbell intercepted it for Texas.

The statistics are accurate in indicating how even this perform-

Defensive tackle Mike McCoy about to annihilate a Northwestern quarterback in 1972.

All-American Tom Clements, quarter-backing in a 1973 snow.

ance was. Texas had 448 yards of total offense in seventy-eight plays. Notre Dame 410 yards in seventy plays. By playing this game, Notre Dame had earned the respect of the Texas Longhorns and the rest of the viewing public for its team and over $200,000 for minority scholarships.

At the start of the 1970 season, Notre Dame's team figured to be so good that it would be invited to the bowl game of its choice. And that's exactly how it turned out.

The Irish picked on Northwestern

again in the opener, 35–14, and Purdue's three-game winning streak came to an abrupt halt, 48–0. Notre Dame even beat Michigan State in East Lansing for the first time since 1949 and by the lopsided score of 29–0. Actually, the only negative aspect of the season by this time was the loss of All-America offensive lineman Larry DiNardo to knee surgery.

And things kept going well. Notre Dame crushed Army, Dan Devine's Missouri Tigers, Navy, and Pittsburgh. During that stretch, Theismann passed Terry Hanratty as the all-time total offense leader at Notre Dame.

No sooner had he set it than the offense ran out. The Irish were in for struggles the next two weeks. Georgia Tech decided the way to beat this Notre Dame team was to take away its rushing attack. That strategy had the game 0–0 at halftime. Georgia Tech led 7–3 with nine minutes to play. It was then that Parseghian plotted a way to have the Yellow Jackets' tactics blow up in their faces.

Since Georgia Tech was pulling eight men to the line to shut off the run, Parseghian decided to send four receivers into the secondary against three defenders. This theory produced a forty-six-yard pass completion to Ed Gulyas. Six plays later the Irish scored and held on for a 10–7 win.

"To have a successful season, a team must win the type of game we won today," Parseghian explained to the press after the game. "I was particularly proud of our club the way they continued to come back. They drove eighty yards in the final quarter with the wind in their faces, and that's the sign of a great team. This was the third time this year we've had to come from behind, and we've done it each time."

They weren't behind the next week but with less than three minutes to play in the game the Irish were fighting to break a scoreless tie with LSU. The offense finally got the ball to the LSU 7, and Hempel was called on to attempt a twenty-four-yard field goal. The kick was perfect, and Notre Dame had its ninth win in a row.

Notre Dame teams coached by Ara Parseghian were getting used to being 9–0 on their way to the West Coast to face Southern Cal. So far John McKay's squad had cost Notre Dame one national championship and provided the means for earning another. The 1970 meeting had an interesting twist added; it was played in four inches of rain.

That element proved to be Notre Dame's undoing. Southern Cal took a 21–7 lead after the first quarter, which forced Notre Dame to pass on nearly every play the remainder of the game, a difficult assignment in the pouring rain. The Irish added one more touchdown and USC a field goal for a 24–14 USC halftime lead.

Then came the bad luck on the wet field. Darryll Dewan fumbled

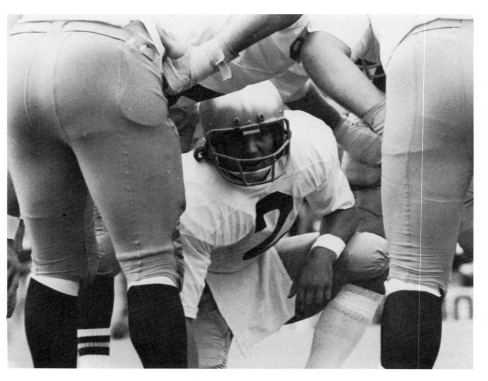

the slippery ball on the ND 17 and the Trojans had an easy touchdown four plays later. The lead became insurmountable moments later when Theismann was blindsided in the end zone and USC recovered for a touchdown. That put the Trojans up, 38–14.

But Joe Theismann was not finished yet. Southern Cal waited for Theismann to throw on every play. He did and completed most of them. That included a forty-six-yard touchdown pass to Larry Parker and a scramble on his own for another score. Notre Dame was now within ten points, but it got no closer.

Theismann did everything that could be expected of a quarterback in such climatic conditions. He completed thirty-three of fifty-eight passes for 526 yards and two touchdowns. Had balloters been able to hold off voting until after this game, Theismann probably would have won the Heisman Trophy instead of finishing second to Stanford quarterback Jim Plunkett.

As a team, Notre Dame had a chance to do better than second. The Irish could do that by knocking off top-ranked Texas, a team that had won its last thirty games, the longest winning streak in the land. It was a dream Cotton Bowl rematch.

To win, Notre Dame would have to find a way to handle the Texas Wishbone. Parseghian designed something called the "Mirror Defense" that figured either to so baffle the Longhorns that they could not cope with it or so confuse the Irish defenders that they could not stop Texas. The concept was to assign specific defensive backs to "tail" specific halfbacks and the quarterback and specific linebackers to shadow the fullback. If the defenders contained the men to whom they were assigned, it would work to perfection. More than most defenses, however, it demanded team play; no free lancing.

Parseghian had to be concerned about his strategy on the very first offensive play of the game. Texas

Quarterback Clements calling a shot against Northwestern in 1972.

Leopardskins. An ND tradition that was terminated in 1976. At the end of the third quarter, a senior would shimmy up a pole and doff his clothes—up to a point.

quarterback Eddie Phillips faked a handoff to fullback Steve Worster but kept the ball himself. Defensive back Mike Crotty had been assigned to Phillips but got sucked in a little too far by the fake. Phillips stepped around Crotty and ran sixty-three yards before Ralph Stepaniak was able to tackle him. The Longhorns scored a field goal on that march.

That, however, was about all they did offensively the rest of the day. Before it was all over Texas fumbled the ball nine times and lost five of them.

Meanwhile, Notre Dame was moving the ball with ease. Theismann threw twenty-six yards to Tom Gatewood for a touchdown. The Irish got a "cheapie" after Texas fumbled on its 13. Theismann carried that one over from the three. The shifty quarterback scored on another run, this one fifteen yards, early in the second quarter.

After Texas mounted another scoring drive, Parseghian called for the most basic of football plays. He sent in his strongest-armed quarterback, Jim Bulger, and his swiftest runner, Clarence Ellis. Ellis, normally a defensive back, ran as fast as he could and Bulger threw as far as he could. Thirty-seven yards later the ball and the receiver met. That put Hempel in field-goal range. His thirty-six-yarder ended the scoring for the half at 24–11 in Notre Dame's favor.

With Theismann protecting an injured finger and Gatewood out with a pulled hamstring, the Irish played conservatively in the second half. Their opponents, though, could not afford that luxury. The wishbone offense is well designed for a ball-control style of play. It is not suited for playing catch up. Texas was forced to its weakness in the second half—passing—and that is exactly what the Irish wanted them to do. The result was that neither team scored in the second half, and the Irish stopped the Longhorns' winning streak.

That put Notre Dame's record at 10–1 and in some contention for the national championship. The Irish needed an assist from LSU in the Orange Bowl that night. The Tigers had to knock off Nebraska to give the Irish clear title to the top ranking. LSU gave it a run but could not pull it off. And just in case anyone at Notre Dame thought they still had a shot at the title anyway, Nebraska coach Bob Devaney put it in perspective in his postgame press conference. "Not even the Pope would vote Notre Dame no. 1." He was right, and the Irish settled for second.

Second was a lot better than Notre Dame would do the next two seasons. There were many reasons for this recession—injuries and personnel deficiencies among them. But the chief factor was the motivation of the players.

College football had lost its lustre in the late sixties. That was not just true at Notre Dame but everywhere. Still, spirit had always been the trademark of Notre Dame football. The players reflected it, and so did the other students. Certainly

there were more important things than football to Notre Dame students. But football and other sports had always united the student body. Supporting the team nurtured pride in the university.

In the late sixties, many students found current events nationally and internationally more worthy of their attention. In the past, it had been unthinkable for a Notre Dame student to miss a football game. During this period, many in the student body thought it unthinkable that their classmates would waste time on sport when they could be

changing the shape of the world.

All this had an effect on the players. While they had always lived in the mainstream of the student body, they were held in higher esteem by their classmates. This was changing in the late sixties. Not only that, but like their classmates, the players were caught up in questioning their country's involvement in the Vietnam War and in such controversial topics as equal rights, pollution, abortion, and racism. Practicing football and, indeed, even playing were not as important

as they once had been for many of them. This definitely had an effect on the way they played, and it required a change in the way they could be coached.

Parseghian and his staff were not only forced to deal with this lack of intensity and complacency from the success of 1970, but they also had to find a replacement for Joe Theismann. There were four men in line for that role. Pat Steenberge, Bill Etter, Cliff Brown, and Jim Bulger each had attributes for the position. Unfortunately, as in 1965, they also had drawbacks.

A jubilant locker room scene after a 24-23 national championship win over Alabama in 1973.

Drew Mahalic grabs a fumble in mid-air during the 1973 Sugar Bowl.

In 1973, Irish students with bitter memories of Anthony Davis dancing on their grave were ready for him, and USC.

Steenberge was chosen for the season opener against Northwestern. Actually, all the quarterbacks got a shot against the Wildcats. The 50–7 outcome would seem to indicate that all or some of them sparkled. Such was not the case.

Steenberge played the whole game against Purdue in a constant downpour. Purdue scored just before the end of the first half on a twenty-six-yard screen pass to take a 7–0 lead. That is the way it stood until Clarence Ellis blocked a Boilermaker punt in the end zone

and Fred Swendsen recovered it for a touchdown with 2:58 to play.

In a more realistic situation than the 1966 Michigan State game to demonstrate whether or not he played for ties, Parseghian sent in a trick play for the two-point conversion attempt. It was known as the "Genuflect Play" because tight end Mike Creaney had to fall to one knee and act like he had slipped out of the play, then sneak into the end zone to await a pass. The play looked better in the game than it did when conceived on the blackboard. Steenberge barely got

the ball off, and it was hardly a spiral, but Creaney was able to catch it, and the Irish had an 8–7 victory.

Steenberge pulled a hamstring in that game and was replaced for Michigan State by Bill Etter. Etter did fine in a conservative approach, completing ten of sixteen short passes and directing the rushing attack. The Irish won 14–2. He started again when Notre Dame and Miami met the next week. Early in the second quarter, he was tackled hard and tore cartilage in his knee, requiring surgery. Cliff Brown came in to replace him.

Brown had an outstanding arm and good speed. He was an exceptional athlete who needed refinement of his skills. But he had one more characteristic that worked against him. He was black. He became the first black to quarterback at Notre Dame team. Some of the team's supporters did not go for that, and they let Cliff know it from the stands and on the telephone. The remarks had their impact.

Brown guided the Irish to victory against Miami and North Carolina. He played well against Southern Cal, but the Trojan offense played better, especially receiver Edesel Garrison. He caught touchdown passes of thirty-one and twenty-four yards and set up another score with a forty-two-yard reception. USC beat the Irish at Notre Dame Stadium, 28–14.

The Irish had no trouble the next three weeks against Navy, Pittsburgh, and Tulane. At 8–1 with one to play, that left them with an opportunity to face Penn State in the Gator Bowl. As had been his policy in the past, Parseghian put it to a vote of the players whether or not to accept the bowl bid.

Unlike the previous two years, the players asked the coaches to leave their meeting after Parseghian described the arrangements. They wanted to discuss the bid privately. Once gone, two of the players took the occasion to snipe at Parseghian and the university. One

accused Parseghian of lying about conditions at the bowl site. Another said the university had not lived up to its promise of bowl proceeds going toward minority scholarships. Other players did not want to participate in the game because they felt the Irish would be outmanned or they would rather have spent the full holidays at home. All this disharmony resulted in a landslide decision to refuse the invitation.

It also resulted in a win for Louisiana State in the season finale. Injuries and this poor attitude were

too much against LSU's outstanding squad, led by Bert Jones at quarterback. The Tigers dumped the Irish, 28–6. For the first time since Parseghian came to Notre Dame, his team finished out of the top ten at no. 15.

Things were going to get worse before they got better. In 1972 Notre Dame would suffer three of its worst defeats ever, including the most stunning upset in college football that season.

The year started well for the Irish. There were opening wins by large margins against North-

western, Purdue, Michigan State, and Pittsburgh. Week five figured to be the easiest test of all. Missouri was the opponent at Notre Dame Stadium. The Tigers, now coached by Al Onofrio, had been humiliated the week before by Nebraska, 62–0. That's 62–0. They stood at 2–3.

But Missouri led 30–14 with ten minutes to play. The Tigers got a big assist from the officials on one of their touchdowns. With fourth and one from the Notre Dame 1, quarterback John Cherry handed off to fullback Don Johnson. Johnson could not get possession of the ball but he continued up the middle and into the end zone. He did not fool the Irish defenders who

Coach Parseghian meets the press after a bowl victory.

Freshman Dave Reeve kicks, and Frank Allocco holds during the 1974 Wildcats game.

Tom Clements directing strategy against Northwestern, 1974.

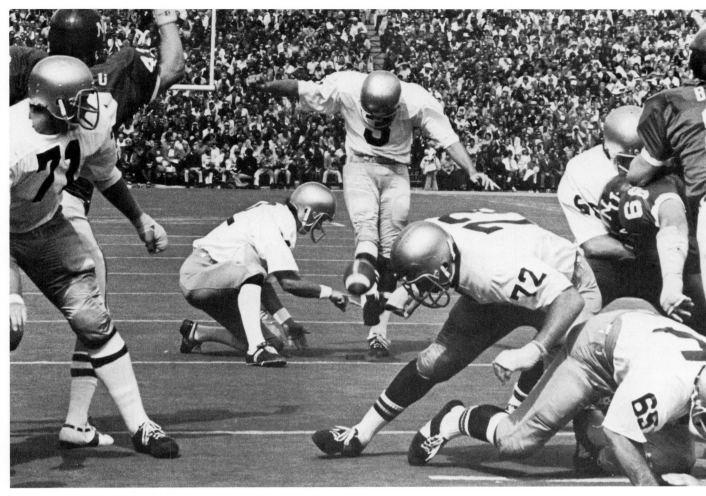

Miami the next week. But the Irish were missing the edge in 1972. And that almost cost them the Orange Bowl bid.

Notre Dame led Miami 20—3, with one extra point missed after holder Brian Doherty was distracted by a snowball thrown by a student just as Bob Thomas was approaching the ball. Then Miami's quarterback, Ed Carney, got the Hurricanes moving in the fourth quarter. He directed two scoring drives to pull Miami to 20—17 with just over three minutes to play.

At that point the Irish were merely trying to maintain possession and were naturally keeping the ball on the ground. That turned out to be literally true when full-

recovered the fumble at the 1, nor did he deceive the thousands of spectators in the stands. What counted, though, he did bluff the officials, and over the protests of Notre Dame they signaled for a touchdown.

The Irish made a strong comeback in the final ten minutes. Sophomore quarterback Tom Clements directed drives of seventy

and eighty yards to make the score 30—26. The Irish got the ball back one more time, but Clements threw an interception, and Missouri had its upset.

"This was a tremendous victory for us, our biggest since I've been coach at Missouri," said Onofrio after the game. "We played a great Notre Dame team, which was demonstrated by their ability to

come back in the fourth quarter. We played the best possible game we could . . . You just never know what will happen in this game."

What happened to the Fighting Irish the rest of the season is that they lost intensity, a watchword in athletics. Oh, they beat TCU, Navy, and Air Force the next three weeks, and the Orange Bowl did extend an invitation, contingent upon beating

back Andy Huff fumbled on a third-down play and Miami recovered at the Notre Dame 34. The Hurricanes were only able to advance the ball five yards but that gave them a chance for a tie if they could hit a forty-six-yard field goal. Fortunately, or as it would later turn out, unfortunately, they missed, and Notre Dame was headed for the Orange Bowl after one last regular-season test.

The Irish were used to this final exam against Southern Cal, but one question they could not figure out in 1972 was how to stop Anthony Davis. The sophomore tailback carried the opening kickoff ninety-seven yards for a touchdown.

Before the day ended he had five more scores, and in case anyone on the Notre Dame sideline failed to notice, he did a little victory dance in the end zone after each one.

Notre Dame pulled within two points at 25–23. But Mr. Davis swung back into action on the next kickoff. For the second time that day, he took it the length of the field and ruined any chance Notre Dame had of winning. From that point on, nothing the Irish did was right. The Trojans finished with a 45–23 win.

"USC has had a lot of good football teams in the past, but this is probably the best balanced team they've ever had," Parseghian told the press. "Davis' two kickoff returns plus the errors in the game really killed us. Fumbles, interceptions, interference calls—you

can't make those mistakes against a team like USC. Just take the two returns, the interference call (40 yards in the end zone), and the fumble at the nine, add it together, and you get twenty-eight points. You just can't give that away. We moved up again to 25–23 and then came the kickoff return. No question about it, that was the turning point of the game."

As though that had not been a bad enough experience for the Irish, they had a worse one waiting for them in the Orange Bowl. The Nebraska Cornhuskers had the Heisman Trophy winner, Johnny Rodgers, and a retiring coach, Bob Devaney, to give them incentive. With two crushing losses, Notre Dame had nothing but pride on the line. That was not enough against the Nebraska attack. When the dust settled the Irish lost 40–6, their worst defeat since 1956. While it was an embarrassing moment, it was a lesson that would prove valuable for 1973.

If any squad could give the 1966 team a run for the title "Parseghian's best," the 1973 group was it. This team did not have the All-Americans of 1966. Tight-end Dave

Running back Al Samuel hit by a Purdue tackler in 1974.

Clements prepares to pass against Northwestern, 1974.

Casper and defensive-back Mike Townsend were the only players so honored. But from top to bottom this was a talented, well-balanced team.

As often had been the case, it was Northwestern's misfortune to catch the Irish in a season opener trying to make amends for the prior year. Such was true in 1973. Notre Dame was nearly flawless on offense and defense, gaining 473 yards and shutting out the Wildcats, 44–0.

Tom Clements played that game with the knowledge that his sister was in a coma, the result of being struck by a car the night before. What he did not know was that she had died just before the game started. Despite Parseghian's encouragement to take the week off, Clements came back to direct the team to a 20–7 win at Purdue the next week.

Michigan State scared Notre Dame in the '73 meeting. Notre Dame was up 14–3 when Clements threw an interception at the Notre Dame 15. The Spartans converted the turnover for a touchdown that brought them to 14–10. The defense saw to it that was as close as they got the rest of the game.

Tulane and Army fell, enabling Notre Dame to host Southern Cal with a 5–0 record. The Trojans had one tie in 1973, against Oklahoma, but they also had gone twenty-three games without losing, longest in the nation. If ever there was a chance to pay back the 1964 defeat in full, this was it.

The Notre Dame enthusiasm of

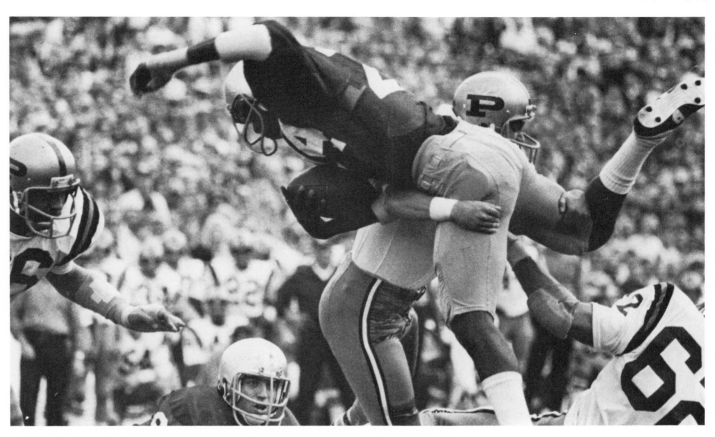

carries. The team outrushed USC 316 to 68. Notre Dame led at the half 13–7, and Eric Penick put the game away at the start of the third quarter. The halfback broke loose for an eighty-five-yard touchdown that stunned the Trojans. Each team scored again, but Notre Dame beat USC for the first time since 1966, 23–14.

"We are delighted to have this game ball," Parseghian beamed after the game. "Because Southern Cal's twenty-three-game streak began here at Notre Dame, I think it is appropriate it has ended here as well. Southern Cal played great football during that streak, and they did so today, but our kids put forth a tremendous effort and deserved to win. They were up all week, and they remembered last year's forty-five points by Southern Cal and six touchdowns by Anthony Davis."

Davis showed his class when interviewed following the game.

"With the poor field position we had, a lot of things can happen, and they did," he said. "I don't think they are as strong inside as they were last year. Notre Dame would

old was well represented on campus for this game. The students were not pleased with Anthony Davis' performance against Notre Dame in the 1972 game, neither the six touchdowns he scored nor his dancing after them. They found a picture of Davis doing his end zone routine and had hundreds of copies made. These were taped to sidewalks around campus, so the students could "walk all over him."

The Irish players did a good job of that as well. Notre Dame held Davis to fifty-five yards in nineteen

Fanning, Nosbusch, and Russell converge for the hit.

A goal-line pileup in a Purdue game.

have its hands full against Oklahoma, and Arkansas was the toughest hitting team we played this year. Tim Rudnick (Notre Dame defensive back) talked to me through the entire game, and that's because he'll never forget me from last year."

Eric Penick was asked why he did not dance after he scored his touchdown. "This is Notre Dame," he responded. "We're not hot dogs."

Despite their 6–0 record and strong showing against USC, the Irish were ranked seventh at this stage. They would progress steadily the remainder of the season with impressive wins against Navy, Pittsburgh, Air Force, and Miami. All of these teams had improved squads in 1973, making Notre Dame's one-sided victories all the more significant.

At regular season's end, Alabama was undefeated and ranked no. 1. Notre Dame was undefeated and ranked no. 3. It was a perfect bowl pairing. The Sugar Bowl was the host for this winner-take-all event. It turned out to be a classic, certainly one of the great games in college football history.

Notre Dame got on the board first with fullback Wayne Bullock plunging over from one yard. A bad snap from center cost Notre Dame the point after.

In the second quarter, Alabama adjusted to the Notre Dame defense and took a 7–6 lead on a

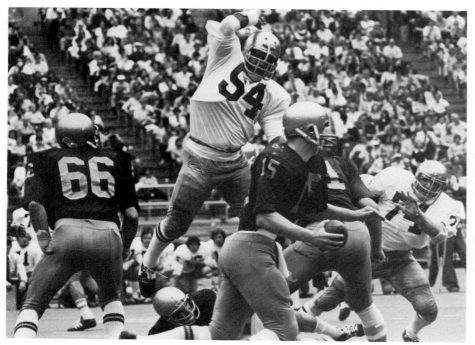

seven-play drive. Moments later, speedy freshman Al Hunter had a chance to use a special kick-return play that had been put in for this game. Hunter caught the ball at the 7, followed a wave of blockers, cut up the middle when seeing daylight, and he was off with his 9.5 speed.

In order to make up for the missed point on the previous touchdown, Parseghian sent in a two-point conversion play. Clements saw Dave Casper, his primary receiver, was covered. He spotted split-end Pete Demmerle with a step on his defender and lofted him the ball. The pass was complete, and Notre Dame had a 14–7 lead.

Alabama kicked a thirty-nine-

yard field goal before the half and came back with a ninety-three-yard touchdown march in the third quarter to go ahead, 17–14. The Irish defense got back on track, with linebacker Greg Collins jarring runningback Willie Shelby so hard he fumbled at the Alabama 12. Drew Mahalic recovered for Notre Dame.

On the first offensive play, Penick cut his way through the Crimson Tide defense and regained the lead for Notre Dame. Bob Thomas made good on this extra point.

That is where the scoring stood until midway through the fourth quarter. Then crafty Bear Bryant sent in a trick play. On a third-and-seven situation Bryant counted on

Parseghian calling for a blitz. Bryant was right, and his play was perfect for the defense. Quarterback Richard Todd handed off to halfback Mike Stock and continued on as a receiver. The Irish had not expected this, and Stock was able to pass to an uncovered Todd for a touchdown. However, the point-after jinx hit Alabama as kicker Bill Davis could not convert after a bad snap, and the Crimson Tide led, 23–21.

Notre Dame had the ball on its own 19 and set off on a drive that would put them back on top. The key play was a reception by Casper on a third-and-one play. Casper was well covered, and Clements really just put the ball up for grabs. Fortunately, the tall, agile Casper was the one to grab it. That gave the Irish the ball on the 'Bama 15. They were able to move it to the two before calling on Thomas. Thomas barely got the ball through, but it did put Notre Dame up, 24–23.

Parseghian questioned Thomas about his accuracy when he returned to the bench. "I was thinking on the way out that if I stuck it right down the pipe nobody

Wayne "The Train" Bullock being derailed in 1974.

Wayne Bullock, nursing an ankle.

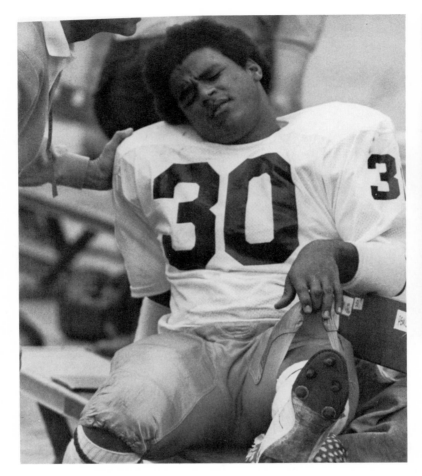

would ever remember it," he quipped. "This way they'll be talking about it for years."

The defense forced Alabama to punt by getting them to fourth-and-twenty. Freshman defensive-end Ross Browner rushed into punter Greg Gantt, but not until he got the ball off. It carried all the way to the Notre Dame 1. The penalty yardage would not have given Alabama a first down, so Bryant refused it and dared Notre Dame to

get out of the hole.

From that spot, it figured Alabama would be able to hold and get the ball back in excellent shape. The Tide stopped Notre Dame on the first two downs, bringing up third and six. Parseghian then made his best call ever. With no one in the stadium expecting it, he told Clements to pass the ball. Running from a two-tight-end formation that would further disguise his intent, Parseghian sent

in a pass play with Casper as the primary receiver.

Casper jumped early, and Notre Dame was penalized, pushing the ball back to the two. Parseghian signaled Clements to let it ride. Clements dropped back, saw that Casper was covered, and released the ball in the direction of Robin Weber, the second tight end. Weber juggled it but gained control before going out of bounds at the 37 for his first Notre Dame reception. The Irish now had room to work and were able to kill the clock.

"The pass from Clements to Weber with seconds to go was the key to the win," Parseghian said to the hordes of media jammed into the locker room. "It was a win-or-punt situation. If we hadn't made the first down, Alabama would surely have been in field-goal position with us punting from our end zone.

"I definitely feel we're the national champions. We beat the leading scoring team in the nation. They are an excellently disciplined team. We beat a great football team, and they lost to a great football team."

The voters in the Associated Press poll agreed and chose Notre Dame number one. The Irish were also presented with the MacArthur Bowl, emblematic of the national football champion.

The great thing about the success of 1973 was that Notre Dame figured to be just as good in 1974. The returning talent and the incoming freshmen made the Irish a favorite to repeat as national champions. But even before the next season started, Notre Dame fans could watch that talent pool diminish.

It began in spring ball when Eric Penick broke his ankle and would have to miss most or all of the season. Defensive-back and punt-returner Tim Simon had his eye

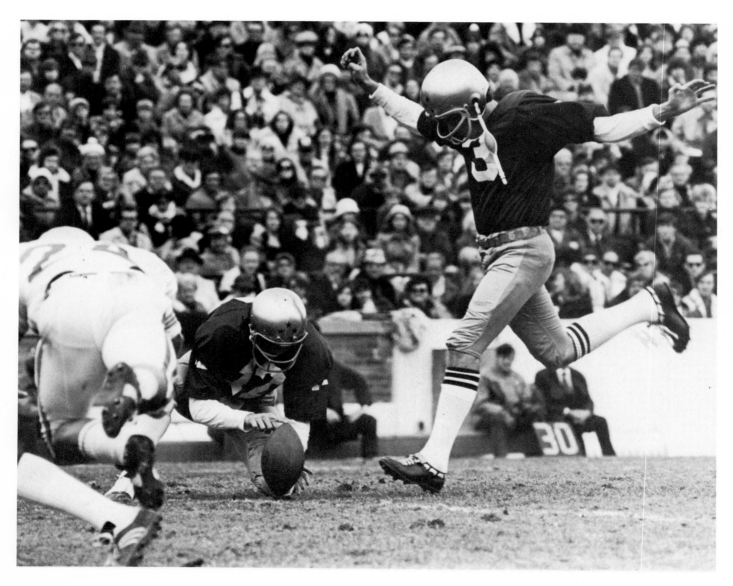

Dave Reeve booting.

poked in a freak accident and would be at least partially blinded. Tight-end Steve Quehl was fortunate to survive an explosion of a truck he was driving. His leg was broken in ten places, and physicians feared he would limp for the rest of his life.

The incident that had the most far-reaching effect occurred during summer school. Defensive-ends Ross Browner and Willie Fry, defensive-back Luther Bradley, and running-back Al Hunter would all be starters in 1974. Running back Dan Knott would be a top reserve. Quarterback Al Henry would be moved to defensive back, and his status was unknown. But after breaking dormitory regulations, none of these players would be permitted to attend school or compete in athletics for *at least* one year.

Finally when practice opened in the fall, defensive-back Bob Zanot suffered a knee injury that put him out for the year.

That added up to ten players, eight probable starters, who were lost unexpectedly. Not only would it be impossible to replace these people in kind, but it would also be difficult to keep morale at the level that could have been expected.

On the surface, Notre Dame opened with two impressive victories. The Irish beat Georgia Tech, 31—7, on national television, then jumped on Northwestern, 49—3. But the anticipated letdown came one week later.

Purdue came to Notre Dame

Stadium with a mediocre squad, and the Boilermakers were heavy underdogs. Like Missouri two years earlier, that made no difference. Purdue shocked Notre Dame by getting ahead 24—0, thanks in part to a fumble recovery and pass interception. Notre Dame finally got its offense going, but it was too late. Purdue had a 31—20 win.

Notre Dame played conservatively the next two weeks and came away with low-scoring wins over Michigan State and Rice. But the Irish blew the next two opponents away, looking like national champs in wins against Army and Miami.

The 1974 Navy—Notre Dame game will never be remembered as a great one, though Navy played better than any time in a decade against Notre Dame. The Irish staggered most of the day, scored offensively in the fourth quarter to take the lead, then put the game away on a forty-yard interception return by Randy Harrison. Notre Dame won, 14—6.

What is important about this game is that Parseghian made up his mind to retire because of it. It was not a snap decision. The pressures of the job finally caught up with him. Parseghian had been taking blood-pressure pills and tranquilizers for many months. Several of his close friends had died in 1974. The off-season developments with the players the past months unnerved him. And now all these things came into focus following the win over Navy. His team won, but *only* 14—6. The

Irish were criticized for such a narrow escape when in reality Navy had a good team that year. Parseghian reached the conclusion it just was not worth it anymore.

He confided only in his wife, Katie, his brother, Jerry, and Father Joyce. He told them that he would probably call it quits after this season.

Pittsburgh fell grudgingly the next week, and Air Force made it easy on Notre Dame in the next game. That left the dreaded Trojans. Parseghian's last game with them would be the strangest in a series marked by the unique.

The Irish looked like they could take on the National Football League in the first half. They led 24–6 at intermission. But then came seventeen minutes of hell for Notre Dame. It was one of the most incredible turnarounds in any football game ever. Southern Cal scored forty-nine points in those seventeen minutes while holding Notre Dame scoreless. Neither team scored in the final thirteen minutes, but the Trojans did not have to, and the Irish were still in shock.

No one on the team could explain what happened. The media tried to. One theory was that the blacks on the team folded in the second half as a way to embarrass Parseghian for his handling of the summer incident involving six black players. Another was that Art Best started a fight in the locker room at halftime. Both ideas were ridiculous. However, it remains a

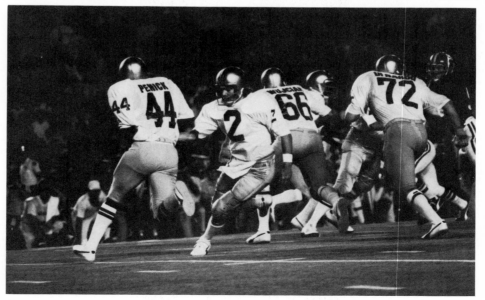

At the Sugar Bowl.

mystery what did cause the dramatic change in the second half.

Parseghian considered changing his mind following this crushing defeat. In the end, his wife and brother convinced him to stick by his plan, and he told Father Joyce he would, indeed, resign following the upcoming Orange Bowl date with Alabama.

The rematch with the Crimson Tide was not the game it had been a year earlier. Still, a victory by Alabama would nail down the national championship.

But a victory by Notre Dame would be oh-so-fitting for a man who brought the Fighting Irish back into national prominence. A victory would give him 170 against 58 defeats and 6 ties to put him among the thirty winningest coaches of all time. It would leave

him second to Knute Rockne at Notre Dame.

All this would not be easy. The Irish were eleven-point underdogs. Several of their top players were banged up or sick. But most of them managed to play at least a few downs in Parseghian's last game. The result was a 13—11 Notre Dame win. The Irish took a 13—0 lead in the first half and then just hung on.

"I've never had a victory in my coaching career with a group of guys so dedicated," Parseghian told the squad as he fought back his tears. "I'll remember this forever. This was my last game at Notre Dame. I'm never going to forget any one of you. What a great football game. You beat an undefeated team that was ranked number one. You were the under-dogs. You showed all those who were down in the mouth about us. Father Toohey, come on over here and say the prayer. We've got a lot to be thankful for."

And Notre Dame could be thankful for having had Ara Parseghian. The Orange Bowl win put the Irish at 10—2 in 1974 and fourth in the final ratings. He had Notre Dame in the running for national titles each of his eleven seasons. More importantly, this "outsider" reminded his players and everyone else at the university what Notre Dame is all about.

Dan Devine at the Helm

Dave Condon

Introduction

The best way I can think of to describe my six seasons at Notre Dame is that they were anything but boring.

Those years turned out their share of victories that don't seem to stick in my mind for any particular reason. They also produced some losses that I *hope* won't stick in my mind for too long.

But most of my fondest memories about Notre Dame involve those games that somehow ended up in the win column after just about everyone was resigned to losing. I'm still not sure exactly how or why some of those amazing rallies came about. I'm sure there was a little luck involved at least a few times. I guess, above all, those games taught me a little bit about that Notre Dame spirit described in the Victory March. The odds might have been great or small, but some of those comebacks made it seem like they simply had been destined to be that way. I didn't have the fortune of attending Notre Dame, but I certainly became a believer in a few short weeks!

It seems that everywhere it's said that people are what make Notre Dame such a great place. I couldn't agree more. From Fathers Hesburgh and Joyce down through the faculty and athletic administration to the students themselves, Notre Dame people are special in their own way. I also was blessed with superb groups of assistant coaches, not to mention an awfully impressive list of young men who wore Notre Dame football uniforms in my years. The university always has emphasized the term student-athlete, and that's probably part of the reason I so enjoyed getting to know those young men as individuals as much as I enjoyed watching their successes on the field.

I'll always remember some of the obvious highlights of the years 1975 through 1980.

That first game in '75 against Boston College on national television was my baptism as far as Notre Dame was concerned. I found out a little bit more about subway alumni that Monday night—and I also came to realize that you can go anywhere on the globe and find Notre Dame fans.

The next year we managed to defeat Bear Bryant and Alabama—and then finished the year by beating a good Penn State team in the Gator Bowl.

The '77 season turned out to be a once-in-a-lifetime experience for all of us connected with that team. That was the year that Southern Cal came back to town armed with a three-year winning streak and hungry to make it four. But we were hungrier. The Trojans were

met by a Fighting Irish football team wearing green, not blue, and playing with the intensity and the drive characteristic of a championship team. It was a week of electricity, a day of glory, and a victory that was among the sweetest.

Winning football games and bowl games is a thrilling experience. But when they add together to equal a national championship title, well, that has to be one of the most amazing experiences in which I have ever been involved.

I don't think any of us will forget the scene in the locker room at the Cotton Bowl after we had beaten undefeated Texas. That was a feeling that would be tough to match, anytime, anywhere. Yet, once you are handed that national champion designation, you become something special for the next year. The reception we received, no matter who was connected with that team, wherever we went over the next year, proved to all of us that there are an awfully large number of people in this country who enjoy college football.

We enjoyed our third straight bowl victory in '78 by defeating Houston in the final seconds of the Cotton Bowl—and we closed out the '79 campaign by traveling to Tokyo where we played Miami in the Mirage Bowl. I'll never forget the reception Vagas Ferguson received in Japan and the way he was treated like some sort of folk hero. The name Notre Dame seemed to stand for something spe-

cial even to those people who had never seen the Golden Dome.

As far as buildup for a single football game, one that impressed me a great deal was our match with Alabama in 1980. We knew months ahead of time that the Alabama people had been waiting years for that game. They tried to let us know what was in store for us in Birmingham, so much so that we felt like Daniel in the lion's den for a few seconds. But I would be the first to credit the Alabama fans—they were some of the greatest fans of college football that I've ever run into. And our young men, to their credit, came up with one of the grittiest efforts I've seen for sixty minutes on a football field.

The loss to USC in Los Angeles in 1978 and our defeat in the Sugar Bowl against Georgia are a couple of games that I'll probably wonder about for a long while. On both those afternoons, it seemed like we somehow should have ended up winning the football game—but it just didn't happen that way.

Despite all those moments, what really stands out most in my mind are some of those come-from-behind wins.

I'll always remember Joe Montana coming off the bench two weeks in a row as a sophomore to help us rally to beat North Carolina and Air Force on the road. He did nearly the same thing two years later against Purdue in West Lafayette in the '77 season—and he even finished his Notre Dame career by doing it against Houston in

the Cotton Bowl. That was the day he helped make chicken soup famous. The effort by the whole team that day, under those weather conditions, deserved more than just a pat on the back. Even if the sun had been out and the dial read 70 degrees, it would have been an astounding performance.

Rusty Lisch caught that same bug the next year with a last minute drive against South Carolina—and even Harry Oliver and Blair Kiel picked it up to beat Michigan in 1980. I guess those are the kinds of games that keep the fans coming back every Saturday. They almost made me wish I could sit up in section 26, eat a hot dog or two and yell, too!

People like Rockne, Leahy, Brennan, and Parseghian took part in plenty of those extra special Saturday afternoons during their stays at Notre Dame—and Gerry Faust and others will be a part of their share of extraordinary moments in the future.

In between there, I hope I was able to do a little something to help make Notre Dame the unique place that it is today. An awful lot of Notre Dame rubbed off on me in six years—and I know I've left a little bit of my heart behind, too.

—DAN DEVINE

Daniel John Devine had built Arizona State into a gridiron powerhouse, revitalized the program at Missouri (taking the Tigers to six bowl games), and served as coach-general manager of the pro Green Bay Packers (National Football Conference Coach of the Year in 1952), when he was officially named to the Notre Dame post on December 17, 1974.

Following the legends of Rockne, Leahy, and Parseghian, Devine would serve six years. He would win fifty-three, lose sixteen, and tie three, while sending the Irish to four bowl games—victories over Penn State, Texas, and Houston, and a seven-point loss to Georgia's national champions on New Year's Day, 1981.

At the time Devine left Notre Dame, his Vagas Ferguson and Jerome Heavens were one-two (ahead of George Gipp) in career rushing yardage records for Irish players. Devine's Ferguson, Phil Carter, Jim Stone, and Heavens were in the records as the only ND athletes to have rushed for two hundred or more yards in at least one game. Ferguson's seventeen career TDs were an all-time Irish high. His Dave Reeve and Harry Oliver had kicked the five longest field goals in Notre Dame history since George Gipp's controversial but legendary sixty-two-yard drop kick. Oliver ranked first, as Dan left the campus, in Notre Dame field goals (eighteen) for a single season. And, at the same time, Joe Montana (1975, 1977-78)

rated high in the passes-completed statistics, both career and single season, and in the career and season records for total offense yards.

Despite the critics, Dan would give Notre Dame a "Devine Era."

Dan, one of nine children, was born in Augusta, Wisconsin, where his father's business did not survive the depression. At the age of six, Dan was living with an aunt and uncle in Proctor, Minnesota, across from Duluth. "The only reason I was away from my parents was because of the depression. My aunt and uncle had only one child, so they took me in." Others in the family also lived with them occasionally. Growing up, Dan accepted whatever jobs were available. Sometimes he unloaded barges of frozen ore, in frigid weather, in Duluth. "You had to break up that ore and ice with a pick," he remembered. As a one hundred thirty-five-pound sophomore at Proctor High School, Dan broke into the all-senior starting lineup by winning the center's post from a two hundred ten-pound vet.

"Yes, I was center and nose guard until the third game, when I intercepted a pass and showed some speed. After that I was a halfback," Devine recalled one time we were visiting at Notre Dame. "But I'll never forget after I took that senior's job—we were travelling in an old school bus, to our first game, and none of the seniors would talk to me. It hurt, because I was a shy and sensitive kid."

Devine paused in that narrative, and came up to the moment, which was in his office in 1978, and said: "Yes, I was a very shy, sensitive kid. I guess I still am."

Dan's studies at University of Minnesota-Duluth were sandwiched between a thirty-month career as an Air Force bombardier. After his post-war return to Minnesota-Duluth, Dan captained both the football and basketball teams, served as student body president, and married Joanne Brookhart. They had seven children. The first were twin daughters, and Dan and Jo packed the twins "and everything else we possessed in the world" into a battered old station wagon when he moved to coach at East Jordan, Michigan, High School. Devine had two unbeaten teams at East Jordan. He

went to Michigan State University to earn his master's degree and find an introduction to big-time football. Biggie Munn signed Dan as a freshman coach; later Munn's successor, Duffy Daugherty, moved him to varsity backfield coach. In 1955, he accepted the top post at Arizona State Teachers (Arizona State University). The Tempe university lost two football games in Dan's first season, lost one his second, and in the third had its first unbeaten campaign in forty-three years. Missouri, looking for a successor after Frank Broyles moved on to Arkansas, snatched Dan from Arizona. He served thirteen seasons with Mizzou, before trying the Green Bay experiment, and his 1960 Tigers were unbeaten in eleven games and highly ranked nationally.

When Devine took over at Notre Dame, it was apparent that he indeed was shy, sensitive, and often had to fight back tears at disappointments or lying, biting criticism. "He looks like a college professor, but there's steel inside," explained a former Missouri athlete.

Dan Devine's Notre Dame debut came before a capacity crowd in Schaefer stadium, Foxboro, Massachusetts, and a nationally televised audience. Boston College, which had lost coach Frank Leahy to Notre Dame more than three decades earlier, was primed for the first battle, ever, against the gridiron Irish. There had been a downtown luncheon rally that drew many of Leahy's former BC and ND players, souvenir glasses imprinted with Leahy's records at both schools, and a Waterford crystal bowl honoring Leahy's memory was put up as a trophy for the contest.

The Eagles played spiritedly in the scoreless first period. In the following quarter, Boston was stopped at the ND 22. A forty-one yard sprint by Mark McLane soon had the Irish headed for a 3–0 lead. Notre Dame had touchdown intentions but settled for Dave Reeve's

Practice under Devine.

An Irish Flag rally.

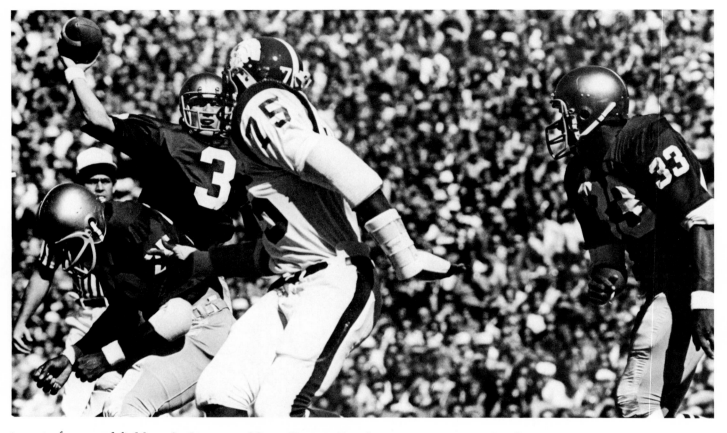

Montana throws against Michigan State in 1975.

Joe Montana calling the signals in 1975.

Montana installed at quarterback. Willie Fry blocked a Wildcat punt to provide opportunity for the next Irish touchdown, which came four plays later on a ten-yard zip into the end zone by Jim Browner, behind Mark McLane's excellent blocking. Ted Burgmeier, almost trapped for a loss, broke free and gained fifty yards. McLane took a fourteen-yard scoring pass from Montana, the extra point was added, and Notre Dame owned an insurmountable 21—7 halftime bulge. Dave Reeve's forty-four-yard field goal also contributed to the final 31—7 margin. Montana passed for eighty yards, including one TD run. Jerome Heavens, the freshman fullback, gained one hundred six yards in fifteen carries.

Michigan State's Tyrone Wilson's seventy-six-yard scoring run broke a 3—3 deadlock with 3:50 to play at Notre Dame. The Spartans' 10—7 conquest was the only Devine loss to Michigan State in six meetings.

twenty-four-yard field goal when the offense sputtered at the BC 4. The Eagles tied it, 3—3, on Fred Steinfort's forty-five-yard field goal only eleven seconds before intermission. In the second half, Ross Browner started things moving with recovery of a BC fumble on his 40. Brother Jim Browner concluded the drive by racing ten yards for a TD. Adding the point, the Irish led, 10—7. Boston College received. The Eagles took to the air on their fourth play, a costly mistake. Willie Fry and Mike Banks tipped the pass and a third

Notre Damer, Randy Harrison, intercepted at the BC 42. Al Hunter scored the touchdown with a twenty-four-yard run down his right sideline. The subsequent conversion left Notre Dame a 17—3 victor. The Browner brothers were awarded the game ball to send to their critically ill father. Coach Devine said: "Pressure? I wouldn't have taken this job if I thought I was going to die in the first game. But I'll be honest. . . . Boston College literally had me dying several times."

Five days later the Irish invaded

Purdue to win, 17—0. Northwestern came to Notre Dame, giving home fans their first look at a team coached by Devine, and established a 7—0 lead with their first TD against the Irish since 1971. The scoring assault started after Wildcat Mike Harlow intercepted a Rick Slager pass and returned to the ND 26. Greg Boykin then carried four times in succession for the Northwestern touchdown. Notre Dame covered seventy-seven yards to get a touchdown, then added the tying point. During this assault, Slager was injured and

The Irish trailed North Carolina by fourteen points going into the last quarter at Chapel Hill. Rick Slager completed passes to three different receivers, for thirty-seven yards, in piloting ND toward the touchdown scored by Al Hunter's two-yard slash. Slager missed a two-point conversion pass to Ken MacAfee. On next possession by the Irish, Slager missed three passes. So when Notre Dame again took over, at its 27, Montana was at quarterback, and Notre Dame scored on its fifth play. Montana's thirty-nine-yard pass to Dan Kelleher was the key maneuver, putting the ball in position for another two-yard TD slant by Hunter. Montana's two-point pass to Doug Buth made it 14—14. The closing two minutes saw the Irish take possession, soon facing second-and-ten on their 20 and intending to use a draw play. Montana called an audible when he spotted a Carolina cornerback playing too deep. So Montana flipped a quick turnout pass to Ted Burgmeier, who had lined up wide and only four yards from the sideline. The cornerback charged in, apparently with intentions to intercept. "I kept running right down the sideline," said Burgmeier. "That only left the safetyman and I got by him with a shoulder fake at about the 50." Burgmeier's TD, with ensuing extra point, gave the Irish a 21—14 victory, though the Tar Heels quickly probed back to the ND 19, only to see the Irish defense stifle third and fourth-down passes.

The visit to Air Force Academy provided another heart-stopper, with the surprising Falcons—who had lost five and tied one in this season—holding a 30—10 edge in the final quarter. Joe Montana, though, came off the bench to spur another of those patent Notre Dame rallies. It wasn't easy. The Irish came up to third-and-five at the Air Force 47. They solved this with a Montana to Ken MacAfee pass that gained twenty-nine yards. The ND touchdown soon came on Montana's three-yard run. Now Notre Dame was fighting both the inspired Falcons and the clock and it looked futile when the Irish were backed up to their own 15; more futile the instant Falcon Jim Miller made his third interception of the afternoon. But Miller fumbled and Ernie Hughes recovered, putting the Irish back in business. Montana passed to MacAfee for two yards, then hurled to Mark McLane, whose running wasn't checked until he reached the Air Force 7. Montana immediately passed to MacAfee for a touchdown with 5:29 still to play.

Notre Dame's defense forced Air Force to punt, ND taking over on the Falcon 45. On first down, Al Hunter swept forty-four yards to the 1, stepping outside a weakside linebacker before cutting back against the flow. Jerome Heavens, who in the third quarter had sped fifty-five yards for a touchdown, plunged the single yard to create a 30—30 tie. Dave

Reeve kicked point for the 31–30 victory, the Irish holding on through the final 3:23.

Jubilance in the dressing room was dampened when Devine was asked about a rumor that this would be his last game as head coach, with Ara Parseghian returning to the helm for the balance of the season. "I just heard the rumor a few moments ago," said Dan. "I don't want to dignify it with any comment. I just cry inside for my family."

The Irish seized a 6–0 first quarter lead, thanks to Al Hunter's early TD jaunt of fifty-two yards, on visiting Southern California. The Trojans had command after a long touchdown pass, plus extra-point kick, within the first minute of the second period. Notre Dame retaliated with cornerback Tom Lopienski gobbling up a blocked Trojan punt and charging on thirteen yards for a touchdown, Kris Haines adding a two-point conversion taking a pass from Al Hunter, so the Irish were in front, 14–7, at intermission. Southern California's

MacAfee blocks against Alabama in 1976.

Willie Fry, 94, signals his mates.

Dave Reeve kicks in 1976. He holds ND records for field goals attempted and made.

1976 cheerleaders.

Ricky Bell, who gained one hundred sixty-five yards in forty rushes, picked up three of those yards with a third quarter TD smash. The Trojans added point, leaving it 14–14 starting the final period. ND regained control as Dave Reeve hit a twenty-seven-yard field goal. USC accepted the kickoff and after seven plays, including four rushes by Bell, was at the ND 1. Bell fumbled but the Trojans' alert Melvin Johnson recovered at the 2. Quarterback Vince Evans feinted Bell into the line, retained the ball and scooted wide left for a TD. Following the point kick, Southern California had a 21–17 bulge. A thirty-five-yard field goal provided the Trojans' 24–17 winning margin. In the winners' dressing room, USC coach John McKay tossed the game ball to Bell.

Navy was beaten (31–10) and Georgia Tech fell (24–3), both games in South Bend, to send Notre Dame off to battle rebuilding Pittsburgh. Junior Tony Dorsett, the one-man gang, gained three hundred three yards, added seventy-one more on three pass receptions, and scored two touchdowns to pace Pitt's 34–20 triumph.

The Irish, knocked out of the bowl game invitation derby by the loss at Pittsburgh, wound up with a night game at Miami (Florida). Notre Dame's opening possession led to a 3–0 advantage on Dave Reeve's twenty-six-yard field goal. The Miami team responded with its own field goal, leaving it 3–3 entering the second quarter. The

Irish picked up sixteen points, and a 19–3 intermission edge, on touchdowns by Jerome Heavens (a two-yard plunge) and Ken MacAfee (short pass from Rick Slager), two extra-point kicks by Reeve, and a safety posted when Ross Browner tackled a Miami runner for a safety. Notre Dame went on to a 32–9 conquest, and Devine had ended his first season with a record of eight victories, three losses.

Pittsburgh, bound for the national championship, appeared at Notre Dame to begin Coach Dan Devine's second season, and again Tony Dorsett gave the Irish more headaches than they could handle. Tony ran for one-hundred eighty-one yards in twenty-two rushes, making his running yardage total seven hundred fifty-four yards in four seasons against ND. Dorsett explained he had a special incentive to always play well against the Irish, who originally had tried to recruit him but who lost interest, he said, after an assistant Notre Dame coach reportedly tabbed him as "just a skinny, little kid who couldn't make it in big-time football."

Notre Dame took the lead with Rick Slager directing an eighty-six-yard touchdown drive. He totalled fifty-two yards in completing all three of his passes, including the twenty-five-yard TD pitch to Ken MacAfee. Dave Reeve kicked the point. Enter Dorsett. On Pitt's first play following the

ensuing kickoff, Tony broke for a sixty-one-yard gain. Two scrimmages later, he scored on a five-yard thrust. With the extra point, the Panthers had tied it, 7–7.

Early in the second period, Pitt's LeRoy Felder intercepted a Slager pass, pitched when Rick was off-balance, and returned twenty-eight yards. This opportunity was turned into a 14–7 lead on Haygood's one-yard scoring rush, and the subsequent extra point. Moments later, Slager hurled another interception and a third Pitt touchdown drive—Dorsett contributed a fourteen-yard run—was underway. Haygood hit the end zone, again with a one-yard plunge, and, with the conversion, Pittsburgh led, 21–7. Notre Dame picked up three points via Reeve's fifty-three-yard field goal prior to halftime. The third quarter was scoreless but in the fourth, Carson Long of Pittsburgh booted a thirty-one-yard field goal. And still the Panthers prowled, with Dorsett's twenty-eight-yard gain setting up Matt Cavanaugh's eight-yard TD burst. The extra point swelled Pitt's final margin to 31–10. But the Irish had seen the last of Tony Dorsett.

"Our job now is to bounce back," said Devine, following Notre Dame's worst opening game loss in history. Bounce back the Irish did, at the expense of three Big Ten foes: Purdue (23–0), Northwestern (48–0), and Michigan State (24–6). Visiting Oregon became a 41–0 victim, but the following week host South Carolina was more stubborn though finally yielding, 13–6.

The South Carolina game was played in front of President Gerald Ford, who saw Notre Dame establish a 13–0 early lead but had to wait until the closing defensive stand to find out why they're indeed the Fighting Irish. Rick Slager passed nine yards to Willard Browner for the opening TD. Dave Reeve added the extra point, then soon came back with a thirty-seven-yard field goal, as the Irish rolled ahead, 10–0. Reeve added a thirty-yard field goal, climaxing a drive highlighted by Al Hunter's twenty-two-yard run, early in the second quarter. The feisty Gamecocks dug in to hold ND scoreless thereafter. South Carolina picked up a field goal prior to intermission, and narrowed the margin to 13–6 with another three-pointer with less than six minutes elapsed in the final period. Yet with 3:32 to play, South Carolina was at the Notre Dame 21. The Gamecocks scented a victory if they could get the touchdown and a two-point conversion, and frenzied home fans were shouting: "We want eight! We want eight!" Willie Fry momentarily quieted the cheering by throwing an SC runner for a three-yard loss. Then the "we want eight" chant was resumed. South Carolina's Ben Cornett had a pass in his grasp at the ND 15, only to find the ball yanked from him by Jim Browner, one of the three Browner brothers in the starting ND lineup. Yet Notre Dame,

backed up to its 15, was in a perilous situation. Al Hunter solved that by streaking for a sixty-one-yard gain, and now the Irish safely could run out the clock.

Navy was high the next Saturday in Cleveland. The Irish, four-touchdown favorites, may have been complacent. The Midshipmen threw forty-six passes and came close to the upset of the season before falling, 27–21.

Disaster came at Georgia Tech after Notre Dame returned from the intermission with a 14–10 lead forged around Al Hunter's two short touchdown runs. The Rambling Wrecks did not throw a pass throughout, but assaulted the Irish with a running attack that netted three hundred sixty-eight yards compared to only one hundred seven ground out by ND rushers.

A series of weird events prevented Notre Dame from going into the third quarter with a comfortable 14–3 lead. Georgia Tech faced third and seven at its 36 when Notre Dame stopped the clock by calling time-out with forty seconds left in the second quarter. As soon as play resumed, the Yellow Jackets' Drew Hill scooted forty-six yards before being knocked out of bounds. When Hill was halted, the clock showed nineteen seconds left, but officials agreed that actually twenty-nine seconds remained. A personal foul against Luther Bradley subsequently moved the ball to the Irish 8, from where Gary Lanier ran it into the end zone. Georgia Tech added the point, and

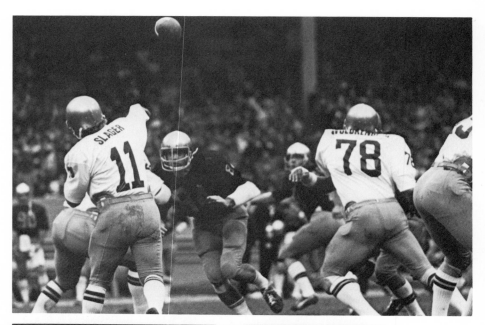

Rick Slager, 11; Harry Woelkenberg, 78; Ernie Hughes, 65.

Ross Browner and Willie Fry close in on talented Navy QB Bob Lezcynski, 1976.

1976 Cotton Bowl. Slager, 11; MacAfee, 81; Willard Browner, 24; Tom Domin, 26; Slager passing.

added thirteen more in the second half to triumph, 23—14, terminating a six-game ND winning streak.

So the Irish geared for Alabama's invasion, the first Notre Dame-Crimson Tide encounter outside the bowl game arenas. The Irish scored all their points in the second quarter. Rick Slager completed fifteen of twenty-three aerials, including a fifty-six-yard gainer to Dan Kelleher for Notre Dame's opening touchdown. Freshman Vagas Ferguson, making his first start, rushed one hundred and seven yards including a seventeen-yard touchdown dash. Ken MacAfee caught six passes for ninety-two yards. Ross Browner was a defensive standout all afternoon, but brother Jim came up with the spectacular that prevented possible defeat when Alabama was going-for-broke in the closing four minutes. Jim ended that threat by intercepting a pass by Jeff Rutledge. Coach Devine praised the Irish for not being overcome by the adversity of two missed opportunities, the failure of a "chip shot" field goal attempt, and a fumble into the end zone.

Miami (Florida) sustained a 40—27 loss at Notre Dame and the Irish were off to Southern California in high spirits. They nearly pulled an upset, and Devine did some masterful coaching, before yielding 17—13 to the Trojan team that finished No. 2 to Pittsburgh in the national rankings.

This led to Notre Dame's first bowl trip under Devine—a Gator Bowl duel with Penn State in Jacksonville, Florida. Joe Paterno's Nittany Lions drove to Notre Dame's 10 the first time they had possession, but had to settle for a 3—0 lead on a twenty-six-yard field goal. Terry Eurick returned the following kickoff for sixty-five yards, igniting an advance that took the Irish to a fourth-down-and-foot-to-go situation at the State 16. Al Hunter made fifteen feet on the try, and later ran one yard for the touchdown sending Notre Dame ahead.

The Irish were not so successful the next time they disdained the field goal to seek a touchdown, failing a fourth-down pass from the Nittany Lions' 2. They quickly picked up those three points, and a 10—3 lead, as Steve Heimkreiter forced State's Mike Guman to fumble, Jim Browner recovering. This break led to Dave Reeve's twenty-three-yard field goal.

Notre Dame fielded a short Penn State punt on the Irish 49. The attack produced a 17—3 advantage on the conversion that followed Hunt-

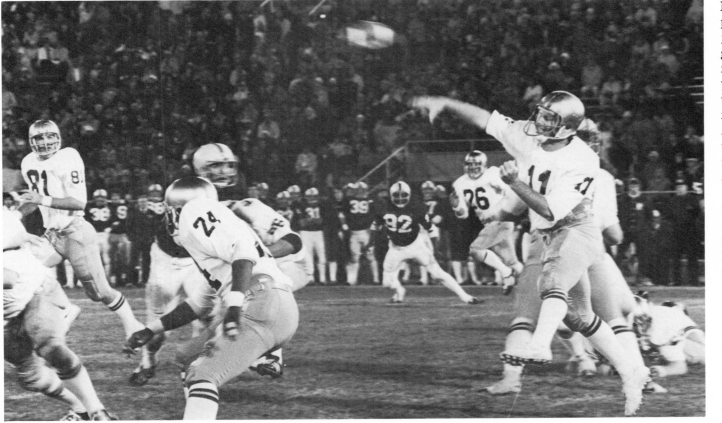

er's second TD burst. Reeve's field goal, another twenty-three-yarder, mounted the lead to 20–3 on the last play of the half. Penn State picked up a consolation six points by marching eight yards to the touchdown after blocking Joe Restic's punt.

Notre Dame was to graduate only quarterback Slager and wide receiver Dan Kelleher from its squad of twenty-two starters and celebrated the Penn State game by chanting "wait until next year." The 1976 record of eight won, three lost was good for a No. 12 national ranking. Ross Browner was a unanimous All-American, Ken MacAfee made it on many teams, and Luther Bradley and Willie Fry did not go unnoticed when various All-American squads were chosen.

And next year was coming!

This was next year! This was a great season, the season of the Green Machine. This was "the championship season." It didn't start out impressively, of course, but all's well that ends well.

The campaign opened at Pittsburgh, home of the defending national champions. The first serious Irish drive was roadblocked when the Panthers intercepted a pass that Rusty Lisch had intended for Ken MacAfee. Here Pitt moved into position for Matt Cavanaugh, its outstanding quarterback, to hurl a touchdown aerial that, coupled with an extra-point kick, pushed the Panthers ahead, 7–0.

Notre Dame's Willie Fry crashed into Cavanaugh on the scoring throw and Cavanaugh, nursing a severe wrist injury, was through for the afternoon. Pitt wasn't. The Panthers boosted their edge by two points when ND's Joe Restic, back to punt, had butterfingers grabbing the ball, didn't get off the kick, and was charged with a safety. Rusty Lisch rallied the Irish with five pass completions, the fifth a short touchdown pitch snared by MacAfee. So Pitt led 9–6 at the half; by the same margin going into the fourth period. Dave Reeve's thirty-five-yard field goal created no more than a tie score, but Reeve hit a twenty-six-yard three-pointer and Notre Dame had its lead. As insurance, Terry Eurick added a TD on a four-yard thrust shortly after Jim Browner's recovery of a fumble at the Panther 11. (Reeve converted.) Final: Irish 19, Panthers 9.

In Jackson, Mississippi led after one quarter, 3–0, after a twenty-nine-yard field goal by Hoppy Langley. Jim Browner's pass interception on the first play following Mississippi's recovery of Terry Eurick's fumble, set the Irish moving from the southerners' 26. Jerome Heavens' two-yard touchdown run, plus Dave Reeve's conversion kick, changed the score to 7–3, Notre Dame. Ole Miss altered that, gaining almost sixty-five yards of a seventy-five-yard scoring advance via the airlines. A ten-yard air mail touchdown delivery to Jim Storey, and the extra point, gave Ole

Miss a 10–7 bulge until Jay Case recovered a Mississippi fumble in the fourth quarter. This opportunity led to no more than a forty-four-yard Reeve field goal that brought a 10–10 stalemate. Another fumble recovery started marching the Irish toward the rebel goal line, but Mississippi wasn't yielding any more touchdowns. They did yield to Reeve, whose twenty-eight-yard goal pushed ND in front, 13–10. Less than five minutes remained, time enough for Ole Miss to tally another ten points for a 20–13 upset conquest. Storey caught a second TD pass, the point was added by Langley, and now the rebel yells signalled a 17–13 Mississippi lead. The clock showed 3:23 left. Would Notre Dame dramatically pull out another one? Not today. Ole Miss recovered Jerome Heavens' fumble at the ND 14, an opportunity the southerners finally cashed on Langley's three-point kick. With time precious, the Irish tried for the miracle. All hopes were dashed through interception of a Rusty Lisch pass.

Notre Dame now had won one and lost one and hadn't looked spectacular either time. Coach Dan Devine recalled years later: "I remember it vividly. We were back at Notre Dame and had a squad meeting at 4 P.M. Sunday. I told the players, 'I know we're a better team than we've been so far.' In meetings, I can rant and holler, and about ten times I must have raved loudly, 'I know you're a great football team!' I told them

they were good enough to bounce back. I said we'd play one game at a time, and we'd play tough, so that if the time came when something good might happen to us, we would have done our part to set up the opportunity."

Yet the following Saturday, at Purdue, the Irish trailed 10–0 after one quarter, and 24–14 entering the last period. Freshman Mark Hermann had hurled three touchdown passes for the Boilermakers; Rusty Lisch had made pitches to Terry Eurick for the two Irish touchdowns up to this point. Gary Forystek, replacing Lisch at quarterback, began engineering a fourth-quarter ND rally. Forystek himself ran thirteen yards to the Purdue 17, where a mass tackle fractured his collarbone. Joe Montana rushed off the bench but the new quarterback did not work immediate miracles. Dave Reeve finally kicked a twenty-four-yard field goal that still left the Boilermakers with a 24–17 edge that was vulnerable because the Irish could go ahead with a touchdown and two-point conversion. Plenty of time remained, and Luther Bradley's pass interception on Mark Hermann, just on the Purdue side of midfield, set up a Notre Dame opportunity. And Montana was the tonic the Irish needed. Joe passed with super-marksmanship, ultimately finding Ken MacAfee with a touchdown aerial. Confident they could score again, the Irish disdained the two-point conversion and let Reeve's kick make it 24–24.

Less than four minutes remained as Montana began a victory march from the ND 30. MacAfee and Kris Haines each caught two of Montana's flips while the Irish were progressing to Purdue's 10. Here Montana forgot the air lanes and called on his infantry, with two rushes—the second a five-yarder by Dave Mitchell—producing the go-ahead touchdown. Reeve kicked the final point in a 31–24 victory. The Fighting Irish were on their way.

Michigan State was next, and its defense stopped two early Notre Dame drives. The Spartans were backed to their 3-yard line on an Irish thrust highlighted by Joe Montana's long-distance aerial to Ken MacAfee, when they gained a reprieve by recovering a Dave Mitchell fumble. The Irish soon rampaged again, but were frustrated on interception of a Montana pass. There was more frustration for ND as Michigan State took a 3–0 lead on Hans Nielsen's thirty-eight-yard field goal. The frustration was compounded by a third Irish bobble—Jerome Heavens dropped Montana's pass when Jerome had an open route to the goal line.

The scoreboard showed 3–3 following Dave Reeve's forty-two-yard field goal. Reeve's extra point, after Mitchell's nine-yard touchdown run, produced a 10–3 Irish halftime lead. The Spartans scored a third-period field goal but not until Reeve had picked a pair of three-pointers, forty and

All-American Ken MacAfee gathers the ball.

fifty-one yards, respectively. After this 16–6 success (Bob Golic, Ted Burgmeier, and Ross Browner were defensive stars), the Irish had an off Saturday before going to East Rutherford, N.J., to renew rivalry with Army. Jerome Heavens carried thirty-four times against the Cadets, scoring one touchdown, in Notre Dame's 24–0 victory. Terry Eurick's two short slashes scored the other touchdowns while Dave Reeve was three-for-three on extra points, besides a twenty-nine-yard field goal. Clearly, the Army-Notre Dame games no longer held the glamour of old. Army had challenged the Irish seven times since Col. Earl Blaik's 1958 Cadets triumphed at Notre Dame, 14–2, and in those seven losses had scored just thirteen points (only one touchdown) to two-hundred eighty-two points for ND. (And, following their eighth game against the Fighting Irish in 1980, Coach Dan Devine's last season, the West Pointers were in arrears, three hundred-twelve points to sixteen, in the matches after 1958.)

Yet if the Army series had lost its glitter, there was continued in-

Mike Whittington, 54, tackling in 1977.

Cheerleaders, 1978.

Devine celebrates a squeaker victory over Clemson in 1977.

creasing luster to the Notre Dame–Southern California duels that had started in 1926. So there was great fanfare when the Trojans, who had won six of the previous seven challenges from the Irish, appeared in South Bend. But Devine had been plotting for Southern California for months. He was going to use typically Rockne psychology. With almost the same secrecy that surrounded the Manhattan project, Devine placed an order for green jerseys, which seldom or never had been worn since the eras of Frank Leahy and Terry Brennan. Devine knew it was essential his strategy not be tipped in advance. The cat almost escaped the bag when athletic director Ed "Moose" Krause approached Devine's platform, where the coach was supervising a pre-season practice, and inquired: "Dan, what about those green jerseys you've ordered?" Devine motioned to Krause to forget the whole thing, and Moose did. Equipment manager Gene O'Neill, of course, eventually had to be told. Assistant coaches remained in the dark.

Dandy Dan had a busy Friday. He gave his athletes a pep talk much longer than Rock's win-for-the-Gipper brainstorm, yet it was as effective. Recently, Devine recalled anew: "I talked to them of Irish history and pointed out that the Irish are noted for courage and integrity. I spoke of Irish adversities, and I think I touched everyone because there were so many minority groups represented on our team.

"I explained it was because of courage, integrity, and winning against the odds that we were called The Fighting Irish. I said I wanted our black-American athletes, approximately one-third of the squad, to be truly aware of the cultural heritage of this great university . . . . I also let them know I was certain if the good Lord helped Alabama and old Bear Bryant beat Southern California (21—20), He certainly wasn't going to let down Irish Catholics and their teammates."

As another touch, Devine produced the golden-throated tennis coach, Tom Fallon, to favor the squad with a selection of revered Irish songs, including, of course, "Wearin' o' the green." Finally, Devine revealed his secret to the four co-captains, Ross Browner, Terry Eurick, Willie Fry, and Steve Orsini, impressing them that the confidence must be kept.

Notre Dame warmed up wearing blue, before a capacity crowd and the Southern California athletes, in Saturday's pre-game drills. The players returned to the dressing room, each discovering a green jersey in his locker. They quickly shucked the blue garb and donned the green. Alumni, students, everyone, gasped as the Green Machine charged from the tunnel to start the battle. Trojan players gasped. In the stands, the president of the company that sold Notre Dame its jerseys turned to his sales manager and said, "why aren't they wearing our outfits?" The sales manager, who had kept the secret, responded: "Those ARE our jerseys."

Notre Dame led after one period, 7—0, on Dave Mitchell's four-yard TD run and Dave Reeve's conversion. Southern Cal tied it when Mario Celotto grabbed Terry Eurick's fumble and sprinted five yards to the goal line, Frank Jordan kicking the point. Now Notre Damers proved themselves, once again, the Fighting Irish. Montana scored a touchdown on a single-yard thrust, Tom Domin added a two-point conversion by clutching a pass from Ted Burgmeier. Ken MacAfee took a thirteen-yard scoring aerial from Montana, Reeve kicking the point, to establish a 22—7 lead going into intermission. The Irish added thirteen points in the third period. Jay Case picked up the loose football following Bob Golic's block of a USC punt, and ambled thirty yards for a TD. Reeve kicked point. Montana's one-yard flip to MacAfee concluded a lengthy drive for the second touchdown of this quarter,

but the kick for extra point failed. So the Green Machine led, 35—7, entering the final period, when each team would tally two touchdowns. Southern Cal failed its conversion attempts, but Reeve hit the conversion bullseye after Montana's one-yard TD plunge and after Rusty Lisch's four-yard scoring aerial to Kevin Hart. Notre Dame's 49—19 conquest brought frenzied celebrating outside the Irish locker room, where Coach Devine—noblest Irishman of them all—said: "I realized the electric shock that the nostalgic sight of those green jerseys would give Notre Dame fans. But more important were the big hearts that beat under those green jerseys. If there ever was a team win, this was it."

A 43—10 Notre Dame victory spoiled Navy's visit, and with the previous season's upset still in mind, the Irish were prepared for Georgia Tech's arrival. The opening period was scoreless. The first ND drive to get on the boards went awry as Reeve missed a field goal attempt. Reeve also failed the point-after kick following Joe Montana's one-yard TD burst. Reeve kicked off deep to the Yellow Jackets' Dave Hillman, who lateraled to Eddie Lee Ivery, with Ivery running more than ninety yards for a touchdown. Adding the point, Georgia Tech led, 7—6. The lead lasted only until Terry Eurick grabbed an eight-yard scoring pass from Montana. Montana ran for a two-point conversion, making up

for the missed Reeve extra-point, and the Irish were off to a 21—7 lead at the half. The margin was boosted to 69—7 before Georgia Tech could tally the seven points reducing the final ND edge to 69—14.

Notre Dame traveled to Clemson, whose tough Tigers were girding for an upset and apparently were headed for one after overcoming an early 7—0 deficit arranged by Jerome Heavens' five-yard TD run and Dave Reeve's extra-point kick. Entering the fourth quarter in front of a most partisan home crowd, the Tigers were in front, 17—7. Coach Devine, fuming over the officiating, felt better following Joe Montana's two-yard scoring smash on the final period's first play, Reeve converting. Still Clemson held a three point bulge, but that was jeopardized the instant that Mike Calhoun pounced on a Clemson fumble. This surge carried to the Tigers' 1, where Montana needed two carries for the go-ahead touchdown. Reeve's extra point iced the 21—17 victory.

Air Force (beaten 49—0) and Miami of Florida (a 48—10 victim) were no trouble. Now the 10—1 Irish had almost a month to prepare for the Cotton Bowl shoot-out with unbeaten, No. 1-ranked Texas. There were dire predictions, mainly from Texas, that Notre Dame was overmatched and that the game would be one-sided. The prognostication that the game would be one-sided proved accurate. Yet Coach Devine had his worries in the work-

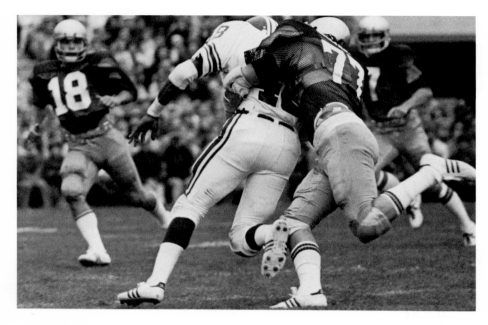

outs in Dallas, and was infuriated to read that ND linebacker Bob Golic had stated the game would not even be close—that Texas would be blown out.

Addressing his squad before the next practice, Devine said: "You're right. The game won't be close. But we're the ones who are going to be blown off." He reminded the players they had fallen into careless habits. To cool off, Dan absented himself from the first twenty minutes of practice. Recalled Golic: "Coach Devine really tore into us. It was one of the best speeches I ever heard. He said there was no way we could stay in the same stadium with them . . . . He came up to me later and told me he hoped I hadn't minded being singled out." Ken MacAfee would remember: "He

said the way we were practicing we didn't stand a chance. He really did a psyche job on us." By kickoff hour, Willie Fry, who shared the tri-captaincy with Ross Browner and Terry Eurick, was convinced the Irish would win handily. Afterwards, Fry said, "I attribute the 38—10 score to the fact that we were thoroughly ticked off."

Notre Dame was first in the scoring columns, thanks to Dave Reeve's forty-seven-yard field goal. Russell Erxleben, the Longhorns' long distance kicking specialist, matched that to send the contest into the second period knotted 3—3. The haughty Texans figured it was only a question of time before their Earl Campbell, the Heisman trophy winner, began running roughshod over the ND defense. Before those fans could

realize what was happening, the Irish had a 24—3 lead, and would have gone to intermission with that margin except for some weird happenings in the waning seconds. On what should have been the last play of the half, Texas missed a desperation pass but gained a reprieve—time for one more play with time at 0:00—because Jim Browner drew a pass-interference penalty. Longhorn Mike Lockett snared a thirteen-yard scoring aerial, and the extra point was good. Texas seemed revived by the points that left it behind only 24—10 at the half. Notre Dame rooters were nervous. Could the powerful Longhorns come back, as Southern California had done in 1974, to win in a rout?

Texas did return charging, not realizing they were through scoring for the afternoon, but their early third-quarter assault finally found ND digging in and the Longhorns had to settle for a field-goal attempt that failed. Vagas Ferguson, who had taken a TD pass from Joe Montana after Eurick's pair of scoring runs during that second-quarter broadside, scored on a three-yard run in the third period and, in the last stanza, sped twenty-six yards for the final touchdown following Steve Heimkreiter's fumble recovery. Reeve kicked both extra points but, before his second rolled the final figures to 38—10, disgusted Texas fans were stampeding from the Cotton Bowl. Ferguson and Jerome Heavens each had rushed for one hun-

dred yards or better. Golic, Ross Browner, and Fry were the defensive standouts. Right guard Ernie Hughes was an offensive ace. At the game's end, one Notre Dame standout—a native of Dallas—knelt and kissed the fifty-yard line and said: "If the Associated Press writers don't rate us No. 1, it will be a contradiction because we beat the raters' No. 1 team . . . and beat them in every way possible."

Now the long wait for the final rating began. Would Notre Dame's early loss to Mississippi be an unfavorable factor? Would Texas, with its great record, hold on to No. 1? What about Alabama, which finished at 11—1 with an impressive shellacking of Ohio State (35—6) in the Sugar Bowl? Or Arkansas, also 11—1 after an awesome 31—6 Orange Bowl conquest of Oklahoma?

About 2 A.M., Devine accompanied by Joe Montana, perched on a staircase at the Marriott hotel and informed celebrating fans, friends, and alumni, that Notre Dame had just been voted the National Football Foundation's MacArthur Bowl, symbolic of the national championship. It would not be until 4 P.M., though, that the wire service balloting results would be known.

Devine was eating a bowl of cornflakes in his suite as the zero hour approached. The telephone had been ringing incessantly, so Dan told the operators to shut off all calls except any from the wire services. At seven minutes to four

Kris Haines, 1977-78.

P.M., the phone jingled. Jill, Dan's daughter, reached for it. "I'll take this one myself," said Dan. He answered, "Yes, this is Dan Devine. Well, thank you very much." Sarah, another Devine daughter, said, "It shows on his face. We're No. 1." Dan nodded, and said, "Yes, in the UPI coaches poll." Now players joined the writers and friends in the Devine suite. Soon there was another telephone call. There was only a single ring before the coach had the instrument to his ear. This had to be the Associated Press. Devine listened a moment, then lifted his arm and extended the right index finger. No. 1! To make a sweep, the Irish also were awarded the Grantland Rice championship trophy from the Football Writers Association. Four seasons after Ara Parseghian's last success, Notre Dame again was at the top of the roost, and *Chicago Tribune* columnist Robert Markus wrote: "It's time to give the man [Devine] his due." Ross Browner and Ken MacAfee were unanimous All-American choices. Others singled out for All-American recognition were Luther Bradley, Ernie Hughes, Bob Golic, Willie Fry, and

Ted Burgmeier. Ross Browner won both the Maxwell and Vince Lombardi trophies; MacAfee was tabbed "player of the year" by the Walter Camp Foundation. MacAfee, Dave Vinson, and Joe Restic were Academic All-Americans.

The early part of the 1978 campaign made fans forget the jubilance of the 1977 championship season. The Irish lost to Missouri and Michigan and were thoroughly scared by Purdue, in their first three games, all at home. Missouri's Jeff Brockhaus kicked a thirty-three-yard field goal in the

final quarter to give the Tigers a 3–0 decision, Notre Dame's first shutout in 131 games. Michigan, back on the schedule after thirty-five years, trailed 7–0 after one quarter (Dennis Grindinger scored on a pass from Joe Montana), and 14–7 at halftime (Vagas Ferguson tallied the second quarter TD by running four yards). The Midwest titans were deadlocked, 14–14, with fifteen minutes to play. Ricky Leach, who had run for Michigan's first TD and passed for the second, hit the bullseye with two scoring aerials at the close. It was not one of Joe Montana's better days. Montana yielded interceptions setting

up both final Michigan scoring opportunities, then was tackled in the end zone for the safety capping Michigan's 28–14 triumph. Purdue led at the intermission, 6–0, after kicking two field goals. The Irish won it, 10–6, with a third period rally highlighted by Jerome Heavens' twenty-six-yard TD run, and a field goal by little Joe Unis, who also had kicked an extra point.

At Michigan State, the Spartans trailed 22–6 following the opening two periods, and were behind, 29–13, early in the fourth. The Spartans pulled near with a pair of late TDs, missed both attempts at two-point conversions, and the

Montana fumbles against Missouri in 1978.

Irish salvaged a 29—25 decision.

The invading Pitt Panthers spotted Notre Dame a seven-point lead, then found themselves in charge, 17—7, with the last quarter underway. Time for a Joe Montana comeback. Joe found Kris Haines with an eight-yard TD pass but missed hitting Pete Holohan on the air attempt for a two-point conversion. Montana ran a yard for another touchdown, and though Joe Unis had a bad center snap and

never got off the extra-point kick, Notre Dame had charged in front, 19—17. Montana apparently didn't find that margin too comfortable and soon pitched a short scoring pass to Vagas Ferguson, Unis adding the point. Final: Irish, 26, Panthers, 17. Jerome Heavens (tri-captain with Bob Golic and Montana) rushed for one hundred twenty yards, erasing George Gipp's career total of 2,341 yards from the record book.

Chuck Male, the walk-on long-distance kicker, booted a forty-yard field goal to open the scoring at Air Force. Montana had two short touchdown runs, and completed a pair of scoring aerials— the one to Kris Haines a fifty-six-yard play—to spark the 38—15 shootdown of the Falcons. Miami of Florida made the trip to Notre Dame for nothing; the Hurricanes were blanked, 20—0. Vagas Ferguson had short runs for ND's only

touchdowns. Chuck Male added both extra points and contributed a pair of tape-measure field goals. Male also scored a pair of marathon field goals as Navy sank, 27—7, at Cleveland, in a game that spoiled the Middies' 7—0 record and saw Vagas Ferguson rush for two hundred nineteen yards. Ferguson's picturebook play was an eighty-yard touchdown bolt.

Mighty Tennessee came in for its first battle with the Fighting Irish, ever, and led after one quarter, 7—3, and after two, 7—6. An eighteen-point ND third quarter, while the Vols were scoreless, put the game away. Each team scored seven points in the final period of the 31—14 Notre Dame victory.

The crowd at Georgia Tech was unruly, and toward the end, when Joe Unis was preparing to kick the extra point that would give the Irish a 38-15 edge, began pelting the Notre Dame bench with bottles, ice, and fish. Coach Dan Devine delayed the game and moved his squad to a safer position in midfield, where the players stood around. Georgia Tech offered a haven alongside its own bench, but

Calhoun, 77, tackles Missouri player. Jay Case, 75.

Kris Haines dives for the loose ball, against Missouri, 1978.

finally some calm prevailed and ND went on to a 38–21 conquest. Joe Montana passed for two touchdowns, and ran one yard for another. With the victory came an invitation for Notre Dame, 8–2 following their shaky start, to face Houston in the Cotton Bowl.

But first, there was the trip to Southern California for one of the most exciting matches of the long intersectional series. USC led, 6–3 after one, 17–3 at the half, and 24–6 early in the fourth quarter. So far, the Irish had tallied only via Joe Unis field goals. Time for Joe Montana to spur another of the fabled Fighting Irish rallies.

Montana reached Dean Masztak with a pass. Now at the ND 43, Joe orbited a long one to Kris Haines. Kris made the catch near the SC 15 and had no traffic as he sprinted on to touchdown territory. Montana could not click on a two-point conversion attempt via the air lanes.

Notre Dame's next possession came at its own 2. Montana quickly showed the Trojans more slight of hand. Haines was his chief target, but Masztak got in the catching act, too. Montana crossed up the Trojans by running the football himself clear to the USC 3. On second down, Pete Buchanan thrust one yard for another touchdown. Unis kicked point, paring the Southern Cal edge to 24–19. The final three minutes were more hectic. Notre Dame's defense contained the Trojans following the kickoff and, following a short SC

punt, the Irish were at their 43. The clock was at 1:35. Montana moved by air and ground, and assisted by a pass-interference call on the Trojans, moved to the SC 2. Pete Holohan took Montana's pass to put ND in front for the first time, 25–24. Montana missed a two-point conversion pass. Southern California had about forty-five seconds, and the luck of the Irish on one official's call that will be debated as long as the series continues.

Irish fans moaned the conversion failure that would have given ND a three-point edge. Soon they were cheering, then again moaning and moaning. Paul McDonald of SC went behind his own 40-yard line to attempt a pass on the second play after kick-off. Jeff Weston crashed the SC line and wasn't feinted by McDonald faking a pass. McDonald seemed to be starting a run, and under Weston's attack, the football fell loose. Weston pounced on it. Notre Dame had recovered a fumble and could run out time for a one-point victory. But what's that? An official ruled it was not a fumble, but an incomplete pass. Southern Cal still had possession. The Trojans attacked anew and had reached the ND 20 before calling time out with six seconds to go. Frank Jordan kicked the thirty-seven yard field goal to provide the 27–25 Southern California victory. The crowd had been so emotionally drained by the fourth quarter's thrills that it could respond to the winning three-

pointer with only minimal cheering.

So to Dallas and the Cotton Bowl assignment against a first-time foe for the Irish, Bill Yeoman's Houston Cougars, who had lost only to Memphis State and Texas Tech. The game was sold out, but after a previous night's freezing rain, which toppled trees and power lines and made driving and walking hazardous, only an announced 32,500—probably less—made it to the Dallas arena. Those who did brave the elements saw the all-time thriller, one that inspired athletic director Ed "Moose" Krause to declare, "This beats the Army game of '32. It surpasses the win of '35 at Ohio State. It beats everything."

Notre Dame quickly established a 12–0 advantage, failing conversion after both touchdowns. Houston responded with a four-touchdown, two-field goal broadside that left the Cougars in front, 34–12, after three periods. They still held that lead when forced to punt with 7:37 on the clock. Writers already were leaving the press box to make the ice-covered trek to the dressing rooms. One writer quipped, "I hate to miss the rally that'll make everyone at Notre Dame forget about the finish against Ohio State."

Tony Belden blocked the Houston kick and Steve Cichy, a freshman Notre Dame defender, seized the loose ball and carried it thirty-three yards for a touchdown. Joe Montana made a two-point conversion pass to Vagas Ferguson. Hous-

ton, 34; Notre Dame, 20. Time left, 7:25.

Now it was Montana time again. No sooner had Houston surrendered possession against demon Irish defenders than Joe tossed long-distance aerials to Dean Masztak and Jerome Heavens. Pete Holohan missed catching a pass, but interference on Houston advanced ND to the Cougar 3. Those were a difficult three yards, Montana finally running two yards for the touchdown. He found Kris Haines with an air delivery good for two extra points. Houston, 34; Notre Dame, 28. Time left, 4:15.

The Cougars received and had to punt. Montana was ready to shake down the thunder and guided the Irish to Houston's 36. Montana had no receivers and broke for a lengthy gain, but fumbled. Houston recovered. The Cougars, determined to run out the clock, soon faced fourth-and-six. Punt time, and again fortune favored the Cougars. Notre Dame drew an offside penalty in attempting to block the kick and the punt was called back. Now Houston faced fourth-and-one and went for it. Joe Gramke and Mike Calhoun stood out in the mass surge to deny Houston the needed yard. Notre Dame's ball on Houston's 29, but no more times out, and so little time.

Montana ran for eleven, and Haines, taking a ten-yard pass, fled out of bounds to stop the clock at 0:06. The Cougars regrouped to defend at their 8. Montana missed Haines in the end zone and the

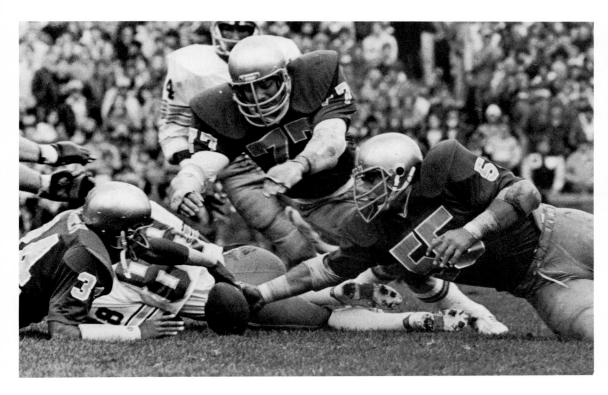

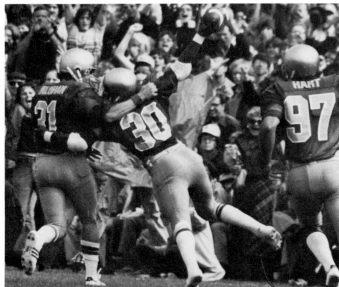

Loose ball. Pouncing are Golic, 55; Waymer, 34; Gibbons, 27; Calhoun, 77.

Kris Haines gathers in a TD ball.

Jerome Heavens, 30; Pete Holohan, 31; Kevin Hart, 97.

Bob Golic, 1978 All-American.

clock was halted at 0:02. Montana called the same play. This time Haines pulled the TD aerial to his bosom. Houston, 34; Notre Dame, 34. Time, 0:00. But Notre Dame had its extra-point attempt coming. This put the burden on little Joe Unis, a native Dallasite who prior to the season had asked the Rev. Gilbert Graham to make a Novena to St. Jude because, said Joe, he knew he would face some testing assignments in the impending season.

Before the previous year's Cotton Bowl game with Texas, Joe had a dream that he would kick the winning point. But for that game, Joe was not needed; Dave Reeve was in charge of the kicking.

And in 1978, Joe started out shaky and lost the kicking job to Chuck Male, who was unavailable on Cotton Bowl day. Now Joe would fulfill a dream—or be a goat. He had had one chance to kick on this frigid day, following Notre Dame's opening TD, but a bad center snap and a bobble by the holder prevented Joe from even getting his foot to the ball. Joe had been nervous lining up for that first kick, but now, staring at the moment of truth, he was calm. He had to be, remembering later "I told myself this was time to take care of business."

Joe kicked straight and true through the uprights. Notre Dame was offside and penalized five yards. Joe had to go through it again. "I didn't take time to think of pressure," Unis said. "I made

my sight, lined up, and kicked." Another bullseye. Fighting Irish, 35; Houston, 34.

"What a glorious way to go out," exclaimed the graduating Jerome Heavens. Notre Dame's president, the Rev. Theodore Hesburgh, who was wearing a green knit cap, paused to lift a finger on each hand in the "We're No. 1" salute as he led the band in the "Victory March." Once inside the dressing room, Father Hesburgh hugged Coach Dan Devine and said, "This is a real Notre Dame victory."

Notre Dame finished 9–3, seventh in the final Associated Press poll, tied with Clemson for No. 6 in United Press International balloting. Bob Golic and Dave Huffman were All-American selections.

Fighting Irish vs. Michigan's Wolverines. What an opener. What a thriller for 105,111 jamming the stadium in Ann Arbor, and the millions watching television. What an afternoon for Notre Dame kicker Chuck Male. All week long Male had fantasized about beating Michigan with his talented toes. Little did he realize how much demand would be asked of him to make the fantasy reality.

Michigan opened with a field goal. Male, who had returned to Notre Dame after originally being turned down and studying at Western Michigan to get his grades in order, retaliated with a forty-yard field goal, and it was 3–3 ending the

opening period. Michigan scored a touchdown and extra point in the second period, before Male hit another three-pointer that covered almost forty-four yards, and the Wolverines had a 10–6 halftime lead. During intermission, Coach Dan Devine told his ND athletes to pray hard, and to play harder in the second half "because you can't play catchup football with Michigan."

Male kicked a twenty-two-yard goal in the third period, paring the Irish deficit to a single point. He returned in the same quarter to hit his fourth consecutive field goal, from thirty-nine yards out, and Notre Dame led, 12–10. There was 18:46 to go, and they were nerve-tingling. The Irish checked a Wolverine probe that produced a first down on the ND 38, and Michigan asked Ali Haji-Sheikh, a long distance booter, to give it a go-ahead field goal. Ali missed from fifty yards. The Wolverines came back and were close to field goal range before Don Kidd stifled the attack by sacking Michigan's quarterback for a seven-yard loss. Mike Courey, coming in as Irish quarterback, immediately tossed an interception. Three pass completions by John Wangler, a Michigan replacement at quarterback, were instrumental in a drive from the ND 44 to first down at the 23. Only fifty-four seconds remained. "We were all conscious of Michigan's field goal position and that they were threatening to go ahead and leave us little time for recovery,"

ND's Bob Crable remembered later.

Michigan lost five yards by penalty, but surged back to the ND 20 and facing third-and-seven. Crable threw Wolverine Stanley Edwards for a five-yard loss. Now the Wolverines were through running for the afternoon and went for a field goal in a final attempt to win the cliff-hanger. Instead of Haji-Sheikh, they called back Bryan Virgil, author of their first period field goal, for the forty-two-yard attempt. The distance could have been only two yards, or two hundred. No matter. Crable charged and catapulted over a Michigan protector to block Virgil's kick with his thigh. "I'm glad we won it with the block rather than have Michigan lose it by missing the kick," said Devine. "We're going to be tough to stop after taking this one." But the next Saturday the Irish were stopped by their old nemesis at Purdue.

The Irish led the Boilermakers, 20–7, on touchdown passes by Greg Knafelc and Tim Koegel, and Chuck Male's two field goals and pair of extra points. Here Purdue's brilliant quarterback, Mark Herrmann, took charge. Herrmann completed four passes for sixty-two yards in a touchdown drive that narrowed Notre Dame's edge to six points. They were still in the third period when Tim Koegel, ND's third quarterback, threw an interception that Marcus McKinnie returned to the Irish 8. Purdue ran in for the touchdown and kicked point to go ahead, 21—20. Herrmann returned to flip a short TD pass to Bart Burrell, and when the point was kicked, the Boilermakers were in front by eight. The Irish picked up an additional two points on a safety after a bad snap to the Purdue punter. The Irish still could tie with a touchdown and win with a point-after. But the final assault fizzled when they were forced to punt. Dick Boushka's kick backed the Boilermakers to their 6, but they responded by moving to a first down and retaining possession until the clock sealed their 28—22 upset conquest.

Tony Hunter took a fourteen-yard touchdown pass from Rusty Lisch, tri-captain Vagas Ferguson scored twice on sprints of twenty-four and forty-eight yards, while Chuck Male kicked two field goals, to highlight the 27-3 victory over visiting Michigan State.

There were tornado warnings and rain when Georgia Tech took the Notre Dame turf. The Irish led by a slim 14—13 in the fourth period before Vagas Ferguson ran for his second touchdown, a seventeen-yard burst, following a controver-

That's blockbuster Willie Fry, 89, bombing Georgia Tech's Head and Brown.

sial fumble recovery on the part of Bob Crable. Officials ruled that Crable had pounced on a loose and free lateral pass; Georgia Tech argued that it was an incomplete forward pass that had been deflected back. Georgia Tech lost the argument and the ball game, 21—13.

At Air Force, Notre Dame was so dominant in soaring to a 38—13 victory that Coach Dan Devine benched Vagas Ferguson, who already had rushed for eighty-four yards and two touchdowns, late in the second period. "Ferguson could have rushed for four hundred yards," said Devine, "but we wanted to hold down the score."

Southern California was a spoil-

Celebrating Harry Oliver's winning field goal against Michigan in 1980.

er at South Bend, though it was scoreless in the first period and 7—7 at halftime. The Trojans' Charles White, heading for the Heisman trophy, rushed for four touchdowns and two hundred sixty-one yards in SC's 42—23 win. Notre Dame's Vagas Ferguson, who did not carry in the last period as the Irish sought to rally via the air, had two touchdowns and one hundred eighty-five yards rushing. Vagas broke a seventy-nine-yard (non-scoring) run in the first quarter to pass Jerome Heavens as ND's all-time ground gainer.

Rusty Lisch pulled off the come-from-behind heroics that provided Notre Dame's 18—17 victory over invading South Carolina. Chuck Male's early forty-yard field goal gave the Irish a 3—0 lead they held at half. South Carolina moved in front 17—3 in the third quarter. Vagas Ferguson's twenty-six-yard scoring run, and Male's point-after, with seventeen seconds to go in the period, narrowed that. The Irish still trailed, 17—10, and time had become precious, when Lisch generaled a drive from the ND 20.

Lisch completed six of seven passes—one to himself when he retrieved a deflected aerial—to cover all eighty yards to the Gamecock goal. The touchdown came on a fourteen-yard Lisch to Dean Masztak air delivery with the stadium timepiece at 0:42. The Irish were within a point and not about to settle for a tying kick. Not with Lisch's passing so hot. Rusty pitched to Pete Holohan for the necessary two-point icing.

Navy was blanked 14—0 at South Bend, leaving three southern foes to face. A crowd of 86,489 turned out to see Notre Dame at Tennessee. This time Johnny Majors' Volunteers were set for the slaughter. The only solace for the Irish was that they briefly held a 6—0 advantage after the first of Vagas Ferguson's three touchdown runs. The Volunteers made touchdown drives of sixty-one, forty-seven, fifty-four, and sixty-six yards the first four times they had the ball, and sandwiched between two points when Rusty Lisch was trapped for a safety. Tennessee led at the intermission, 30—12, and had banked its fortieth point before Ferguson's closing TD reduced the final score to 40—18. The loss dropped Notre Dame from major bowl contention.

Back home against Clemson, the Irish had another jolt. The bad news came following the intermission, which began with Notre Dame leading, 10—0, on Chuck Male's field goal, plus his conversion kick that followed Vagas Fer-

guson's two-yard TD run. Though Rusty Lisch was just out of the sick bed, he paced Notre Dame's offense to a gain of two hundred ninety-five yards in that first half. By intermission, ND might have had an insurmountable edge, but Male had missed two field goal attempts and Lisch's ten-yard touchdown sprint was nullified by penalty. "That call on Lisch changed the momentum," said Devine.

The final two quarters were all Clemson. The Tigers controlled the ball for 21:39 total, getting off forty-nine plays to twenty-two for ND. The third quarter produced two Clemson field goals and quarterback Billy Lott's lengthy scoring dash. Obed Ariri, a former soccer player in Nigeria, kicked the point after Lott's TD and in the last quarter added his third field goal, in the Tigers' 16—10 conquest. Clemson, now eight-and-two for the season, accepted a bowl date against Baylor. Notre Dame, suffering its fourth defeat, did have sort of a bowl game ahead—against Miami in a contest moved from Florida to the Tokyo "Mirage Bowl."

Vagas Ferguson closed his Notre Dame career with glory in the rain in Japan, running for one hundred and seventy-four yards and three touchdowns. Tri-captain Dave Waymer returned two pass interceptions for TDs and Notre Dame concluded with a 40—15 conquest and a seven won, four lost overall record. Ferguson and tri-captain Tim Foley were picked on some

first team All-Americans.

Coach Dan Devine came up with a shocker early in 1980 pre-season practice by telling his squad that this would be his last year at Notre Dame. Dan cited many reasons, and believed the revelation had to be made early in fairness to younger players who when they were recruited had the idea they would be playing their careers under him. Then the Irish settled to business. The schedule was difficult, yet the season offered promise.

Senior Mike Courey was brilliant as regular quarterback in the opening 31—10 triumph over Purdue at Notre Dame. The awesome performance alerted Michigan that its visit to Notre Dame, two Saturdays hence, would be a memorable one. Indeed, the battle with Michigan would be one of the most memorable victories ever achieved by ND.

Phil Carter's six-yard TD run, and Mike Courey's ten-yard touchdown pass to Pete Holohan, coupled with Harry Oliver's extra-point kicks, sent Notre Dame into a 14—0 lead in the second period. But they were playing Bo Schembechler's Wolverines, and by halftime the game was tied, 14—14, after two scoring passes by John Wangler.

Anthony Carter's sixty-seven-yard return was the catalyst for a touchdown drive that sent the Wolverines ahead, 21—14, in the

third period. The Fighting Irish fought back, John Krimm intercepting on Wangler and running forty-nine yards for a touchdown that cut the Notre Dame deficit to one point. Harry Oliver missed the extra point that would have tied things again. Once more the Irish struck, Phil Carter smashing for a TD from four yards out. A pass for a two-point conversion failed, but, cheer, cheer, the Irish were in front, 26—21. Only 3:03 left to play.

Yet ND was playing Michigan! And, with only forty-one seconds to go, the Wolverines scored on Craig Dunaway's first reception in college football. Dunaway was not meant to get the TD aerial from Wangler, but salvaged the crucial catch when the ball was deflected off the grasp of Butch Woolfolk, intended receiver. Michigan attempted a two-point conversion pass that failed, yet at this late hour could be smug with a 27—26 advantage. To shake down the thunder, Devine replaced quarterback Mike Courey with Blair Kiel, the confident freshman. Tony Hunter missed Kiel's first pass but officials penalized Michigan for interference and ND was advanced thirty-two yards to Michigan's 48. Kiel's second pass was almost intercepted. The next was dropped by Dean Masztak. Eleven seconds were left after Kiel's short completion to Phil Carter. Tony Hunter grabbed Kiel's next air delivery, stepping out of bounds to stop the clock at 0:04. Oliver, a left-footed kicker whose longest previous field goal success was a thirty-eight yarder in junior varsity competition, was asked to attempt a fifty-one yard goal effort against a fifteen miles-per-hour wind. Oliver remembered: "I prayed a lot and told myself to plant my toe into the ball." Prior to trying for the miracle, Oliver anxiously asked tri-captain Bob Crable: "What should I do?" Crable said: "Kick the heck out of it, and kick it straight!" That Oliver did. The football cleared the uprights as time expired and the scoreboard rolled to the final: Notre Dame, 29; Michigan, 27.

Tim Koegel, who had held for the winning kick, declared: "Just as I placed the ball down, the wind died. Almost stopped. I knew then we'd make it." Rev. Theodore Hesburgh, Notre Dame's president, appeared in the joyous locker room and said: "I told you in practice that you're part of the ongoing history here. Today, you wrote a great chapter. You did what everybody said was impossible." As Oliver clutched the game ball, Coach Devine told the squad: "I knew we weren't ever going to give up. There isn't a quitter in this room."

At Michigan State, the Spartans became the third consecutive Big Ten victim of these 1980 Irish, 26–21. Miami and Army appeared at Notre Dame and lost, 32–14 and 30–3, respectively. The Irish triumphed at Arizona, 20–3, in a game highlighted by Blair Kiel's eighty-yard touchdown run on a fake punt.

Jim Stone, the backup for injured tailback Phil Carter, rushed for one hundred forty-seven yards in the first period alone, and finished with a total of two hundred eleven yards (becoming the first Irish back to ever exceed one hundred yards running in four consecutive games) in the 33–0 rout of Navy in Giants' Stadium at East Rutherford, New Jersey. Two inci-dents dampened enthusiasm over this impressive conquest that left Notre Dame with a seven won, none lost record and national championship candidates: All-American guard nominee Tim Huffman suffered a recurrence of a bone fracture in his foot, and Alabama—scheduled to oppose the Fighting Irish in Birmingham on November 15 in a game crucial for the rank-ings—had been dropped from the undefeated ranks by Mississippi State, 6–3. Alabama's loss left Notre Dame and Georgia as the only major teams with perfect records. But, returning from Navy, coach Dan Devine said: "I'm not thinking of Alabama, yet. I'm concentrating on next Saturday's game at Georgia Tech." Devine's concern proved valid.

Phil Carter holds the TD ball. 1980 MSU game.

One of the greatest moments. Harry Oliver boots a 51-yard field goal to win against Michigan as time expires.

Georgia Tech's host Yellow Jackets, coached by newcomer Bill Curry, had won only once in eight 1980 games when they encountered Notre Dame, but the psychological factors favored Tech: Notre Dame was ranked No. 1 nationally, and everywhere there was talk that this game would be only a warm-up for the showdown at Alabama. Ken Whisenhunt, a freshman walk-on quarterback who didn't even have a locker in the team dressing room, completed the Tech pass that set up Jimmy Smith's thirty-nine-yard field goal and a 3—0 intermission lead. The Irish were guilty of five turnovers, and the first was costly. Notre Dame had just recovered a fumble at the Tech 21 to set up a touchdown threat. The Irish fumbled back on the next play, and had to wait until 4:44 remained in the game before getting the forty-seven-yard Harry Oliver field goal that accounted for the 3—3 final. "We simply got beat by a better football team that was better coached," said Coach Dan Devine, ignoring the tie.

Salvaging the tie against Georgia Tech kept the Irish in contention for national honors, and now it was the week of the Big Game. Notre Dame vs. Alabama. The Crimson Tide, who had lost all three previous battles against the Irish by a scant total of six points, were aroused. This was going to be their year—and a conquest of ND could make the pollsters forget that upset by Mississippi State.

In Tuscaloosa, students and fans sported bumper stickers reading "Notre Who?", and wore T-shirts proclaiming: "This is an Official Alabama Beat Hell Out of Notre Dame T-shirt." Gary DeNiro, a 'Bama defensive end from Yankeeland, said the Tide would be fired up with support from 80,000 fans (actually 82,633) in Birmingham's Legion Field. "Those 80,000 will put more pressure on Notre Dame," said DeNiro. "It happened when we played Louisiana State. We came out early and walked around Legion Field and the people went crazy."

The game matched two great coaches, Bear Bryant, the winningest active mentor fast closing in on Amos Alonzo Stagg's all-time record, and Dan Devine, the second highest winner among coaches still working the college circuit. Devine did not share the Alabama sentiment that Notre Dame would be overwhelmed by the vast, red-jacketed crowd at Birmingham. Tuesday of game week he conferred with the Rev. Edmund P. Joyce, executive vice-president and chairman of the faculty board in control of athletics, and guaranteed that the Fighting Irish would, in Frank Leahy's old words, "emerge triumphant."

Alabama got the message on their first play from scrimmage when Scott Zettek smashed Tide runner Major Ogilvie for a two-yard loss. Tri-captain Bob Crable, who made eleven tackles in the game, said later that Zettek's tack-

le "set the tempo." Ogilvie afterwards related: "I don't know if one play can set the tempo, but that first play showed me Notre Dame was ready to play football."

Alabama was also ready to play, and dug in as soon as John Hankerd recovered a fumble on the Crimson Tide 12 yard-line. The Irish advanced against a stubborn defense and, after five plays,

Harry Oliver's up in the air after The Kick.

Phil Carter prowling against MSU, 1980.

Tom Gibbons tackling MSU player in 1980.

1980 USC game. Joe Gramke, 92; Joe Radzinski, 51; Scott Zettek, 70, digging up turf.

Blair Kiel, 5, with ball, in 1980 USC game.

sensed they were set for the touchdown thrust. Quarterback Blair Kiel, over-eager, dropped the center snap. 'Bama's Warren Lyles recovered the ball a foot short of the goal line. But Alabama was penned deep, getting off only one play before its Don Jacobs fumbled, with Zettek, the executioner, recovering for Notre Dame. Two plays later Phil Carter, who gained only eighty-four yards in thirty-one carries, burst across for the TD as tri-captain John Scully budged in front of him. Adding the point, Notre Dame led, 7–0. Now it was to be a defensive classic, Kiel twice punting on third down to assure the ND defenders better field position.

The Irish offense, with help from a pass interference penalty, threatened again in the last quarter, advancing to fourth down on the Alabama 1. ND tried to take a delay of game penalty to give Harry Oliver more working room for a field goal kick. Alabama declined the penalty (Bryant and Devine were playing gridiron chess) and called time out to pressure the kicker. Oliver slipped getting off the kick, and it was blocked. Alabama subsequently responded with its own advance, coming up to fourth down, with a yard needed, at the ND 37. Linnie Patrick tried a sweep, only to be stopped for no gain by Crable. The Irish took over, 3:26 remaining. Final: ND, 7; 'Bama, 0.

"It's an understatement to say that the better team won," declared Bryant. "Alabama is not used to playing against a team as strong as Notre Dame. Their offense controlled the ball. . . . I'm proud of our defense for not letting them score more. Dan Devine had Notre Dame prepared. He did a much better job at that than I did. . . ."

Alabama accepted an invitation to the Cotton Bowl. The Irish, before Devine met with reporters, announced they would go to the Sugar Bowl to challenge Georgia's still perfect record.

Why had Devine ordered Oliver to try a field goal with more than eight minutes remaining and the Irish within feet of the touchdown stripe? "Ordinarily, we'd have gone for the TD," said Devine. "We had been struggling to get a second touchdown, because when we scored in the second period I didn't think 7–0 would win it. Now, though, time is running out. I know that Kiel wants us to go for the TD. The fans want it. I want it. But I'm darned certain that at this point 10–0 is sure to win it. I have to try to buy that 10–0 insurance. Too bad the kick was blocked—I didn't think Alabama would take the delay of game penalty, but we tried it because Oliver doesn't explode the ball up in the air real quick."

A week later Air Force was stopped, 24–10, in South Bend, and by this time it was certain that Gerry Faust, the sensational coach at Cincinnati Moeller High School, would be named Devine's successor. All that remained was the official announcement. The Irish, thirty-four-point favorites, were sluggish against the Falcons; perhaps spent from the ordeal in Birmingham. So they were forced to rally from a 3–3 deadlock in the third quarter. Devine explained the sluggishness by suggesting, "It's hard to think of Air Force when everybody on campus talks Southern Cal and Georgia twenty-two hours a day." With Kiel's passing and his receivers ineffective, Notre Dame finally resorted to its proven running game; Phil Carter rushed for one hundred eighty-one yards, Jim Stone for seventy-one.

The following Monday Father Hesburgh revealed that Faust had accepted the head coaching job. Faust was on campus the next day. Devine was preparing for Southern Cal and Georgia, optimistic about chances of winning his second national championship at Notre Dame but wary that, in all the furore about Faust's genius, the athletes' concentration might be divided.

The trip to Los Angeles is a long one. Notre Dame's trip back home was even longer as they returned licking wounds of a 20–3 defeat by Southern California and knowing that the national championship chances were remoter than remote. Southern Cal, ineligible for the Rose Bowl, was fired up because, as one Trojan explained, "Notre Dame is our bowl game for the year."

In the first half, the Irish didn't make a first down until only ten seconds remained, and saw the Trojans cart a 10–0 lead into the intermission. Phil Carter's fumble at the USC 31 yard line gave the winners their first TD opportunity, and Mike Harper ultimately cashed it with a six-yard run. Eric Hipp's twenty-two-yard field goal came after a roughing-the-kicker penalty on Tony Belden opened the

doors for a scoring assault. The Irish were held for four downs inside the Trojan 4 in the third period. Soon Harry Oliver kicked the thirty-yard field goal that was to avert a shutout. ND recovered a fumble at the Trojan 27, where Mike Courey—replacing Blair Kiel—was intercepted with Southern Cal returning clear to the Irish 1. With the Irish bracing, the Trojans settled for a field goal increasing their lead to 13–3. Harper's second touchdown run, this ten yards, sealed the decision. The Irish were held to ninety-five yards rushing, forty-two of those by Phil Carter. With some players in tears afterwards, Carter shook his head and said: "We have a winning attitude at Notre Dame. A loss is hard to take."

Georgia, paced by its great runner, Herschel Walker, was 11–0, and ranked No. 1 nationally in both wire service polls, going into the Sugar Bowl on January 1, 1981. The Irish (9–1–1) were rated No. 7 by the Associated Press and No. 8 by United Press International. Still there was confidence that Georgia could be handled in the meeting in the New Orleans Superdome. No one knew that Irish luck was on a New Year's holiday, nor that Georgia would be so capable of exploiting breaks in the patent Notre Dame fashion. President Jimmy Carter, on hand to cheer the Bulldogs, watched Walker rush for one hundred fifty yards while the touted ND defense was limiting the Dawgs' other runners to a minus-

Dan Devine, shellshocked after Oliver's 1980 field goal.

Coin toss at Sugar Bowl, New Year's Day, 1981.

thirty. The Irish defense also did a job on Bulldog quarterback Buck Belue, limiting his air gains to seven yards with one completion in twelve attempts and sacking him five times for a loss of forty-eight yards. Yet the defense failed to intercept on Georgia, and the Bulldogs did not lose the football once by fumble. Georgia intercepted three times and recovered one Notre Dame bobble. Unbelievably, all of Georgia's seventeen points came within a span of two minutes, fifty-six seconds during the first half.

Harry Oliver's fifty-yard field goal, set up by Blair Kiel passes to Phil Carter and Dean Masztak that netted thirty-eight yards, gave Notre Dame a 3–0 lead. Were the Irish en route to another great upset of a potential national cham-

pion? Georgia thought no, tying the score on Rex Robinson's field goal with 13:15 elapsed in the opening period. Robinson kicked off deep to the Irish. Jim Stone and Ty Barber were waiting; Georgia's Kelly brothers, Steve and Bob, chased downfield. Stone called for Barber to make the catch. Barber, amidst the roar from 77,895, did not hear him. The ball fell free, rolling to the ND 2. Stone attempted a retrieve but could not

claim the ball under Steve Kelly's charge. Bob Kelly fell on the free ball. On second down, Walker ran a yard for the TD, Robinson adding the extra point to push the George edge to 10–3. And 1:04 was still left in the first quarter.

Notre Dame received again, and again. . . . hit by lightning. This came after Chris Welton's recovery of John Sweeney's fumble on the ND 22, a bobble resulting from Frank Ros's hard tackle on Sweeney. Georgia needed only three plays, and seventeen seconds, for another TD. Walker ran for twelve yards on the first thrust, and made his three-yard touchdown dash on the third. Robinson kicked Georgia's lead to 17–3 and the Bulldogs scoring was over. What could the Irish do?

They were frustrated in the second quarter when Mike Courey's thirteen-yard pass, aimed for Pete Holohan, was intercepted in the end zone by Bob Woerner. In the third quarter Tony Hunter snared a thirteen-yard pass from Blair Kiel for an apparent touchdown— officials ruled that the aerial was caught barely out of bounds. Kiel pitched into the end zone, and the pesty Woerner tipped the ball from Holohan's reach. Notre Dame rallied to march fifty-seven yards, including Phil Carter's single-yard TD slash, and Oliver kicked point, putting the Irish within seven points of the Bulldogs late in that third period.

The Fighting Irish would not concede, of course, and attacked strongly in the fourth quarter. They envisioned winning with a TD and two-point conversion. But Georgia would not yield, though Woerner admitted, "I knew Notre Dame had momentum. That's why we needed the big play. We got another one on Mike Fisher's interception." Georgia rode the 17–10 triumph to the national championship. The 9–2–1 Irish were ranked No. 9 by Associated Press, No. 10 by United Press International. Michigan and Alabama, both Notre Dame victims, were rated fourth and sixth, respectively, in both final polls. And Notre Dame had the edge in everything except final score and alertness in the thrilling Georgia duel that would up Dan Devine's coaching career at Notre Dame. John Scully, Bob Crable, and Scott Zettek all received first team All-American positions; Scully was unanimous.

It had, indeed, been a Devine era. The great coach almost went out with another national championship, but that's the way the football bounces. Still, he will be remembered with Rock, Leahy, and Parseghian.

An Afterword

Gerry Faust

There's a mystique about Notre Dame that needs to be experienced over a period of time. It cannot be expressed in words. The school means excellence to many Americans—excellence not only in sports, but in attitude, spirit, character, academic achievement, and the arts. It is that quality of striving for greatness that has won Notre Dame an affectionate place in the hearts of most Americans.

Football is the focal point that allows so many people to feel they are a part of Notre Dame. Through years and decades, great teams, great players, and great coaches have brought joy to our alumni as well as subway alumni everywhere. I've met many of these people—who've lived and died with the team through many a Saturday afternoon broadcast. Notre Dame is "their" university and they love it as fiercely and as completely as any alumnus who spent four or more years on our gracious green campus. When they talk about Notre Dame, they recall the names of its historic greats as readily as the school's own graduates.

In the spring of '81 I directed my first practice session as head coach, and it turned out to be a moment I'll never forget. It was a splendid Saturday afternoon with the sun glowing brightly upon Cartier Field. I was with Brian Boulac looking at some walk-ons trying out for a kicking slot.

Notre Dame has a tradition: just as practice is to begin, the captains lead the team onto the field.

I wanted to get over there, but was so engrossed working with kickers that I didn't pay much attention to them. When I finally did look up, I saw the team trotting to the calisthenics area. This was my first practice—I took off at a run to be with them. As I crossed the field, I glanced up and simultaneously saw the sun glinting from the helmets of Notre Dame players and illuminating the Golden Dome in the background. It brought tears to my eyes. At that moment I thanked God and the Blessed Mother for giving me the opportunity to be here.

Maybe this little story of what happened to me on my first day can serve as a small example of what Notre Dame is all about. From the great era of Rockne to the end of the Devine years, there has been an indomitable spirit, a quest for excellence, that have resulted in thrilling moments and glory.

It is a tremendous responsibility and honor to try to carry on a tradition so rich and priceless that it has made Notre Dame number one.

GERRY FAUST

Notre Dame Statistics

DATE W-L-T OPPONENT SCORE SITE

1887
Coach: None
Captain: Henry Luhn
| N.23 | L | Michigan | 0-8 | H |

(0-1-0)

1888
Coach: None
Captain: Edward C. Prudhomme
Apr.20	L	Michigan	6-26	H
Apr.21	L	Michigan	4-10	H
D.6	W	Harvard School (Chi.)	20-0	H

(1-2-0) 30-36

1889
Coach: None
Captain: Edward C. Prudhomme
| N.14 | W | Northwestern | 9-0 | A |

(1-0-0)

1890-1891 — No team

1892
Coach: None
Captain: Patrick H. Coady
| O.19 | W | South Bend H.S. | 56-0 | H |
| N.24TH | T | Hillsdale | 10-10 | H |

(1-0-1) 66-10

1893
Coach: None
Captain: Frank M. Keough
O.25	W	Kalamazoo	34-0	H
N.11	W	Albion	8-6	H
N.23	W	DeLaSalle (S)	28-0	H
N.30TH	W	Hillsdale (S)	22-10	H
J.1'94	L	Chicago	0-8	A

(4-1-0) 92-24

1894
Coach: James L. Morison
Captain: Frank M. Keough
O.13	W	Hillsdale	14-0	H
O.20	T	Albion	6-6	H
N.15	W	Wabash	30-0	H
N.22	W	Rush Medical	18-6	H
N.29TH	L	Albion	12-19	H

(3-1-1) 80-31

1895
Coach: H. G. Hadden
Captain: Daniel V. Casey
O.19	W	Northwestern Law	20-0	H
N.7	W	Illinois Cycling Club	18-2	H
N.22	L	Indpls. Artillery (S)	0-18	H
N.28TH	W	Chicago Phys. & Surg.	32-0	H

(3-1-0) 70-20

1896
Coach: Frank E. Hering
Captain: Frank E. Hering
O.8	L	Chicago Phys. & Surg.	0-4	H
O.14	L	Chicago	0-18	H
O.27	W	S.B. Commercial A.C.	46-0	H
O.31	W	Albion	24-0	H
N.14	L	Purdue	22-28	H
N.20	W	Highland Views	82-0	H
N.26TH	W	Beloit (R)	8-0	H

(4-3-0) 182-50

1897
Coach: Frank E. Hering
Captain: John I. Mullen
O.13	T	Rush Medical	0-0	H
O.23	W	DePauw	4-0	H
O.28	W	Chicago Dental Surg.	62-0	H
N.6	L	Chicago	5-34	A
N.13	W	St. Viator	60-0	H
N.25TH	W	Michigan State (R)	34-6	H

(4-1-1) 165-40

1898
Coach: Frank E. Hering
Captain: John I. Mullen
O.8	W	Illinois	5-0	A
O.15	W	Michigan State	53-0	H
O.23	L	Michigan	0-23	A
O.29	W	DePauw	32-0	H
N.11	L	Indiana	5-11	H
N.19	W	Albion	60-0	A

(4-2-0) 155-34

1899
Coach: James McWeeney
Captain: John I. Mullen
S.27	W	Englewood H.S.	29-5	H
S.30	W	Michigan State	40-0	H
O.4	L	Chicago	6-23	A
O.14	W	Lake Forest	38-0	H
O.18	L	Michigan	0-12	A
O.23	W	Indiana	17-0	H
O.27	W	Northwestern (R)	12-0	H
N.4	W	Rush Medical	17-0	H
N.18	T	Purdue	10-10	A
N.30TH	L	Chicago Phys. & Surg.	0-5	H

(6-3-1) 169-55

1900
Coach: Pat O'Dea
Captain: John F. Farley

S.29	W	Goshen	55-0	H
O.6	W	Englewood H.S.	68-0	H
O.13	W	S.B. Howard Park	64-0	H
O.20	W	Cincinnati	58-0	H
O.25	L	Indiana	0-6	H
N.3	T	Beloit	6-6	H
N.10	L	Wisconsin	0-54	A
N.17	L	Michigan	0-7	A
N.24	W	Rush Medical (R)	5-0	H
N.29TH	W	Chicago Phys. & Surg.	5-0	H

(6-3-1)   261-73

1901
Coach: Pat O'Dea
Captain: Albert C. Fortin

S.28	T	South Bend A.C.	0-0	H
O.5	W	Ohio Medical U.	6-0	A
O.12	L	Northwestern (R)	0-2	A
O.19	W	Chicago Medical Col.	32-0	A
O.26	W	Beloit	5-0	A
N.2	W	Lake Forest	16-0	H
N.9	W	Purdue	12-6	H
N.16	W	Indiana (R)	18-5	H
N.23	W	Chicago Phys. & Surg.	34-0	H
N.28TH	W	South Bend A.C.	22-6	H

(8-1-1)   145-19

1902
Coach: James F. Faragher
Captain: Louis J. Salmon

S.27	W	Michigan State	33-0	H
O.11	W	Lake Forest	28-0	H
O.18	L	Michigan	0-23	N
O.25	W	Indiana	11-5	A
N.1	W	Ohio Medical U.	6-5	A
N.8	L	Knox	5-12	A
N.15	W	American Medical	92-0	H
N.22	W	DePauw	22-0	H
N.27TH	T	Purdue	6-6	A

(6-2-1)   203-51

N—at Toledo

1903
Coach: James F. Faragher
Captain: Louis J. Salmon

O.3	W	Michigan State	12-0	H
O.10	W	Lake Forest	28-0	H
O.17	W	DePauw (R)	56-0	H
O.24	W	American Medical	52-0	H
O.29	W	Chicago Phys. & Surg.	46-0	H
N.7	W	Missouri Osteopaths	28-0	H
N.14	T	Northwestern	0-0	A
N.21	W	Ohio Medical U.	35-0	A
N.26TH	W	Wabash	35-0	H

(8-0-1)   292-0

1904
Coach: Louis J. Salmon
Captain: Frank J. Shaughnessy

O.1	W	Wabash	12-4	H
O.8	W	American Medical	44-0	H
O.15	L	Wisconsin	0-58	N
O.22	W	Ohio Medical U.	17-5	A
O.27	W	Toledo A.A.	6-0	H
N.5	L	Kansas	5-24	A
N.19	W	DePauw	10-0	H
N.24TH	L	Purdue	0-36	A

(5-3-0)   94-127

N—at Milwaukee

1905
Coach: Henry J. McGlew
Captain: Patrick A. Beacom

S.30	W	N. Division H.S. (Chi.)	44-0	H
O.7	W	Michigan State	28-0	H
O.14	L	Wisconsin	0-21	N
O.21	L	Wabash	0-5	H
O.28	W	*American Medical	142-0	H
N.4	W	DePauw	71-0	H
N.11	L	Indiana	5-22	A
N.18	W	Bennett Med. Col. Chi.	22-0	H
N.24	L	Purdue	0-32	A

(5-4-0)   312-80

N—at Milwaukee

*After a 25-minute first half, with Notre Dame leading, 121-0, the second half was shortened to only 8 minutes to permit the "Doctors" time to eat before catching a train to Chicago. Notre Dame scored 27 touchdowns, but missed 20 extra points.

1906
Coach: Thomas A. Barry
Captain: Robert L. Bracken

O.6	W	Franklin	26-0	H
O.13	W	Hillsdale	17-0	H
O.20	W	Chi. Phys. & Surg.	28-0	H
O.27	W	Michigan State	5-0	H
N.3	W	Purdue	2-0	H
N.10	L	Indiana	0-12	N
N.24	W	Beloit (R)	29-0	H

(6-1-0)   107-12

N—at Indianapolis

1907
Coach: Thomas A. Barry
Captain: Dominic L. Callicrate

O.12	W	Chi. Phys. & Surg. (R)	32-0	H
O.19	W	Franklin	23-0	H
O.26	W	Olivet	22-4	H
N.2	T	Indiana	0-0	H
N.9	W	Knox	22-4	H
N.23	W	Purdue	17-0	H
N.28TH	W	St. Vincent's (Chi.)	21-12	A

(6-0-1)   137-20

1908
Coach: Victor M. Place
Captain: M. Harry Miller

O.3	W	Hillsdale	39-0	H
O.10	W	Franklin	64-0	H
O.17	L	Michigan	6-12	A
O.24	W	Chicago Phys. & Surg.	88-0	H
O.29	W	Ohio Northern	58-4	H
N.7	W	Indiana	11-0	N
N.13	W	Wabash	8-4	H
N.18	W	St. Viator	46-0	H
N.26TH	W	Marquette	6-0	A

(8-1-0)   326-20

N—at Indianapolis

1909
Coach: Frank C. Longman
Captain: Howard Edwards

O.9	W	Olivet	58-0	H
O.16	W	Rose Poly	60-11	H
O.23	W	Michigan State	17-0	H
O.30	W	Pittsburgh	6-0	A
N.6	W	Michigan (U)	11-3	A
N.13	W	Miami (Ohio)	46-0	H
N.20	W	Wabash	38-0	H
N.25TH	T	Marquette	0-0	A

(7-0-1)   236-14

1910
Coach: Frank C. Longman
Captain: Ralph Dimmick

O.8	W	Olivet	48-0	H
O.22	W	Butchel (Akron)	51-0	H
N.5	L	Michigan State	0-17	A
N.12	W	Rose Poly	41-3	A
N.19	*W	Ohio Northern	47-0	H
N.24TH	T	Marquette	5-5	A

(4-1-1)   192-25

*Notre Dame's 100th victory

1911
Coach: John L. Marks
Captain: Luke L. Kelly

O.7	W	Ohio Northern	32-6	H
O.14	W	St. Viator	43-0	H
O.21	W	Butler (R)	27-0	H
O.28	W	Loyola (Chi.)	80-0	H
N.4	T	Pittsburgh	0-0	A
N.11	W	St. Bonaventure	34-0	H
N.20	W	Wabash	6-3	A
N.30TH	T	Marquette	0-0	A

(6-0-2)   222-9

1912
Coach: John L. Marks
Captain: Charles E. (Gus) Dorais

O.5	W	St. Viator	116-7	H
O.12	W	Adrian	74-7	H
O.19	W	Morris Harvey	39-0	H
O.26	W	Wabash	41-6	H
N.2	W	Pittsburgh (S)	3-0	A
N.9	W	St. Louis	47-7	A
N.28TH	W	Marquette	69-0	N

(7-0-0)   389-27

N—at Chicago

1913
Coach: Jesse C. Harper
Captain: Knute K. Rockne

O.4	W	Ohio Northern	87-0	H
O.18	W	South Dakota	20-7	H
O.25	W	Alma	62-0	H
N.1	W	Army (U)	35-13	A
N.7	W	Penn State (R)	14-7	A
N.22	W	Christian Bros. (St.L.)	20-7	A
N.27TH	W	Texas	30-7	A

(7-0-0)   268-41

1914
Coach: Jesse C. Harper
Captain: Keith K. Jones

O.3	W	Alma	56-0	H
O.10	W	Rose Poly	103-0	H
O.17	L	Yale	0-28	A
O.24	W	South Dakota	33-0	N1
O.31	W	Haskell	20-7	H
N.7	L	Army	7-20	A
N.14	W	Carlisle	48-6	N2
N.26TH	W	Syracuse	20-0	A

(6-2-0)   287-61

N1—at Sioux Falls; N2—at Chicago

1915
Coach: Jesse C. Harper
Captain: Freeman C. Fitzgerald

O.2	W	Alma	32-0	H
O.9	W	Haskell	34-0	H
O.23	L	Nebraska	19-20	A
O.30	W	South Dakota	6-0	H
N.6	W	Army	7-0	A
N.13	W	Creighton	41-0	A
N.25TH	W	Texas	36-7	A
N.27	W	Rice	55-2	A

(7-1-0)   230-29

1916
Coach: Jesse C. Harper
Captain: Stan Cofall

S.30	W	Case Tech	48-0	H
O.7	W	Western Reserve	48-0	A
O.14	W	Haskell	26-0	H
O.28	W	Wabash	60-0	H
N.4	L	Army	10-30	A
N.11	W	South Dakota	21-0	N
N.18	W	Michigan State	14-0	A
N.25	W	Alma	46-0	H
N.30TH	W	Nebraska	20-0	A

(8-1-0)   293-30

N—at Sioux Falls

1917
Coach: Jesse C. Harper
Captain: James Phelan

O.6	W	Kalamazoo	55-0	H
O.13	T	Wisconsin	0-0	A
O.20	L	Nebraska	0-7	A
O.27	W	South Dakota (R)	40-0	H
N.3	W	Army (U)	7-2	A
N.10	W	Morningside	13-0	A
N.17	W	Michigan State	23-0	H
N.24	W	Wash. & Jefferson	3-0	A

(6-1-1)   141-9

1918

Coach: Knute K. Rockne
Captain: Leonard Bahan

S.28	W	Case Tech	26-6	A	
N.2	W	Wabash	67-7	A	
N.9	T	Great Lakes	7-7	H	
N.16	L	Mich. State (U) (R)	7-13	A	
N.23	W	Purdue	26-6	A	
N.28TH	T	Nebraska (S)	0-0	A	

(3-1-2) 133-39

1919

Coach: Knute K. Rockne
Captain: Leonard Bahan

O.4	W	Kalamazoo	14-0	H		5,000
O.11	W	Mount Union	60-7	H		4,000
O.18	W	Nebraska	14-9	A		10,000
O.25	W	Western St. Nor.	53-0	H		2,500
N.1	W	Indiana (R)	16-3	N		5,000
N.8	W	Army	12-9	A		8,000
N.15	W	Michigan State	13-0	H		5,000
N.22	W	Purdue	33-13	A		7,000
N.27TH	W	Morningside (S)	14-6	A		10,000

(9-0-0) 229-47 56,500

N—at Indianapolis

1920

Coach: Knute K. Rockne
Captain: Frank Coughlin

O.2	W	Kalamazoo	39-0	H		5,000
O.9	W	Western St. Nor.	42-0	H		3,500
O.16	W	Nebraska	16-7	A		9,000
O.23	W	Valparaiso	28-3	H		8,000
O.30	W	Army	27-17	A		10,000
N.6	W	Purdue (HC)	28-0	H		12,000
N.13	W	Indiana	13-10	N		14,000
N.20	W	*Northwestern	33-7	A		c20,000
N.25TH	W	Michigan State	25-0	A		8,000

(9-0-0) 251-44 89,500

N—at Indianapolis
*George Gipp's last game. He contracted a strep throat and died from complications of the disease on December 14 at the age of 25.

1921

Coach: Knute K. Rockne
Captain: Edward N. Anderson

S.24	W	Kalamazoo	56-0	H		8,000
O.1	W	DePauw	57-10	H		8,000
O.8	L	Iowa (U)	7-10	A		7,500
O.15	W	Purdue	33-0	A		7,500
O.22	W	Nebraska (HC)	7-0	H		14,000
O.29	W	Indiana	28-7	N1		10,000
N.5	W	Army	28-0	A		7,000
N.8	W	Rutgers	48-0	N2		12,000
N.12	W	Haskell	42-7	H		5,000
N.19	W	Marquette	21-7	A		11,000
N.24TH	W	Michigan State	48-0	H		15,000

(10-1-0) 375-41 105,000

N1—at Indianapolis; N2—at Polo Grounds, New York City, on Election Day

1922

Coach: Knute K. Rockne
Captain: Glen Carberry

S.30	W	Kalamazoo	46-0	H		5,000
O.7	W	St. Louis	26-0	H		7,000
O.14	W	Purdue	20-0	A		9,000
O.21	W	DePauw	34-7	H		5,000
O.28	W	Georgia Tech	13-3	A		20,000
N.4	W	Indiana (HC)	27-0	H		c22,000
N.11	T	Army	0-0	A		15,000
N.18	W	Butler	31-3	A		12,000
N.25	W	Carnegie Tech (S)	19-0	A		30,000
N.30TH	L	Nebraska	6-14	A		16,000

(8-1-1) 222-27 141,000

1923

Coach: Knute K. Rockne
Captain: Harvey Brown

S.29	W	Kalamazoo	74-0	H		10,000
O.6	W	Lombard	14-0	H		10,000
O.13	W	Army	13-0	N		c30,000
O.20	W	Princeton	25-2	A		30,000
O.27	W	Georgia Tech	35-7	H		20,000
N.3	W	Purdue (HC)	34-7	H		20,000
N.10	L	Nebraska (U)	7-14	A		30,000
N.17	W	Butler	34-7	H		10,000
N.24	W	Carnegie Tech	26-0	A		30,000
N.29TH	W	St. Louis (R)	13-0	A		9,000

(9-1-0) 275-37 197,000

N—at Ebbets Field, Brooklyn

1924

Coach: Knute K. Rockne
Captain: Adam Walsh

O.4	W	Lombard	40-0	H		8,000
O.11	W	Wabash	34-0	H		10,000
O.18	W	Army	13-7	N1		c55,000
O.25	W	Princeton	12-0	A		40,000
N.1	*W	Georgia Tech (HC)	34-3	H		c22,000
N.8	W	Wisconsin	38-3	A		28,425
N.15	W	Nebraska	34-6	A		c22,000
N.22	W	Northwestern	13-6	N2		45,000
N.29	W	Carnegie Tech	40-19	A		35,000

(9-0-0) 258-44 265,425

ROSE BOWL

Jan.1	W	Stanford	27-10	N3	c53,000

N1—at Polo Grounds; N2—at Soldier Field; N3—at Pasadena, Calif.

*Notre Dame's 200th victory

1925

Coach: Knute K. Rockne
Captain: Clem Crowe

S.26	W	Baylor (R)	41-0	H		13,000
O.3	W	Lombard	69-0	H		10,000
O.10	W	Beloit	19-3	H		10,000
O.17	L	Army	0-27	YS		c65,000
O.24	W	Minnesota	19-7	A		c49,000
O.31	W	Georgia Tech (R)	13-0	A		12,000
N.7	T	Penn State (R)	0-0	A		c20,000
N.14	W	Carnegie Tech (HC)	26-0	H		c27,000
N.21	W	Northwestern	13-10	A		c27,000
N.26TH	L	Nebraska (U)	0-17	A		c45,000

(7-2-1) 200-64 278,000

1926

Coach: Knute K. Rockne
Co-Captains: Eugene Edwards and Thomas Hearden

O.2	W	Beloit	77-0	H		8,000
O.9	W	Minnesota	20-7	A		c48,648
O.16	W	Penn State (R)	28-0	H		18,000
O.23	W	Northwestern	6-0	A		c41,000
O.30	W	Georgia Tech (R)	12-0	H		11,000
N.6	W	Indiana	26-0	H		20,000
N.13	W	Army	7-0	YS		c63,029
N.20	W	Drake (HC) (S)	21-0	H		20,000
N.27	L	Carnegie Tech (U)	0-19	A		c45,000
D.4	W	So. Calif. (2:00)	13-12	A		c74,378

(9-1-0) 210-38 349,055

1927

Coach: Knute K. Rockne
Captain: John P. Smith

O.1	W	Coe (R)	28-7	H		10,000
O.8	W	Detroit	20-0	A		c28,000
O.15	W	Navy	19-6	N1		45,101
O.22	W	Indiana	19-6	A		16,000
O.29	W	Georgia Tech	26-7	H		17,000
N.5	T	Minn. (S) (1:00-M)	7-7	H		25,000
N.12	L	Army	0-18	YS		c65,678
N.19	W	Drake	32-0	A		8,412
N.26	W	So. California	7-6	N2*c120,000		

(7-1-1) 158-57 335,191

*Paid attendance: 99,573
N1—at Baltimore; N2—at Soldier Field

1928

Coach: Knute K. Rockne
Captain: Frederick Miller

S.29	W	Loyola (N.O.)	12-6	A		15,000
O.6	L	Wisconsin	6-22	A		29,885
O.13	W	Navy	7-0	N1*c120,000		
O.20	L	Georgia Tech	0-13	A		c35,000
O.27	W	Drake	32-6	H		12,000
N.3	W	Penn State (R)	9-0	N2		30,000
N.10	W	Army (U) (2:30)	12-6	YS		c78,188
N.17	L	Carnegie Tech (R)	7-27	H†		c27,000
D.1	L	So. California	14-27	A		c72,632

(5-4-0) 99-107 419,705

*Paid attendance: 103,081
†First defeat at home since 1905
N1—at Soldier Field; N2—at Philadelphia

1929†

Coach: Knute K. Rockne
Captain: John Law

O.5	W	Indiana	14-0	A	16,111
O.12	W	Navy	14-7	N1	c64,681
O.19	W	Wisconsin	19-0	N2	90,000
O.26	W	Carnegie Tech	7-0	A	c66,000
N.2	W	Georgia Tech	26-6	A	22,000
N.9	W	Drake	19-7	N2	50,000
N.16	W	So. California	13-12	N2*c112,912	
N.23	W	Northwestern	26-6	A	c50,000
N.30	W	Army	7-0	YS	c79,840

(9-0-0) 145-38 551,112

†No home games; Notre Dame Stadium was under construction
*Paid attendance: 99,351
N1—at Baltimore; N2—at Soldier Field

1930

Coach: Knute K. Rockne
Captain: Thomas Conley

O.4	W	S.M.U. (4:00)	20-14	H	14,751
O.11	W	Navy†	26-2	H	40,593
O.18	W	Carnegie Tech	21-6	H	30,009
O.25	W	Pittsburgh	35-19	A	c66,586
N.1	W	Indiana	27-0	H	11,113
N.8	W	Pennsylvania	60-20	A	c75,657
N.15	W	Drake	28-7	H	10,106
N.22	W	Northwestern	14-0	A	c44,648
N.29	W	Army (R-S) (3:30)	7-6	N1*	c110,000
D.6	W	So. California (U)	27-0	A	c73,967

(10-0-0) 265-74 477,430

†Dedication of Notre Dame Stadium
*Paid attendance: 103,310
N1—at Soldier Field

1931†

Coach: Heartley W. (Hunk) Anderson
Captain: Thomas Yarr

O.3	W	Indiana	25-0	A	12,098
O.10	T	Northwestern (R)	0-0	N1	65,000
O.17	W	Drake	63-0	H	23,835
O.24	W	Pittsburgh	25-12	H	37,394
O.31	W	Carnegie Tech	19-0	A	42,271
N.7	W	Pennsylvania	49-0	H	39,173
N.14	W	Navy	20-0	N2	56,861
N.21	L	So. Calif. (U) (1:00)	14-16	H	*50,731
N.28	L	Army (U)	0-12	YS	c78,559

(6-2-1) 215-40 405,922

*First capacity crowd in Notre Dame Stadium
N1—at Soldier Field; N2—at Baltimore
†Coach Knute K. Rockne, 43, and seven other persons were killed in a plane crash near Bazaar, Kansas, on March 31, 1931.

1932

Coach: Heartley W. (Hunk) Anderson
Captain: Paul A. Host

O.8	W	Haskell	73-0	H	8,369
O.15	W	Drake	62-0	H	6,663
O.22	W	Carnegie Tech	42-0	H	16,015
O.29	L	Pittsburgh (U)	0-12	A	55,616
N.5	W	Kansas	24-6	A	18,062
N.12	W	Northwestern	21-0	H	31,853
N.19	W	Navy	12-0	N	61,122
N.26	W	Army	21-0	YS	c78,115
D.10	L	So. California	0-13	A	93,924

(7-2-0) 255-31 369,739

N—at Cleveland

1933

Coach: Heartley W. (Hunk) Anderson
Co-captains: Hugh J. Devore and Thomas A. Gorman

O.7	T	Kansas	0-0	H	9,221
O.14	W	Indiana	12-2	A	15,152
O.21	L	Carnegie Tech (U)	0-7	A	45,890
O.28	L	Pittsburgh	0-14	H	16,627
N.4	L	Navy	0-7	N	34,579
N.11	L	Purdue	0-19	H	27,476
N.18	W	Northwestern	7-0	A	31,182
N.25	L	So. California	0-19	H	25,037
D.2	W	Army (U)	13-12	YS	c73,594

(3-5-1) 32-80 278,758

N—at Baltimore

1934

Coach: Elmer F. Layden
Captain: Dominic M. Vairo

O.6	L	Texas	6-7	H	20,353
O.13	W	Purdue	18-7	H	34,263
O.20	W	Carnegie Tech (R)	13-0	H	11,242
O.27	W	Wisconsin	19-0	H	25,354
N.3	L	Pittsburgh	0-19	A	56,556
N.10	L	Navy (R)	6-10	N	54,571
N.17	W	Northwestern	20-7	A	38,413
N.24	W	Army (4:00)	12-6	YS	c78,757
D.8	W	So. California	14-0	A	45,568

(6-3-0) 108-56 365,077

N—at Cleveland

1935

Coach: Elmer F. Layden
Captain: °Joseph G. Sullivan

S.28	W	Kansas	28-7	H	11,102
O.5	W	Carnegie Tech	14-3	A	27,542
O.12	W	Wisconsin	27-0	A	19,863
O.19	W	Pittsburgh (3:00)	9-6	H	39,989
O.26	W	Navy	14-0	N	c57,810
N.2	W	Ohio St. (U) (0:32)	18-13	A	c81,018
N.9	W	Northwestern (U)	7-14	H	34,430
N.16	T	Army (0:29-ND)	6-6	YS	c78,114
N.23	W	So. California	20-13	H	38,305

(7-1-1) 143-62 388,173

°Died from complications of pneumonia, March, 1935
N—at Baltimore

1936

Coach: Elmer F. Layden
Captain: °William R. Smith—John P. Lautar

O.3	W	Carnegie Tech	21-7	H	15,673
O.10	W	Washington (St. L.)	14-6	H	9,879
O.17	W	Wisconsin (R)	27-0	H	16,423
O.24	L	Pittsburgh	0-26	A	c66,622
O.31	W	Ohio State (R)	7-2	H	50,017
N.7	L	Navy (U)	0-3	N	51,126
N.14	W	Army	20-6	YS	c74,423
N.21	W	Northwestern (U)	26-6	H	52,131
D.5	T	So. California	13-13	A	71,201

(6-2-1) 128-69 407,495

°Captain-elect. Smith resigned his captaincy because
of illness and Lautar was elected Acting Captain.
N—at Baltimore

1937

Coach: Elmer F. Layden
Captain: Joseph B. Zwers

O.2	W	Drake	21-0	H	14,955
O.9	T	Illinois	0-0	A	42,253
O.16	L	Carnegie Tech (U)	7-9	A	30,418
O.23	W	Navy (S) (2:00)	9-7	H	45,000
O.30	W	Minnesota (U)	7-6	A	c63,237
N.6	L	Pittsburgh	6-21	H	c54,309
N.13	W	Army (R)	7-0	YS	c76,359
N.20	W	Northwestern	7-0	A	42,573
N.27	W	So. California (1:45)	13-6	H	28,920

(6-2-1) 77-49 398,024

1938

Coach: Elmer F. Layden
Captain: James J. McGoldrick

O.1	W	Kansas	52-0	H	25,615
O.8	W	Georgia Tech	14-6	A	26,533
O.15	W	Illinois	14-6	H	29,142
O.22	W	Carnegie Tech	7-0	H	25,934
O.29	W	Army	19-7	YS	c76,338
N.5	W	Navy (R)	15-0	N	58,271
N.12	°W	Minnesota	19-0	H	c55,245
N.19	W	Northwestern	9-7	A	c46,348
D.3	L	So. California (U)	0-13	A	c97,146

(8-1-0) 149-39 440,572

N—at Baltimore
°Notre Dame's 300th victory

1939

Coach: Elmer F. Layden
Captain: John F. Kelly

S.30	W	Purdue	3-0	H	31,341
O.7	W	Georgia Tech	17-14	H	17,322
O.14	W	S.M.U.	20-19	H	29,730
O.21	W	Navy	14-7	N	c78,257
O.28	W	Carnegie Tech (S)	7-6	A	c61,420
N.4	W	Army	14-0	YS	c75,632
N.11	L	Iowa (U)	6-7	A	c42,380
N.18	W	Northwestern (3:30)	7-0	H	49,204
N.25	L	So. California	12-20	H	c54,799

(7-2-0) 100-73 440,085

N—at Cleveland

1940

Coach: Elmer F. Layden
Captain: Milt Piepul

O.5	W	Col. of Pacific	25-7	H	22,670
O.12	W	Georgia Tech	26-20	H	32,492
O.19	W	Carnegie Tech	61-0	H	29,515
O.26	W	Illinois	26-0	A	c68,578
N.2	W	Army (R)	7-0	YS	c75,474
N.9	W	Navy (4:00)	13-7	N	c61,579
N.16	L	Iowa (5:00) (U)	0-7	H	45,960
N.23	L	Northwestern	0-20	A	c46,273
D.7	W	So. California	10-6	A	85,808

(7-2-0) 168-67 468,349

N—at Baltimore

1941

Coach: Frank Leahy
Captain: Paul B. Lillis

S.27	W	Arizona	38-7	H	19,567
O.4	W	Indiana (R)	19-6	H	34,713
O.11	W	Georgia Tech	20-0	A	c28,986
O.18	W	Carnegie Tech (R)	16-0	A	17,208
O.25	W	Illinois	49-14	H	34,896
N.1	T	Army (R)	0-0	YS	c75,226
N.8	W	Navy	20-13	N	c62,074
N.15	W	Northwestern	7-6	A	c46,211
N.22	W	So. California	20-18	H	c54,967

(8-0-1) 189-64 373,848

N—at Baltimore

1942

Coach: Frank Leahy
Captain: George E. Murphy

S.26	T	Wisconsin	7-7	A	23,243
O.3	L	Georgia Tech (U)	6-13	H	20,545
O.10	W	Stanford	27-0	H	22,374
O.17	W	Iowa Pre-Flight (U)	28-0	H	26,800
O.24	W	Illinois	21-14	A	43,476
O.31	W	Navy (R)	9-0	N1	66,699
N.7	W	Army	13-0	YS	c74,946
N.14	L	Michigan	20-32	H	c54,379
N.21	W	Northwestern	27-20	H	26,098
N.28	W	So. California	13-0	A	94,519
D.5	T	Great Lakes (S)	13-13	N2	19,225

(7-2-2) 184-99 472,304

N1—at Cleveland; N2—at Soldier Field

1943

Coach: Frank Leahy
Captain: Patrick J. Filley

S.25	W	Pittsburgh	41-0	A	43,437
O.2	W	Georgia Tech	55-13	H	26,497
O.9	W	Michigan	35-12	A	c86,408
O.16	W	Wisconsin	50-0	H	16,235
O.23	W	Illinois (R)	47-0	H	24,676
O.30	W	Navy	33-6	N	c77,900
N.6	W	Army	26-0	YS	c75,121
N.13	W	Northwestern	25-6	A	c49,124
N.20	W	Iowa Pre-Flight	14-13	H	39,446
N.27	L	Gt. Lakes (U) (0:33)	14-19	A	c23,000

(9-1-0) 340-69 461,844

N—at Cleveland

1944

Coach: Edward C. McKeever
Captain: Patrick J. Filley

S.30	W	Pittsburgh	58-0	A	46,069
O.7	W	Tulane	26-0	H	32,909
O.14	W	Dartmouth (R)	64-0	N1	c38,167
O.21	W	Wisconsin	28-13	H	36,086
O.28	W	Illinois	13-7	A	57,122
N.4	L	Navy	13-32	N2	c60,938
N.11	L	Army	0-59	YS	c75,142
N.18	W	Northwestern	21-0	H	39,701
N.25	W	Georgia Tech	21-0	A	28,662
D.2	W	Great Lakes	28-7	H	36,900

(8-2-0) 272-118 451,696

N1—at Fenway Park, Boston; N2—at Baltimore

1945

Coach: Hugh J. Devore
Captain: Frank J. Dancewicz

S.29	W	Illinois	7-0	H	41,569
O.6	W	Georgia Tech	40-7	A	30,157
O.13	W	Dartmouth	34-0	H	34,645
O.20	W	Pittsburgh	39-9	A	c57,542
O.27	W	Iowa	56-0	H	42,841
N.3	T	Navy	6-6	N	c74,621
N.10	L	Army	0-48	YS	c46,294
N.17	W	Northwestern	34-7	A	51,368
N.24	W	Tulane	32-6	A	51,368
D.1	L	Great Lakes	7-39	A	c23,000

(7-2-1) 255-122 484,057

N—at Cleveland

1946

Coach: Frank Leahy
New Captain Each Game

S.28	W	Illinois	26-6	A	c75,119
O.5	W	Pittsburgh	33-0	H	50,350
O.12	W	Purdue	49-6	H	c55,452
O.26	W	Iowa	41-6	A	52,311
N.2	W	Navy	28-0	N	c63,909
N.9	T	Army	0-0	YS	c74,121
N.16	W	Northwestern (R)	27-0	H	c56,000
N.23	W	Tulane	41-0	A	65,841
N.30	W	So. California	26-6	H	c55,298

(8-0-1) 271-24 548,401

N—at Baltimore

1947

Coach: Frank Leahy
Captain: George Connor

O.4	W	Pittsburgh	40-6	A	c64,333
O.11	W	Purdue	22-7	A	42,000
O.18	W	Nebraska	31-0	H	c56,000
O.25	W	Iowa	21-0	H	c56,000
N.1	W	Navy	27-0	N	c84,070
N.8	W	Army	27-7	H	c59,171
N.15	W	Northwestern (R)	26-19	A	c48,000
N.22	W	Tulane	59-6	H	c57,000
D.6	W	So. California	38-7	A	c104,953

(9-0-0) 291-52 571,527

N—at Cleveland

1948
Coach: Frank Leahy
Captain: William Fischer

S.25	W	Purdue	28-27	H	c59,343
O.2	W	Pittsburgh	40-0	A	c64,000
O.9	W	Michigan State	26-7	H	c58,126
O.16	W	Nebraska	44-13	A	c38,000
O.23	W	Iowa	27-12	A	c53,000
O.30	W	Navy	41-7	N	c63,314
N.6	W	Indiana (R)	42-6	A	c34,000
N.13	W	Northwestern	12-7	H	c59,305
N.27	W	Washington	46-0	H	50,609
D.4	T	So. Calif. (0:35-ND)	14-14	A	c100,571
		(9-0-1)	320-93		580,268

N—at Baltimore

1949
Coach: Frank Leahy
Co-Captains: Leon J. Hart and James E. Martin

S.24	W	Indiana	49-6	H	53,844
O.1	W	Washington	27-7	A	c52,000
O.8	W	Purdue	35-12	A	c52,000
O.15	W	Tulane	46-7	H	c58,196
O.29	W	Navy	40-0	N	c62,000
N.5	W	Michigan State	34-21	A	c51,277
N.12	W	North Carolina	42-6	H	c67,000
N.19	W	Iowa	28-7	H	c56,790
N.26	W	So. California	32-0	H	c57,214
D.3	W	S.M.U.	27-20	A	75,457
		(10-0-0)	360-86		575,278

N—at Baltimore

1950
Coach: Frank Leahy
Captain: Jerome P. Groom

S.30	W	No. Carolina (2:40)	14-7	H	c56,430
O.7	L	Purdue (U) (R)	14-28	H	c56,746
O.14	W	Tulane	13-9	A	73,159
O.21	L	Indiana (U)	7-20	A	c34,000
O.28	L	Michigan State	33-36	H	c57,866
N.4	W	Navy (R-S)	19-10	N	71,074
N.11	W	Pittsburgh	18-7	H	c56,966
N.18	T	Iowa	14-14	A	c52,863
D.2	L	So. California	7-9	A	70,177
		(4-4-1)	139-140		529,281

N—at Cleveland

1951
Coach: Frank Leahy
Captain: Jim Mutscheller

S.29	W	Indiana	48-6	H	55,790
O.5	W	Detroit (Nt)	40-6	N1	52,331
O.13	L	S.M.U. (U)	20-27	H	c58,240
O.20	W	Pittsburgh	33-0	A	c60,127
O.27	W	Purdue	30-9	H	c57,890
N.3	W	Navy	19-0	N2	44,237
N.10	L	Michigan State	0-35	A	c51,296
N.17	W	North Carolina	12-7	A	c44,500
N.24	T	Iowa (0:55-ND)	20-20	H	40,685
D.1	W	So. California (R)	19-12	A	55,783
		(7-2-1)	241-122		520,879

N1—at Briggs Stadium, Detroit; N2—at Baltimore
*Notre Dame's 400th victory

1952
Coach: Frank Leahy
Captain: James F. Alessandrini

S.27	T	Pennsylvania	7-7	A	c74,518
O.4	W	Texas (U)	14-3	A	c67,666
O.11	L	Pittsburgh (U)	19-22	H	45,507
O.18	W	Purdue	26-14	A	49,000
O.25	W	North Carolina	34-14	H	54,338
N.1	W	Navy	17-6	N	61,927
N.8	W	Oklahoma (U)	27-21	H	c57,446
N.15	L	Michigan State	3-21	A	c52,472
N.22	W	Iowa	27-0	A	46,600
N.29	W	So. California (U)	9-0	H	c58,394
		(7-2-1)	183-108		567,868

N—at Cleveland

1953
Coach: Frank Leahy
Captain: Donald Penza

S.26	W	Oklahoma	28-21	A	c59,500
O.3	W	Purdue	37-7	A	49,135
O.17	W	Pittsburgh	23-14	H	c57,998
O.24	W	Georgia Tech	27-14	H	c58,254
O.31	W	Navy	38-7	H	c58,154
N.7	W	Pennsylvania	28-20	A	c74,711
N.14	W	North Carolina	34-14	A	c43,000
N.21	T	Iowa (0:06-ND)	14-14	H	c56,478
N.28	W	So. California	48-14	H	97,952
D.5	W	S.M.U.	40-14	H	55,522
		(9-0-1)	317-139		610,704

1954
Coach: Terry Brennan
Co-Captains: Paul A. Matz and Daniel J. Shannon

S.25	W	Texas	21-0	H	c57,594
O.2	L	Purdue (U)	14-27	H	c58,250
O.9	W	Pittsburgh	33-0	A	c60,114
O.16	W	Michigan State (R)	20-19	H	c57,238
O.30	W	Navy	6-0	N	c60,000
N.6	W	Pennsylvania	42-7	A	61,189
N.13	W	North Carolina	42-13	H	55,410
N.20	W	Iowa	34-18	A	c56,576
N.27	W	So. Calif (R) (5:57)	23-17	H	c56,438
D.4	W	S.M.U.	26-14	A	c75,501
		(9-1-0)	261-115		598,310

N—at Baltimore

1955
Coach: Terry Brennan
Captain: Raymond E. Lemek

S.24	W	S.M.U.	17-0	H	c56,454
O.1	W	Indiana	19-0	H	c56,494
O.7	W	Miami (Fla.) (Nt)	14-0	A	c75,685
O.15	L	Michigan State	7-21	A	c52,007
O.22	W	Purdue	22-7	A	c55,000
O.29	W	Navy (R)	21-7	H	c59,475
N.5	W	Pennsylvania	46-14	A	45,226
N.12	W	North Carolina	27-7	A	38,000
N.19	W	Iowa (2:15)	17-14	H	c59,955
N.26	L	So. California (U)	20-42	A	94,892
		(8-2-0)	210-112		593,188

1956
Coach: Terry Brennan
Captain: James A. Morse

S.22	L	S.M.U. (U) (Nt) (1:50)	13-19	A	61,000
O.6	W	Indiana	20-6	H	c58,372
O.13	L	Purdue	14-28	H	c58,778
O.20	L	Michigan State	14-47	H	c59,378
O.27	L	Oklahoma	0-40	H	c60,128
N.3	L	Navy (R)	7-33	N	57,773
N.10	L	Pittsburgh	13-26	A	c58,697
N.17	W	No. Carolina (1:16)	21-14	H	c56,793
N.24	L	Iowa	8-48	A	c56,632
D.1	L	So. California	20-28	A	64,538
		(2-8-0)	130-289		592,089

N—at Baltimore

1957
Coach: Terry Brennan
Co-Captains: Richard Prendergast and
Edward A. Sullivan

S.28	W	Purdue	12-0	A	52,108
O.5	W	Indiana	26-0	H	54,026
O.12	W	Army	23-21	N	95,000
O.26	W	Pittsburgh	13-7	H	c58,775
N.2	L	Navy (R)	6-20	H	c58,922
N.9	L	Michigan State	6-34	A	c75,391
N.16	W	Oklahoma (U) (3:50)	7-0	A	c63,170
N.23	L	Iowa	13-21	H	c58,734
N.30	W	So. California (S)	40-12	H	54,793
D.7	W	S.M.U.	54-21	A	51,000
		(7-3-0)	200-136		621,919

N—at Philadelphia

1958
Coach: Terry Brennan
Co-Captains: Allen J. Ecuyer and
Charles F. Puntillo

S.27	W	Indiana	18-0	H	49,347
O.4	W	S.M.U.	14-6	A	61,500
O.11	L	Army	2-14	H	c60,564
O.18	W	Duke	9-7	H	c59,068
O.25	L	Purdue (R)	22-29	H	c59,563
N.1	W	Navy	40-20	N	c57,777
N.8	L	Pittsburgh (0:11)	26-29	H	55,330
N.15	W	North Carolina	34-24	H	c56,839
N.22	L	Iowa	21-31	A	c58,230
N.29	W	So. California	20-13	A	66,903
		(6-4-0)	206-173		585,117

N—at Baltimore

1959
Coach: Joseph L. Kuharich
Captain: Kenneth M. Adamson

S.26	W	North Carolina (R)	28-8	H	56,746
O.3	L	Purdue	7-28	A	c50,362
O.10	W	California	28-6	H	68,500
O.17	L	Michigan State	0-19	H	73,480
O.24	L	Northwestern (R)	24-30	H	c59,078
O.31	W	Navy (0:32)	25-22	H	c58,652
N.7	L	Georgia Tech (4:27)	10-14	H	c58,775
N.14	L	Pittsburgh (R)	13-28	H	52,337
N.21	W	Iowa (3:25)	20-19	A	c58,500
N.28	W	So. California (U)	16-6	H	48,684
		(5-5-0)	171-180		584,914

1960
Coach: Joseph L. Kuharich
Captain: Myron Pottios

S.24	W	California	21-7	H	49,286
O.1	L	Purdue	19-51	H	c59,235
O.8	L	North Carolina (R)	7-12	A	41,000
O.15	L	Michigan State	0-21	H	c59,133
O.22	L	Northwestern	6-7	A	c55,682
O.29	L	Navy	7-14	N	63,000
N.5	L	Pittsburgh	13-20	H	55,696
N.12	L	Miami (Fla.) (Nt)	21-28	A	58,062
N.19	L	Iowa	0-28	H	45,000
N.26	W	So. Cal. (U) (R)	17-0	A	54,146
		(2-8-0)	111-188		540,240

N—at Philadelphia

1961
Coach: Joseph L. Kuharich
Co-Captains: Norbert W. Roy and
Nicholas A. Buoniconti

S.30	W	Oklahoma	19-6	H	55,198
O.7	W	Purdue	22-20	A	c51,295
O.14	W	So. California	30-0	H	50,427
O.21	L	Michigan State	7-17	A	c76,132
O.28	L	Northwestern	10-12	H	c59,075
N.4	L	Navy	10-13	H	c59,075
N.11	W	Pittsburgh	26-20	H	50,527
N.18	L	Syracuse (0:00)	17-15	H	49,246
N.25	L	Iowa	21-42	A	c58,000
D.2	L	Duke	13-37	A	35,000
		(5-5-0)	175-182		543,975

1962
Coach: Joseph L. Kuharich
Captain: Mike Lind

S.29	W	Oklahoma	13-7	A	c60,500
O.6	L	Purdue	6-24	H*	c61,296
O.13	L	Wisconsin	8-17	A	c61,098
O.20	L	Michigan State (R)	7-31	H	c60,116
O.27	L	Northwestern	6-35	A	c55,752
N.3	W	Navy (R)	20-12	N	35,000
N.10	W	Pittsburgh	43-22	H	52,215
N.17	W	North Carolina	21-7	H	35,553
N.24	W	Iowa	35-12	H	42,653
D.1	L	So. California	0-25	A	81,676
		(5-5-0)	159-192		545,859

N—at Philadelphia
*Notre Dame Stadium record

1963
Coach: Hugh J. Devore
Captain: Joseph Robert Lehmann

S.28	L	Wisconsin (1:07)	9-14	H	56,806
O.5	L	Purdue	6-7	A	c51,723
O.12	W	So. Cal. (U) (6:28)	17-14	H	c59,135
O.19	L	U.C.L.A.	27-12	H	42,948
O.26	L	Stanford (U)	14-24	A	55,000
N.2	L	Navy	14-35	H	c59,362
N.9	L	Pittsburgh	7-27	H	41,306
N.16	L	Michigan State	7-12	A	70,128
N.23	..	Iowa*			
N.28	L	Syracuse (3:28)	7-14	YS	56,972
		(2-7-0)	108-159		493,380

*Game cancelled because of the death of President Kennedy

1964

Coach: Ara Parseghian
Captain: James S. Carroll

S.26	W	Wisconsin (R)	31-7	A	c64,398
O.3	W	Purdue	34-15	H	c59,611
O.10	W	Air Force	34-7	A	c44,384
O.17	W	U.C.L.A.	24-0	H	58,335
O.24	W	Stanford	28-6	H	56,721
O.31	W	Navy	40-0	N	66,752
N.7	W	Pittsburgh	17-15	A	56,628
N.14	W	Michigan State	34-7	H	c59,265
N.21	W	Iowa	28-0	H	c59,135
N.28	L	So. Calif. (U)(1:33)	17-20	A	83,840

(9-1-0) 287-77 609,069

N—at Philadelphia

1965

Coach: Ara Parseghian
Captain: Philip F. Sheridan

S.18	W	California	48-6	A	53,000
S.25	L	Purdue	21-25	H	c61,291
O.2	W	Northwestern	38-7	H	c59,273
O.9	W	Army (Nt)	17-0	N	c61,000
O.23	W	So. California (R)	28-7	H	c59,235
O.30	W	Navy	29-3	H	c59,206
N.6	W	Pittsburgh	69-13	A	c57,169
N.13	W	North Carolina	17-0	H	c59,216
N.20	L	Michigan State	3-12	H	c59,291
N.27	T	Miami (Fla.) (Nt)	0-0	A	68,077

(7-2-1) 270-73 596,758

N—at Shea Stadium, New York

1966

Coach: Ara Parseghian
Captain: James R. Lynch

S.24	W	Purdue	26-14	H	c59,075
O.1	W	Northwestern	35-7	A	c55,356
O.8	W	Army	35-0	H	c59,075
O.15	W	North Carolina	32-0	H	c59,075
O.22	W	Oklahoma	38-0	A	c63,439
O.29	W	Navy	31-7	N	70,101
N.5	W	Pittsburgh	40-0	H	c59,075
N.12	W	Duke	64-0	H	c59,075
N.19	T	Michigan State	10-10	A	c80,011
N.26	W	So. California	51-0	A	88,520

(9-0-1) 362-38 652,802

N—at Philadelphia

1967

Coach: Ara Parseghian
Captain: Robert P. (Rocky) Bleier

S.23	W	California	41-8	H	c59,075
S.30	L	Purdue	21-28	A	c62,316
O.7	W	Iowa	56-6	H	c59,075
O.14	L	So. California	7-24	H	c71,227
O.21	W	Illinois	47-7	A	c59,075
O.28	W	Michigan State	24-12	H	c59,075
N.4	W	Navy	43-14	H	c59,075
N.11	W	Pittsburgh	38-0	A	54,075
N.18	°W	Georgia Tech	36-3	A	c60,024
N.24	W	Miami (Fla.) (Nt)	24-22	A	c77,265

(8-2-0) 337-124 620,282

°Notre Dame's 500th victory

1968

Coach: Ara Parseghian
Co-Captains: George J. Kunz and Robert L. Olson

S.21	W	Oklahoma	45-21	H	c59,075
S.28	L	Purdue	22-37	H	c59,075
O.5	W	Iowa	51-28	A	58,043
O.12	W	Northwestern	27-7	H	c59,075
O.19	W	Illinois	58-8	H	c59,075
O.26	L	Michigan State	17-21	A	c77,339
N.2	W	Navy	45-14	N	63,738
N.9	W	Pittsburgh	56-7	H	c59,075
N.16	W	Georgia Tech	34-6	H	c59,075
N.30	T	So. California	21-21	A	82,659

(7-2-1) 376-170 636,229

N—at Philadelphia

1969

Coach: Ara Parseghian
Co-Captains: Robert L. Olson and Michael Oriard

S.20	W	Northwestern	35-10	H	c59,075
S.27	L	Purdue	14-28	A	c68,179
O.4	W	Michigan State	42-28	H	c59,075
O.11	W	Army	45-0	N1	c63,786
O.18	T	Southern California	14-14	A	c59,075
O.25	W	Tulane (Nt)	37-0	A	40,250
N.1	W	Navy	47-0	H	c59,075
N.8	W	Pittsburgh (R)	49-7	A	44,084
N.15	W	Georgia Tech (Nt)	38-20	H	41,104
N.22	W	Air Force	13-6	H	c59,075

(8-1-1) 334-113 552,778

COTTON BOWL
Jan. 1 L Texas (1:08) 17-21 N2 c73,000
N1 — at Yankee Stadium, New York
N2 — at Dallas, Texas

1970

Coach: Ara Parseghian
Co-Captains: Larry DiNardo and Tim Kelly

S.19	W	Northwestern	35-14	A	50,049
S.26	W	Purdue	48-0	H	c59,075
O.3	W	Michigan State	29-0	A	c76,103
O.10	W	Army	51-10	H	c59,075
O.17	W	Missouri	24-7	A	c64,200
O.31	W	Navy	56-7	N1	45,226
N.7	W	Pittsburgh	46-14	H	c59,075
N.14	W	Georgia Tech (6:28)	10-7	H	c59,075
N.21	W	Louisiana State (2:54)	3-0	H	c59,075
N.28	L	Southern Cal(R)(U)	28-38	A	64,694

(9-1-0) 330-97 595,647

COTTON BOWL
Jan. 1 W Texas 24-11 N2 c73,000
N1 — at Philadelphia
N2 — at Dallas, Texas

1971

Coach: Ara Parseghian
Co-Captains: Walter Patulski and Thomas Gatewood

S.18	W	Northwestern	50-7	H	c59,075
S.25	W	Purdue (2:58) (R)	8-7	A	c69,765
O.2	W	Michigan State	14-2	H	c59,075
O.9	W	Miami (Fla.) (Nt)	17-0	A	66,039
O.16	W	North Carolina	16-0	H	c59,075
O.23	L	So. California (U)	14-28	H	c59,075
O.30	W	Navy	21-0	H	c59,075
N.6	W	Pittsburgh	56-7	A	55,528
N.13	W	Tulane	21-7	H	c59,075
N.20	L	Louisiana State (Nt)	8-28	A	c66,936

(8-2-0) 225-86 612,718

1972

Coach: Ara Parseghian
Co-Captains: John Dampeer and Greg Marx

S.23	W	Northwestern	37-0	A	c55,155
S.30	W	Purdue	35-14	H	c59,075
O.7	W	Michigan State	16-0	A	c77,828
O.14	W	Pittsburgh	42-16	H	c59,075
O.21	L	Missouri (U) (R)	26-30	H	c59,075
O.28	W	TCU	21-0	H	c59,075
N.4	W	Navy	42-23	N1	43,089
N.11	W	Air Force	21-7	A	c48,671
N.18	W	Miami (Fla.)	20-17	H	c59,075
D.2	L	Southern Cal	23-45	A	75,243

(8-2-0) 283-152 595,361

ORANGE BOWL
J.1 L Nebraska (Nt) 6-40 N2 c80,010
N1—at Philadelphia; N2—at Miami

1973

Coach: Ara Parseghian
Tri-Captains: Dave Casper, Frank Pomarico (Off.)
and Mike Townsend (Def.)

S.22	W	Northwestern	44-0	H	c59,075
S.29	W	Purdue	20-7	A	c69,391
O.6	W	Michigan State	14-10	H	c59,075
O.13	W	Rice (Nt)	28-0	A	50,321
O.20	W	Army	62-3	A	c42,503
O.27	W	Southern Cal (R)	23-14	H	c59,075
N.3	W	Navy	44-7	H	c59,075
N.10	W	Pittsburgh (S)	31-10	A	c56,593
N.22TH	W	Air Force	48-15	H	57,236
D.1	W	Miami (Fla.)(Nt)	44-0	A	42,968

(10-0-0) 358-66 555,312

SUGAR BOWL
D.31 W Alabama 24-23 N1 c85,161
(4:26) (Nt)
N1—at New Orleans

1974

Coach: Ara Parseghian
Co-Captains: Tom Clements and Greg Collins

S.9	W	Georgia Tech	31-7	A	45,228
S.21	W	Northwestern	49-3	A	c55,000
S.28	L	Purdue (U) (R)	20-31	H	c59,075
O.5	W	Michigan State	19-14	A	c77,431
O.12	W	Rice (3:08)	10-3	H	c59,075
O.19	W	Army (S)	48-0	H	c59,075
O.26	W	Miami (Fla.)	38-7	H	c59,075
N.2	W	Navy	14-6	N1	48,634
N.16	W	Pitt (2:49)	14-10	H	c59,075
N.23	W	Air Force (R)	38-0	H	c59,075
N.30	L	Southern Cal	24-55	A	83,522

(9-2-0) 305-136 664,265

ORANGE BOWL
J.1 W Alabama (U) 13-11 N2 71,801
N1—at Philadelphia; N2—at Miami

1975

Coach: Dan Devine
Co-Captains: Ed Bauer and Jim Stock

S.15	W	Boston College	17-3	N	c61,501
S.20	W	Purdue	17-0	A	c69,795
S.27	W	Northwestern	31-7	H	c59,075
O.4	L	Michigan State (3:50)	3-10	H	c59,075
O.11	W	No. Carolina (1:03)	21-14	A	c49,500
O.18	W	Air Force (3:23)	31-30	A	43,204
O.25	L	Southern Cal	17-24	H	c59,075
N.1	W	Navy (R)	31-10	H	c59,075
N.8	W	Georgia Tech	24-3	H	c59,075
N.15	L	Pittsburgh (U)	20-34	A	c56,480
N.22	W	Miami (Fla.) (Nt)	32-9	A	24,944

(8-3-0) 244-144 600,799

N—at Foxboro

1976

Coach: Dan Devine
Co-Captains: Mark McLane and Willie Fry

S.11	L	Pittsburgh	10-31	H	c59,075
S.18	W	Purdue	23-0	H	c59,075
S.25	W	Northwestern	48-0	A	44,396
O.2	W	Michigan State	24-6	A	c77,081
O.16	W	Oregon	41-0	H	c59,075
O.23	W	South Carolina	13-6	A	c56,721
O.30	W	Navy	27-21	N1	61,172
N.6	L	Georgia Tech (U)	14-23	A	50,079
N.13	W	Alabama	21-18	H	c59,075
N.20	W	Miami (Fla.)	40-27	H	c59,075
N.27	L	Southern Cal	13-17	A	76,561

(8-3-0) 274-149 661,925

GATOR BOWL
D.27 W Penn State (Nt) 20-9 N2 67,827
N1—at Cleveland; N2—at Jacksonville

1977

Coach Dan Devine
Tri-Captains:
Ross Browner, Terry Eurick and Willie Fry

S.10	W	Pittsburgh	19-9	A	c56,500
S.17	L	Mississippi (U)(3:28)	13-20	N1	c48,200
S.24	W	Purdue	31-24	A	c68,966
O.1	W	Michigan State	16-6	H	c59,075
O.15	W	Army	24-0	N2	c72,594
O.22	W	Southern Cal	49-19	H	c59,075
O.29	W	Navy	43-10	H	c59,075
N.5	W	Georgia Tech	69-14	H	c59,075
N.12	W	Clemson	21-17	A	c54,189
N.19	W	Air Force	49-0	H	c59,075
D.3	W	Miami (Fla.)	48-10	A	35,789

(10-1-0) 382-129 631,613

COTTON BOWL
J.2 W Texas (U) 38-10 N3 c76,701
N1—Jackson; N2—Giants Stadium, East Rutherford, N.J.;
N3—Dallas

1978

Coach: Dan Devine
Tri-Captains:
Bob Golic, Jerome Heavens and Joe Montana

S.9	L	Missouri (12:50)	0-3	H	c59,075
S.23	L	Michigan	14-28	H	c59,075
S.30	W	Purdue	10-6	H	c59,075
O.7	W	Michigan State	29-25	A	c77,087
O.14	W	Pittsburgh	26-17	H	c59,075
O.21	W	Air Force	38-15	A	35,425
O.28	W	Miami (Fla.)	20-0	H	c59,075
N.4	W	Navy	27-7	N1	63,780
N.11	W	Tennessee	31-14	H	c59,075
N.18	W	Georgia Tech	38-21	A	54,526
N.25	L	Southern Cal	25-27	A	84,256

(8-3-0)   258-163   669,524

COTTON BOWL

| J.1 | *W | Houston (0:00) | 35-34 | N2 | 32,500 |

N1—at Cleveland; N2—at Dallas
*—Notre Dame's 600th victory

1979

Coach: Dan Devine
Tri-Captains:
Vagas Ferguson, Tim Foley and Dave Waymer

S.15	W	Michigan	12-10	A	c105,111
S.22	L	Purdue	22-28	A	c70,567
S.29	W	Michigan State	27-3	H	c59,075
O.6	W	Georgia Tech (R)	21-13	H	c59,075
O.13	W	Air Force	38-13	A	34,881
O.20	L	Southern Cal	23-42	H	c59,075
O.27	W	South Carolina (0:42)	18-17	H	c59,075
N.3	W	Navy	14-0	H	c59,075
N.10	L	Tennessee	18-40	A	c86,489
N.17	L	Clemson	10-16	H	c59,075
N.24	W	Miami (Fla.) (R)	40-15	N	62,574

(7-4-0)   243-197   714,072

N—National Olympic Stadium, Tokyo, Japan

1980

Coach: Dan Devine
Tri-Captains
Bob Crable, Tom Gibbons and John Scully

S.6	W	Purdue	31-10	H	c59,075
S.20	W	Michigan (0:00)	29-27	H	c59,075
O.4	W	Michigan State	26-21	A	c76,821
O.11	W	Miami	32-14	H	c59,075
O.18	W	Army	30-3	H	c59,075
O.25	W	Arizona	20-3	A	c56,211
N.1	W	Navy	33-0	N1	c76,891
N.8	T	Georgia Tech (N.D. 4:44)	3-3	A	41,266
N.15	W	Alabama	7-0	A	c78,873
N.22	W	Air Force	24-10	H	c59,075
D.6	L	Southern Cal	3-20	A	82,663

(9-1-1)   238-111   708,100

SUGAR BOWL

| J.1 | L | Georgia | 10-17 | N2 | c77,895 |

N1—Giants Stadium, East Rutherford, N.J.;
N2—Superdome, New Orleans, La.

1981

Coach: Gerry Faust
Tri-Captains:
Bob Crable, Phil Carter and Tony Belden

S.12		Louisiana State	27-9	H	c59,075
S.19		Michigan	7-25	A	c105,888
S.26		Purdue	14-15	A	c70,007
O.3		Michigan State	20-7	H	c59,075
O.10		Florida State	13-19	H	c59,075
O.24		Southern Cal	7-14	H	c59,075
O.31		Navy	38-0	H	c59,075
N.7		Georgia Tech	35-3	H	c59,075
N.14		Air Force	35-7	A	36.700
N.21		Penn State	21-24	A	c84,175
N.28		Miami (Fla.)	15-37	A	58,681

(5-6)   217-123   651,220

Individual Records

TOTAL OFFENSE
(Rushing and Passing Combined)

Plays
Game: 75—Terry Hanratty vs. Purdue, 1967 (420 yards)
     71—Joe Theismann vs. Southern Cal, 1970 (512 yards)
Season: 391—Joe Theismann, 1970 (2813 yards)
     332—Joe Montana, 1978 (2114 yards)
     310—Tom Clements, 1974 (1918 yards)
     308—Joe Theismann, 1969 (1909 yards)
Career: 807—Joe Theismann, 1968-70 (5432 yards)
     760—Tom Clements, 1972-74 (4664 yards)
     731—Terry Hanratty, 1966-68 (4738 yards)

Plays Per Game
Season: 39.1—Joe Theismann, 1970 (391 in 10)
Career: 28.1—Terry Hanratty, 1966-68 (731 in 26)

Yards Gained
Game: 512—Joe Theismann vs. Southern Cal, 1970 (526 passing, minus 14 rushing)
     420—Terry Hanratty vs. Purdue, 1967 (366 passing, 54 rushing)
Season: 2813—Joe Theismann, 1970 (384 rushing, 2429 passing)
     2114—Joe Montana, 1978 (104 rushing, 2010 passing)
     2069—John Huarte, 1964 (7 rushing, 2062 passing)
Career: 5432—Joe Theismann, 1968-70 (1021 rushing, 4411 passing)
     4738—Terry Hanratty, 1966-68 (586 rushing, 4152 passing)

Yards Per Game
Season: 281.3—Joe Theismann, 1970 (2813 in 10)
     249.3—Terry Hanratty, 1968 (1745 in 7)
Career: 187.3—Joe Theismann, 1968-70 (5432 in 29)
     182.2—Terry Hanratty, 1966-68 (4738 in 26)

Games Gaining 200 Yards or More
Season: 8—Joe Theismann, 1970; 7—John Huarte, 1964
Career: 11—Joe Theismann, 1968-70; 10—Terry Hanratty, 1966-68

Yards Gained and Average Per Game Against One Opponent
Career: 1031 and 343.7—Terry Hanratty vs. Purdue, 1966-68
(National Records)

Yards Per Play
Game: (Min. 20 plays) 13.7—John Huarte vs. Navy, 1964 (20 for 273)
Season: (Min. 1000 yards) 9.37—George Gipp, 1920 (164 for 1536)
     8.55—John Huarte, 1964 (242 for 2069)
Career: (Min. 2000 yards) 7.46—John Huarte, 1962-64 (306 for 2283)
     7.39—George Gipp, 1917-20 (556 for 4110)

Points Responsible For (Points scored and passed for)
Game: 35—Art Smith vs. Loyola, Chicago, 1911 (7 TDs, 5 points each)
Season: 126—John Mohardt, 1921 (scored 12 TDs, passed for 9)
     124—Joe Theismann, 1970 (scored 26 points, passed for 98)
Career: 280—Joe Theismann, 1968-70 (scored 92 points, passed for 31 TDs and one 2-point conversion)
     264—Terry Hanratty, 1966-68 (scored 98 points, passed for 27 TDs and two 2-point conversions)

Points Responsible For Per Game
Season: 12.4—Joe Theismann, 1970 (124 in 10)
     11.8—John Huarte, 1964 (118 in 10)
Career: 10.2—Terry Hanratty, 1966-68 (264 in 26)
     9.7—Joe Theismann, 1968-70 (280 in 29)

RUSHING

Carries
Game: 40—Phil Carter vs. Michigan State, 1980 (254 yards)
39—Vagas Ferguson vs. Georgia Tech, 1979 (177 yards)
38—Jim Stone vs. Miami, 1980 (224 yards)
36—Wayne Bullock vs. Michigan State, 1974 (127 yards)
Season: 301—Vagas Ferguson, 1979 (1437 yards)
Also holds per-game record at 27.4 (301 in 11)
233—Al Hunter, 1976 (1058 yards)
229—Jerome Heavens, 1977 (994 yards)
211—Vagas Ferguson, 1978 (1192 yards)
Career: 673—Vagas Ferguson, 1976-79 (3472 yards)
Also holds per-game record at 16.4 (673 in 41)
590—Jerome Heavens, 1975-78 (2682 yards)
476—Neil Worden, 1951-53 (2039 yards)

Consecutive Carries by Same Player
Game: 8—Phil Carter vs. Air Force, 1980
8—Larry Conjar vs. Army, 1965
8—Neil Worden vs. Oklahoma, 1952

Yards Gained
Game: 255—Vagas Ferguson vs. Georgia Tech, 1978 (30 carries)
254—Phil Carter vs. Michigan State, 1980 (40 carries)
224—Jim Stone vs. Miami, 1980 (38 carries)
219—Vagas Ferguson vs. Navy, 1978 (18 carries)
211—Jim Stone vs. Navy, 1980 (32 carries)
Season: 1437—Vagas Ferguson, 1979 (301 carries)
1192—Vagas Ferguson, 1978 (211 carries)
1058—Al Hunter, 1976 (233 carries)
Career: 3472—Vagas Ferguson, 1976-79 (673 carries)
2682—Jerome Heavens, 1975-78 (590 carries)
2341—George Gipp, 1917-20 (369 carries)

Yards Gained Per Game
Season: 130.6—Vagas Ferguson, 1979 (1437 in 11)
117.4—Phil Carter, 1980 (892 in 7)
108.4—Vagas Ferguson, 1978 (1192 in 11)
103.4—George Gipp, 1917-20 (827 in 8)
Career: 86.7—George Gipp, 1917-20 (2341 in 27)
84.7—Vagas Ferguson, 1976-79 (3472 in 41)
74.3—Don Miller, 1922-24 (1933 in 26)

Games Gaining 100 Yards or More
Season: 7—Vagas Ferguson, 1979
5—George Gipp, 1920
Career: 13—Vagas Ferguson, 1976-79

Consecutive Games Gaining 100 Yards or More
Season: 4—Jim Stone, 1980 (Miami, Army, Arizona, Navy)

Games Gaining 200 Yards or More
Season: 2—Jim Stone, 1980 (Miami and Navy)
2—Vagas Ferguson, 1978 (Navy and Georgia Tech)

Yards Gained by a Freshman
Game: 148—Jerome Heavens vs. Georgia Tech, 1975 (18 carries)
Season: 756—Jerome Heavens, 1975 (129 carries)

Yards Gained by a Quarterback
Game: 146—Bill Etter vs. Navy, 1969 (11 carries)
Season: 384—Joe Theismann, 1970 (123 carries)
Career: 1070—Tom Clements, 1972-74 (270 carries)
(Joe Theismann, 1968-70, holds per-game record at 35.2)

Average Per Carry
Game: (Min. 10 carries) 17.1—John Petitbon vs. Michigan State, 1950 (10 for 171)
(Min. 5 carries) 24.4—Coy McGee vs. Southern Cal, 1946 (6 for 146)
Season: (Min. 100 carries) 8.1—George Gipp, 1920 (102 for 827)
7.5—Marchy Schwartz, 1930 (124 for 927)
Career: (Min. 150 carries) 6.8—Don Miller, 1922-24 (283 for 1933)
6.4—Christie Flanagan, 1926-28 (285 for 1822)

Touchdowns Scored by Rushing
Game: 7—Art Smith vs. Loyola, Chicago, 1911
6—Bill Downs vs. DePauw, 1905
Season: 17—Vagas Ferguson, 1979
16—Bill Downs, 1905
(Per Game) 1.7—Ray Eichenlaub, 1913 (12 in 7)
Career: 36—Louis (Red) Salmon, 1900-03
32—Vagas Ferguson, 1976-79
30—Stan Cofall, 1914-16
Also holds per-game record at 1.2 (30 in 25)

Longest Rush
92—Bob Livingstone vs. Southern Cal, 1947 (TD)

PASSING

Attempts
Game: 63—Terry Hanratty vs. Purdue, 1967 (completed 29)
58—Joe Theismann vs. Southern Cal, 1970 (completed 33)
Season: 268—Joe Theismann, 1970 (completed 155)
260—Joe Montana, 1978 (completed 141)
215—Tom Clements, 1974 (completed 122)
Career: 550—Terry Hanratty, 1966-68 (completed 304)
515—Joe Montana, 1975, 77-78 (completed 268)
509—Joe Theismann, 1968-70 (completed 290)

Attempts Per Game
Season: 28.1—Terry Hanratty, 1968 (197 in 7)
Career: 21.2—Terry Hanratty, 1966-68 (550 in 26)

Completions
Game: 33—Joe Theismann vs. Southern Cal, 1970 (attempted 58)
29—Terry Hanratty vs. Purdue, 1967 (attempted 63)
Season: 155—Joe Theismann, 1970 (attempted 268)
141—Joe Montana, 1978 (attempted 260)
122—Tom Clements, 1974 (attempted 215)
Career: 304—Terry Hanratty, 1966-68 (attempted 550)
290—Joe Theismann, 1968-70 (attempted 509)

Completions Per Game
Season: 16.6—Terry Hanratty, 1968 (116 in 7)
Career: 11.7—Terry Hanratty, 1966-68 (304 in 26)

Consecutive Passes Completed
Game: 10—Joe Montana vs. Georgia Tech, 1978
10—Angelo Bertelli vs. Stanford, 1942

Consecutive Games Completing a Pass
Career: 34—Ralph Guglielmi; last 4 games of 1951, all 10 of 1952, 1953, 1954

Percent Completed
Game: (Min. 10 comp.) 85.7%—Rick Slager vs. Northwestern, 1976 (12 of 14)
81.3%—Bob Williams vs. Michigan State, 1949 (13 of 16)
Season: (Min. 100 atts.) 58.9%—Terry Hanratty, 1968 (116 of 197)
57.8%—Joe Theismann, 1970 (155 of 268)
Career: (Min. 150 atts.) 57.0%—Joe Theismann, 1968-70 (290 of 509)
55.3%—Terry Hanratty, 1966-68 (304 of 550)

*Highest Passing Efficiency Rating Points
Season: (Min. 50 comp.) 159.1—Bob Williams, 1949 (147 attempts, 83 completions, 7 interceptions, 1374 yards, 15 TD passes)
(Min. 100 comp.) 155.1—John Huarte, 1964 (205 attempts, 114 completions, 11 interceptions, 2062 yards, 16 TD passes)
Career: (Min. 60 comp.) 141.7—Frank Tripucka, 1945-48 (141 attempts, 80 completions, 12 interceptions, 1122 yards, 15 TD passes)
(Min. 100 comp.) 136.1—Joe Theismann, 1968-70 (509 attempts, 290 completions, 35 interceptions, 4411 yards, 31 TD passes)

Passes Had Intercepted
Game: 7—Frank Dancewicz vs. Army, 1944
Season: 16—Joe Theismann, 1969; Angelo Bertelli, 1942; John Niemiec, 1928 (also holds per-game record at 1.8, 16 in 9)
Career: 35—Joe Theismann, .1968-70
(Per Game) 1.3—Terry Hanratty, 1966-68 (34 in 26)

Lowest Percentage Had Intercepted
Season: (Min .100 atts.) 2.2 %—Rick Slager, 1975 (3 of 139)
3.46%—Joe Montana, 1978 (9 of 260)
3.54%—Ralph Guglielmi, 1953 (4 of 113)
Career: (Min. 150 atts.) 4.3 %—John Huarte, 1962-64 (11 of 255)
4.9 %—Joe Montana, 1975, 77-78 (25 of 515)
5.2 %—Rusty Lisch, 1976-1979 (18 of 343)
5.5 %—Ralph Guglielmi, 1951-54 (24 of 436)

Attempts Without Interception
Game: 31—Frank Dancewicz vs. Navy, 1944

Consecutive Attempts Without Interception
Career: 91—John Huarte, all of 1962 and 1963 and first two games of 1964

Yards Gained
Game: 526—Joe Theismann vs. Southern Cal, 1970
366—Terry Hanratty vs. Purdue, 1967
Season: 2429—Joe Theismann, 1970
2062—John Huarte, 1964
Career: 4411—Joe Theismann, 1968-70
4152—Terry Hanratty, 1966-68

Yards Per Game
Season: 242.9—Joe Theismann, 1970 (2429 in 10)
209.4—Terry Hanratty, 1968 (1466 in 7)
Career: 159.7—Terry Hanratty, 1966-68 (4152 in 26)
152.6—Joe Montana, 1975, 77-78 (4121 in 27)
152.1—Joe Theismann, 1968-70 (4411 in 29)

Yards Per Attempt
Game: (Min. 20 atts.) 12.8—George Izo vs. Pittsburgh, 1958 (26 for 332)
Season: (Min. 100 atts.) 10.1—John Huarte, 1964 (205 for 2062)
9.4—Joe Theismann, 1970 (268 for 2529)
Career: (Min. 150 atts.) 9.2—John Huarte, 1962-64 (255 for 2343)
8.7—Joe Theismann, 1968-70 (509 for 4411)

Yards Per Completion
Game: (Min. 10 comp.) 27.4—John Huarte vs. Navy, 1964 (10 for 274)
Season: (Min. 50 comp.) 18.1—John Huarte, 1964 (114 for 2062)
17.8—George Izo, 1958 (60 for 1067)
Career: (Min. 75 comp.) 17.3—George Izo, 1957-59 (121 for 2095)
17.0—John Huarte, 1962-64 (138 for 2343)

Touchdown Passes
Game: 4—Daryle Lamonica vs. Pittsburgh, 1962
4—Angelo Bertelli vs. Stanford, 1942
Season: 16—Joe Theismann, 1970; John Huarte, 1964; Bob Williams, 1949
Career: 31—Joe Theismann, 1968-70
28—Angelo Bertelli, 1941-43

Touchdown Passes Per Game
Season: 1.7—Angelo Bertelli, 1943 (10 in 6)
Career: 1.08—Angelo Bertelli, 1941-43 (28 in 26)
1.07—Joe Theismann, 1968-70 (31 in 29)

Longest Pass Play
91—John Huarte to Nick Eddy vs. Pittsburgh, 1964 (TD)

RECEIVING

Passes Caught
Game: 13—Jim Seymour vs. Purdue, 1966 (276 yards, 3 TD)
12—Tom Gatewood vs. Purdue, 1970 (192 yards, 3 TD)
Season: 77—Tom Gatewood, 1970 (1123 yards)
60—Jack Snow, 1964 (1114 yards)
Career: 157—Tom Gatewood, 1969-71 (2283 yards)
138—Jim Seymour, 1966-68 (2113 yards)

Catches Per Game
Season: 7.7—Tom Gatewood, 1970 (77 in 10)
6.9—Jim Seymour, 1966 (48 in 7)
Career: 5.3—Jim Seymour, 1966-68 (138 in 26)
5.2—Tom Gatewood, 1969-71 (157 in 30)

Passes Caught by a Tight End
Season: 54—Ken MacAfee, 1977 (797 yards)
Career: 128—Ken MacAfee, 1974-77 (1759 yards)

Yards Gained
Game: 276—Jim Seymour vs. Purdue, 1966 (caught 13, 3 TD)
217—Jack Snow vs. Wisconsin, 1964 (caught 9, 2 TD)
Season: 1123—Tom Gatewood, 1970 (caught 77)
1114—Jack Snow, 1964 (caught 60)
Career: 2283—Tom Gatewood, 1969-71 (caught 157)
2113—Jim Seymour, 1966-68 (caught 138)

Yards Per Game
Season: 123.1—Jim Seymour, 1966 (862 in 7)
112.3—Tom Gatewood, 1970 (1123 in 10)
Career: 81.3—Jim Seymour, 1966-68 (2113 in 26)
76.1—Tom Gatewood, 1969-71 (2283 in 30)

Yards Per Catch
Game: (Min. 5) 41.6—Jim Morse vs. Southern Cal, 1955 (5 for 208) **(National Record)**
26.2—Tony Hunter vs. Southern Cal, 1979 (5 for 131)
26.0—Ken MacAfee vs. Navy, 1977 (5 for 130)
Season: (Min. 20) 25.6—Tony Hunter, 1979 (27 for 690)
22.1—Jim Morse, 1956 (20 for 442)
21.8—Kris Haines, 1978 (32 for 699)
18.6—Jack Snow, 1964 (60 for 1114)
Career: (Min. 40) 21.5—Kris Haines, 1975-78 (63 for 1353)
21.2—Jim Morse, 1954-56 (52 for 1102)
19.9—†Tony Hunter, 1979 (50 for 993)
17.7—Jack Snow, 1962-64 (70 for 1242)

Touchdown Passes
Game: 3—Tom Gatewood vs. Purdue, 1970; Jim Seymour vs. Purdue, 1966; Jim Kelly vs. Pittsburgh, 1962; Jim Mutscheller vs. Michigan State, 1950; Bill Barrett vs. North Carolina, 1949; Eddie Anderson vs. Northwestern, 1920
Season: 9—Jack Snow, 1964
Career: 19—Tom Gatewood, 1969-71
16—Jim Seymour, 1966-68
15—Ken MacAfee, 1974-77

Touchdown Passes Per Game
Season: 1.1—Jim Seymour, 1966 (8 in 7)
Career: 0.6—Tom Gatewood, 1969-71 (19 in 30)

PUNTING

Punts
Game: 15—Marchy Schwartz vs. Army, 1931 (509 yards)
Season: 67—Fred Evans, 1941 (2557 yards)
66—Blair Kiel, 1980 (2649 yards)
64—Johnny Lattner, 1952 (2345 yards)
Career: 209—Joe Restic, 1975-78 (8409 yards)
134—Brian Doherty, 1971-73 (5333 yards)
122—Bob Williams, 1948-50 (4606 yards)

Punts Per Game
Season: 7.4—Fred Evans, 1941 (67 in 9)
Career: 5.5—Fred Evans, 1940-42 (105 in 19)

Average Per Punt
Game: (Min. 5) 51.6—Joe Restic vs. Air Force, 1975 (5 for 258)
(Min. 10) 44.8—Paul Castner vs. Purdue, 1921 (12 for 537)
Season: (Min. 30) 43.5—Joe Restic, 1975 (40 for 1739);
42.7—Brian Doherty, 1973 (39 for 1664)
Career: (Min. 50) 40.7—Bill Shakespeare, 1933-35 (91 for 3705)
40.1—†Blair Kiel, 1980 (66 for 2649)
39.6—Paul Castner, 1920-22 (84 for 3329)
(Min. 100) 40.2—Joe Restic, 1975-78 (209 for 8409)
39.8—Brian Doherty, 1971-73 (134 for 5333)

Longest Punt
86—Bill Shakespeare vs. Pittsburgh, 1935

INTERCEPTIONS

Interceptions Made
Game: 3—By 11 players. Last: Mike Townsend vs. Air Force, 1972
Season: 10—Mike Townsend, 1972 (39 yards)
Also holds per-game record at 1.0 (10 in 10)
9—Tom MacDonald, 1962 (81 yards)
Career: 17—Luther Bradley, 1973, 75-77 (218 yards)
15—Tom MacDonald, 1961-63 (167 yards)
Also holds per-game record at 0.6 (15 in 24)

Interceptions by a Linebacker
Season: 5—John Pergine, 1966 (72 yards)
Career: 9—John Pergine, 1965-67 (91 yards)

Yards Gained
Game: 103—Luther Bradley vs. Purdue, 1975 (2 interceptions)
Season: 197—Nick Rassas, 1965 (6 interceptions)
Also holds per-game record at 19.7
151—Frank Carideo, 1929 (5 interceptions)
Career: 226—Tom Schoen, 1965-67 (11 interceptions)
220—Nick Rassas, 1963-65 (7 interceptions)
Also holds per-game record at 10.5 (220 in 21)
218—Luther Bradley, 1973, 75-77 (17 interceptions)
215—Tom Gibbons, 1977-80 (9 interceptions)

Average Per Return
Game: (Min. 2) 51.5—Luther Bradley vs. Purdue, 1975 (2 for 103)
Season: (Min. 4) 33.8—Luther Bradley, 1975 (4 for 135)
32.8—Nick Rassas, 1965 (6 for 197)
Career: (Min. 6) 31.4—Nick Rassas, 1963-65 (7 for 220)
23.9—Tom Gibbons, 1977-80 (9 for 215)
21.7—Ted Burgmeier, 1974-77 (6 for 130)
21.2—Paul Hornung, 1954-56 (10 for 212)

Touchdowns
Game: 2—Dave Waymer vs. Miami, 1979
Season: 2—Tom Schoen, 1966; Randy Harrison, 1974; Bobby Leopold, 1977; Dave Waymer, 1979
Career: 3—Tom Schoen, 1965-67; Bobby Leopold, 1976-78

Longest Interception Return
99—Luther Bradley vs. Purdue, 1975 (TD)

PUNT RETURNS

Punt Returns
Game: 9—Tom Schoen vs. Pittsburgh, 1967 (167 yards)
Season: 42—Tom Schoen, 1967 (447 yards)
Also holds per-game record at 4.7
40—Gene Edwards, 1925 (173 yards)
Career: 92—Frank Carideo, 1928-30 (947 yards)
Also holds per-game record at 3.3 (92 in 28)
88—Harry Stuhldreher, 1922-24 (701 yards)

Yards Gained
Game: 167—Tom Schoen vs. Pittsburgh, 1967 (9 returns)
157—Chet Grant vs. Case Tech, 1916 (3 returns)
Season: 459—Nick Rassas, 1965 (24 returns)
447—Tom Schoen, 1967 (42 returns)
Also holds per-game record at 49.7 (447 in 9)
Career: 947—Frank Carideo, 1928-30 (92 returns)
Also holds per-game record at 33.8 (947 in 28)
701—Harry Stuhldreher, 1922-24 (88 returns)

Average Per Return
Game: (Min. 3) 52.3—Chet Grant vs. Case Tech, 1916 (3 for 157)
(Min. 5) 22.0—Frank Carideo vs. Georgia Tech, 1929 (5 for 110)
Season: (Min. 1.5 rets. per game) 19.1—Nick Rassas, 1965 (24 for 459)
13.4—Andy Puplis, 1937 (21 for 281)
Career: (Min. 1.5 rets. per game) 15.7—Nick Rassas, 1963-65 (39 for 612)
12.6—Bill Gay, 1948-50 (46 for 580)

Touchdowns
Game: 2—Vince McNally vs. Beloit, 1926
Season: 3—Nick Rassas, 1965
Career: 3—Nick Rassas, 1963-65

Longest Punt Return
95—Chet Grant vs. Case Tech, 1916 (TD)
95—Harry (Red) Miller vs. Olivet, 1909 (did not score, 110-yard field)

KICKOFF RETURNS

Kickoff Returns
Game: 8—George Gipp vs. Army, 1920 (157 yards)
6—Mark McLane vs. Southern Cal, 1974 (95 yards)
6—Jack Landry vs. Michigan State, 1951 (112 yards)
Season: 19—Jim Stone, 1979 (493 yards)
17—Jim Stone, 1980 (344 yards)
16—Bill Wolski, 1963 (379 yards)
Also holds per-game record at 1.8 (16 in 9)
16—Paul Hornung, 1956 (496 yards)
Career: 49—Jim Stone, 1977-80 (1,079 yards)
(Also holds per-game record of 1.5 (49 in 33 games)
32—Terry Eurick, 1974-77 (739 yards)
30—Gary Diminick, 1971-73 (711 yards)
24—Bill Wolski, 1963-65 (559 yards)
24—Bob Scarpitto, 1958-60 (493 yards)

Yards Gained
Game: 253—Paul Castner vs. Kalamazoo, 1922 (4 returns)
174—Willie Maher vs. Kalamazoo, 1923 (4 returns)
Season: 496—Paul Hornung, 1956 (16 returns)
(Per Game) 70.0—Paul Castner, 1922 (490 in 7)
493—Jim Stone, 1979 (19 returns)
490—Paul Castner, 1922 (11 returns)

Career: 1079—Jim Stone, 1977-80 (49 returns)
767—Paul Castner, 1920-22 (21 returns)
Also holds per-game record at 29.5 (767 in 26)
739—Terry Eurick, 1974-77 (32 returns)
711—Gary Diminick, 1971-73 (30 returns)
663—Paul Hornung, 1954-56 (23 returns)

Average Per Return
Game: (Min. 2) 74.0—Johnny Lattner vs. Penn, 1953 (2 for 148)
Season: (Min. 0.5 rets. per game) 48.3—Nick Eddy, 1966 (4 for 193)
Career: (Min. 12) 36.5—Paul Castner, 1920-22 (21 for 767)
28.9—Nick Eddy, 1964-66 (14 for 404)

Touchdowns
Game: 2—Paul Castner vs. Kalamazoo, 1922
Season: 2—Nick Eddy, 1966; Johnny Lattner, 1953; Willie Maher, 1923; Paul Castner, 1922
Career: Same as season record

Longest Kickoff Return
105—Alfred Bergman vs. Loyola, Chicago, 1911 (did not score, 110-yard field)
100—Joe Savoldi vs. SMU, 1930 (TD)

TOTAL KICK RETURNS
(Combined Punt and Kickoff Returns)

Kick Returns
Game: 10—George Gipp vs. Army, 1920 (2 punts, 8 kickoffs; 207 yards)
9—Tom Schoen vs. Pittsburgh, 1967 (9 punts; 167 yards)
Season: 43—Gene Edwards, 1925 (40 punts, 3 kickoffs; 213 yards)
42—Tom Schoen, 1967 (42 punts; 447 yards)
Also holds per-game record at 4.7 (42 in 9)
Career: 96—Frank Carideo, 1928-30 (92 punts, 4 kickoffs; 1006 yards). Also holds per-game record at 3.4 (96 in 28)
91—Harry Stuhldreher, 1922-24 (88 punts, 3 kickoffs; 724 yards)

Yards Gained
Game: 254—Willie Maher vs. Kalamazoo, 1923 (80 on punts, 174 on kickoffs)
253—Paul Castner vs. Kalamazoo, 1922 (253 on kickoffs)
Season: 559—Paul Hornung, 1956 (63 on punts, 496 on kickoffs)
Also holds per-game record at 55.9
541—Nick Rassas, 1965 (459 on punts, 82 on kickoffs)
Career: 1079—Jim Stone, 1977-80 (1079 on kickoffs)
1006—Frank Carideo, 1928-30 (947 on punts, 59 on kickoffs)
Also holds per-game record at 35.9 (1006 in 28)
797—Nick Rassas, 1963-65 (612 on punts, 185 on kickoffs)

Average Per Return
Game: (Min. 5) 22.7—Angelo Dabiero vs. Pittsburgh, 1960 (6 for 136)
22.0—Frank Carideo vs. Georgia Tech, 1929 (5 for 110)
Season: (Min. 1.5 rets. per game) 28.0—Paul Hornung, 1956 (20 for 559)
25.9—Jim Stone, 1979 (19 for 493)
Career: (Min. 1.5 rets. per game) 22.0—Jim Stone, 1977-80 (49 for 1079)
17.7—George Gipp, 1917-20 (38 for 671)
17.0—Nick Rassas, 1963-65 (47 for 797)

Touchdowns Scored
Game: 2—Vince McNally vs. Beloit (punt returns)
2—Paul Castner vs. Kalamazoo, 1922 (kickoff returns)
Season: 3—Nick Rassas, 1965 (punt returns)
Career: 3—Nick Rassas, 1963-65 (punt returns)

ALL-PURPOSE RUNNING
(Yardage gained from rushing, receiving and all runbacks)

Yards Gained
Game: 361—Willie Maher vs. Kalamazoo, 1923 (107 rushing, 80 punt returns, 174 kickoff returns)
357—George Gipp vs. Army, 1920 (150 rushing, 50 punt returns, 157 kickoff returns)
Season: 1512—Bob Gladieux, 1968 (717 rushing, 442 receiving, 91 punt returns, 262 kickoff returns)
Also holds per-game record at 151.2
1509—Vagas Ferguson, 1979
Career: 3838—Vagas Ferguson, 1976-79 (3472 rushing, 366 receiving)
3116—Johnny Lattner, 1951-53
3064—George Gipp, 1917-20

Yards Per Game
Career: 113.5—George Gipp, 1917-20 (3064 in 27; 2341 rushing, 52 interceptions, 217 punt returns, 454 kickoffs)
103.9—Johnny Lattner, 1951-53 (3116 in 30)

TOTAL YARDAGE GAINED
(Yardage gained from rushing, passing, receiving and all runbacks)

Yards Gained
Game: 519—Joe Theismann vs. Southern Cal, 1970 (526 passing, 7 receiving, minus 14 rushing)
420—Terry Hanratty vs. Purdue, 1967
Season: 2820—Joe Theismann, 1970 (2429 passing, 384 rushing, 7 receiving). Also holds per-game record at 282.0
2114—Joe Montana, 1978
2080—John Huarte, 1964
Career: 5551—Joe Theismann, 1968-70 (4411 passing, 1021 rushing, 20 receiving, 99 punt returns)
Also holds per-game record at 191.4 (5551 in 29)
4833—George Gipp, 1917-20

SCORING

Points Scored
Game: 35—Art Smith vs. Loyola, Chicago, 1911 (7 TD, 5 points each)
30—Bill Wolski vs. Pittsburgh, 1965 (5 TD); Willie Maher vs. Kalamazoo, 1923 (5 TD); Bill Downs vs. DePauw, 1905 (6 TD, 5 points each)
Season: 105—Louis (Red) Salmon, 1903 (15 TD, 5 points each, 30 PAT)
102—Vagas Ferguson, 1979 (17 TD)
Career: 250—Louis (Red) Salmon, 1900-03 (36 TD, 5 points each, 60 PAT, 2 FG, 5 points each)
247—Dave Reeve, 1974-77 (130 PAT, 39 FG)

Points Per Games
Season: 11.7—Louis (Red) Salmon, 1903 (105 in 9)
11.1—Alvin Berger, 1912 (78 in 7)
Career: 10.3—Stan Cofall, 1914-16 (246 in 24)
7.1—Gus Dorais, 1910-13 (198 in 28)

Touchdowns
Game: 7—Art Smith vs. Loyola, Chicago, 1911
             6—Bill Downs vs. DePauw, 1905
Season: 17—Vagas Ferguson, 1979
            16—Bill Downs, 1905
               Also holds per-game record at 1.8 (16 in 9)
Career: 36—Louis (Red) Salmon, 1900-03
            35—Vagas Ferguson, 1976-79
               (Per Game) 1.3—Stan Cofall, 1914-16 (30 in 24)

First Notre Dame Touchdown
Harry Jewett vs. Michigan, April 20, 1888 (5-yard run)

FIELD GOALS

Field Goals Made
Game: 4—Harry Oliver vs. Miami, 1980 (5 attempts)
             4—Harry Oliver vs. Michigan State, 1980 (4 attempts)
             4—Chuck Male vs. Michigan, 1979 (4 attempts)
Season: 18—Harry Oliver, 1980 (23 attempts)
            13—Chuck Male, 1979 (20 attempts)
            12—Dave Reeve, 1977 (20 attempts)
            11—Dave Reeve, 1975 (16 attempts)
Career: 39—Dave Reeve, 1977 (64 attempts)
            22—Chuck Male, 1978-79 (32 attempts)
            21—Bob Thomas, 1971-73 (38 attempts)

Field Goals Attempted
Game: 7—Gus Dorais vs. Texas, 1913 (made 3)
Season: 23—Harry Oliver, 1980 (made 18)
            20—Chuck Male, 1979 (made 13)
            20—Dave Reeve, 1977 (made 12)
            18—Dave Reeve, 1976 (made 9)
            18—Bob Thomas, 1971-73 (made 9)
Career: 64—Dave Reeve, 1977 (made 39)
            38—Bob Thomas, 1971-73 (made 21)

Percent Made
Season: (Min. 10 Atts.) 80.0%—Joe Azzaro, 1967 (8 of 10)
Career: (Min. 15 Atts.) 72.2%—Joe Azzaro, 1964, 66-67 (13 of 18)
          (Min. 20 Atts.) 78.3%—†Harry Oliver, 1980- (18 of 23)

Most Consecutive Field Goals Made
Season: 8—Chuck Male, 1979
Career: 10—Chuck Male, 1978-79

Longest Field Goal Made
53—Dave Reeve vs. Pittsburgh, 1976

First Notre Dame Field Goal
Mike Daly vs. Chicago, 1897 (35 yards)

EXTRA POINTS

Extra Points Made
Game: 9—By four players. Last: Ken Ivan vs. Pittsburgh, 1965
                                                (10 attempts)
Season: 45—Scott Hempel, 1968 (50 attempts)
               Also holds per-game record at 4.5
            43—Bob Thomas, 1973 (45 attempts)
Career: 130—Dave Reeve, 1974-77 (143 attempts)
           122—Scott Hempel, 1968-70 (132 attempts)
               Also holds per-game record at 4.4 (122 in 28)
            98—Bob Thomas, 1971-73 (101 attempts)

Extra Points Attempted
Game: 12—Frank Winters vs. Englewood H.S., 1900 (made 9)
            10—Ken Ivan vs. Pittsburgh, 1965 (made 9)
Season: 52—Steve Oracko, 1949 (made 38)
            51—Scott Hempel, 1968 (made 45)
Career: 143—Dave Reeve, 1974-77 (made 130)
           132—Scott Hempel, 1968-70 (made 122)
           105—Gus Dorais, 1910-13 (made 96)

Percent Made
Season: (Min. 20 made) 100%—Bob Thomas, 1972, (34 of 34)
                       95.6%—Bob Thomas, 1973 (43 of 45)
                       95.5%—Bob Thomas, 1971 (21 of 22)
Career: (Min. 50 made) 97.0%—Bob Thomas, 1971-73 (98 of 101)
                       92.4%—Scott Hempel, 1968-70 (122 of 132)

Consecutive Extra Points Made
62—Bob Thomas, from Nov. 6, 1971 vs. Pittsburgh to Oct. 20, 1973 vs.
       Army (missed 6th attempt)
30—Scott Hempel, from Nov. 16, 1968 vs. Georgia Tech to Oct. 25,
       1969 vs. Tulane

Points Scored by Kicking (PAT and FG)
Game: 14—Harry Oliver vs. Miami, 1980 (2 PAT, 4 FG)
            14—Harry Oliver vs. Michigan State, 1980 (2 PAT, 4 FG)
            13—Bob Thomas vs. Northwestern, 1972 (4 PAT, 3 FG)
            12—Chuck Male vs. Michigan, 1979 (4 FG)
            12—Dave Reeve vs. Navy, 1977 (3 PAT, 3 FG)
            12—Bob Thomas vs. Air Force, 1973 (6 PAT, 2 FG)
            12—Scott Hempel vs. Purdue, 1970 (6 PAT, 2 FG)
            12—Gus Dorais vs. Texas, 1913 (3 PAT, 3 FG)
Season: 75—Dave Reeve, 1977 (39 PAT, 12 FG)
            73—Harry Oliver, 1980 (19 PAT, 18 FG)
            70—Bob Thomas, 1973 (43 PAT, 9 FG)
               Also holds per-game record at 7.0
            63—Chuck Male, 1979 (24 PAT, 13 FG)
Career: 247—Dave Reeve, 1974-77 (130 PAT, 39 FG)
           164—Scott Hempel, 1968-70 (122 PAT, 14 FG)
               Also holds per-game record at 5.9 (164 in 28)

2-Point Attempts
Game: 3—Joe Theismann vs. Pittsburgh, 1970; Terry Hanratty vs.
               Pittsburgh, 1966; John Huarte vs. Wisconsin and Mich-
               igan State, 1964
Season: 9—John Huarte, 1964; 6—Terry Hanratty, 1966
Career: 10—John Huarte, 1962-64; 8—Terry Hanratty, 1966-68

2-Point Attempts Scored
Season: 2—Bob Minnix, 1971; Bill Wolski, 1965

Successful 2-Point Passes
Season: 2—John Huarte, 1964 (attempted 9)

DEFENSIVE RECORDS

Tackles by a Linebacker (Since 1956)
Season: 187—Bob Crable, 1979; 160—Steve Heimkreiter, 1978;
                154—Bob Crable, 1980
Career: 479—Bob Golic, 1975-78; 398—Steve Heimkreiter, 1975-78;
                369—Bob Olson, 1967-69; 354—†Bob Crable, 1978-

Tackles by a Front Four Lineman (Since 1956)
Season: 113—Steve Niehaus, 1975; 104—Ross Browner, 1977
Career: 340—Ross Browner, 1973, 75-77; 290—Steve Niehaus, 1972-
                75; 264—Jeff Weston, 1974-78

Tackles For Minus Yardage (Since 1967)
Season: 28—Ross Browner, 1976 (203 yards)
            19—Jim Stock, 1974 (120 yards)
Career: 77—Ross Browner, 1973, 75-77 (515 yards)
            40—Walt Patulski, 1969-71 (264 yards)

Passes Broken Up (Since 1956)
Season: 13—Clarence Ellis, 1969; 12—Dave Waymer, 1978
Career: 32—Clarence Ellis, 1969-71; 27—Luther Bradley, 1973, 75-77

Opponent Fumbles Recovered (Since 1952)
Season: 5—Jim Browner, 1977; Jim Musuraca, 1971; Don Penza,
               1953; Dave Flood, 1952
Career: 12—Ross Browner, 1973, 75-77
             8—Jim Stock, 1972-75

Photo Credits

The color photos are by Zenon Bidzinski, Gary Mills, Peter Romzick, Jim Klocke, and Neil Rosini.

We are grateful to Chet Grant; The Dome; the University of Notre Dame; and Notre Dame Sports Information for their contributions.

Photos are credited top left-right; bottom left-right.

Index